Making Preschool Inclusion Work

Making Preschool Inclusion Work

Strategies for Supporting Children, Teachers, and Programs

by

Anne Marie Richardson-Gibbs, M.A.
El Monte City School District
El Monte, California

and

M. Diane Klein, Ph.D., CCC-SLP
Early Childhood Special Education
Division of Special Education and Counseling
California State University, Los Angeles

·P A U L·H·
BROOKES
PUBLISHING C°®

Baltimore • London • Sydney

Paul H. Brookes Publishing Co.
Post Office Box 10624
Baltimore, Maryland 21285-0624
USA

www.brookespublishing.com

Typeset by Cenveo, Baltimore, Maryland.
Manufactured in the United States of America by
Sheridan Books, Chelsea, Michigan.

Cover photos are (from top to bottom): Copyright Inmagine, Unlisted Images, Inc., and istockphoto/ matka_Wariatka.

The photos on page ii are (clockwise from top left): © Veer/Ocean Photography; © Veer/Fancy Photography; © istockphoto/mguttman; © Inmagine; © istockphoto/ktaylorg; © Unlisted Images, Inc.; © Veer/Fancy Photography; and © Getty Images/ Photodisc/Andersen Ross.

Selected photos and clip art are © 2014 Jupiterimages Corporation; © Veer/Fancy Photography; © istockphoto/kate_sept2004; © Veer/Juice Images Photography; and © istockphoto/DegasMM.

The quotation on page 7 is from DEC/NAEYC. (2009). *Early childhood inclusion: A joint position statement of the Division for Early Childhood (DEC) and the National Association for the Education of Young Children (NAEYC)* (p. 2). Chapel Hill: The University of North Carolina, FPG Child Development Institute.

Library of Congress Cataloging-in-Publication Data

Richardson-Gibbs, Anne Marie.
  Making preschool inclusion work: strategies for supporting children, teachers, and programs / by Anne Marie Richardson-Gibbs, M.A. and M. Diane Klein, Ph.D., CCC-SLP.
  pages   cm
  Includes bibliographical references and index.
  ISBN 978-1-59857-211-7 (hardcover)   ISBN 978-1-59857-613-9 (EPUB)
  1. Children with disabilities–Education (Early childhood)–United States. 2. Inclusive education–United States. I. Klein, M. Diane. II. Title.

  C4019.3R53 2014
  371.9–dc23   2013035805

British Library Cataloguing in Publication data are available from the British Library.

2018   2017   2016   2015   2014

10   9   8   7   6   5   4   3   2   1

Contents

About the Authors

Anne Marie Richardson-Gibbs, M.A., is an early childhood special educator and has provided inclusion services for the past 20 years in both community-based preschool and public school settings. Ms. Richardson-Gibbs works for the El Monte City School District, where she provides inclusion support to preschool and early elementary age children with disabilities. Ms. Richardson-Gibbs has been the director of an early intervention program that provides services to infants, toddlers, and their families from East Los Angeles and worked as a statewide early intervention program specialist for the California Department of Education. She was the training coordinator for Project Support, a federally funded personnel training grant. As coordinator she created inclusion-support in-services, training videos, and a manual for early childhood special educators. Ms. Richardson-Gibbs has taught early childhood special education classes at California State University, Los Angeles, and has served as chairperson for both the Infant Development Association of California and the Los Angeles Early Intervention Directors' Forum. She continues to provide training and in-services for Head Start and school district personnel on inclusion support, behavior management, and autism and developmental delays in young children.

M. Diane Klein, Ph.D., CCC-SLP, is a professor of early childhood special education at California State University, Los Angeles, where she has directed the programs in early childhood special education for 30 years. Dr. Klein received her M.A. in speech-language pathology and audiology from Western Michigan University and her Ph.D. in developmental psychology from Michigan State University. In her early career, she worked as a speech-language pathologist with young children with disabilities and their families. She has directed numerous federally funded projects involving caregiver–child interaction, working with infants with low incidence and multiple disabilities, training of early childhood special educators, and training inclusion-support personnel (Project Support). She has coauthored—with colleagues Deborah Chen and Ruth Cook—several journal articles and books. These have included a widely used text in early childhood special education, *Adapting Early Childhood Curricula for Children with Special Needs, Eighth Edition* (Merrill/Prentice Hall, 2012); Project PLAI, a curriculum and training video for working with families of infants with multiple disabilities (Paul H. Brookes Publishing Co., 2002); *Including Children with Special Needs in Early Childhood Settings* (Delmar, 2002); and *Working with Children from Culturally Diverse Backgrounds* (Delmar, 2001). Along with Anne Marie Richardson-Gibbs, Dr. Klein has produced a variety of training videos related to inclusion-support strategies for young children with disabilities in community-based early childhood education settings.

Contributors

Sherwood J. Best, Ph.D.
Professor
California State University,
    Los Angeles
Division of Special Education and
    Counseling
5151 State University Drive
Los Angeles, CA 90032

Michelle Dean, Ph.D.
Post-Doctoral Scholar
University of California, Los Angeles
Kasari Research Lab
760 Westwood Plaza, NPI 68-229
Los Angeles, CA 90024

Kathleen C. Harris, Ph.D.
Retired Professor
California Polytechnic State University
    San Luis Obispo
School of Education, College of
    Science and Mathematics
California Polytechnic State
    University
San Luis Obispo, CA 93407

Sarah Chen Ling, M.A.
Special Education Teacher
Moreno Elementary School
4825 Moreno Street
Montclair, CA 91763

Beth A. Moore, M.A.
Retired Teacher of the Visually
    Impaired Family Resource Specialist
    Center for the Partially Sighted
6101 W. Centinela Ave., Suite 150
Culver City, CA 90230

Janice Myck-Wayne, Ed.D.
Associate Professor
California State University, Fullerton
Department of Special Education
Post Office Box 6868
Fullerton, CA 92384

Sue Parker-Strafaci, M.A.
Director of Child Development Services
Braille Institute
741 N. Vermont Avenue
Los Angeles, CA 90029

Kathryn D. Peckham-Hardin, Ph.D.
Professor
California State University, Northridge
18111 Nordhoff Street
Northridge, CA 91330

Jennifer B.G. Symon, Ph.D., BCBA-D
Associate Professor
California State University, Los Angeles
Special Education and Counseling
5151 State University Drive
Los Angeles, CA 90032

Foreword

In this book, Anne Marie Richardson-Gibbs and M. Diane Klein have addressed the unique challenges of creating and maintaining successful inclusive early education programs. They bring to the text years of hands-on experience in early childhood inclusion support, experience in teacher training, and fieldwork supervision. The authentic voices of key players in the inclusion process are also included: administrators, early childhood educators, special educators, parents, and disability specialists.

The authors emphasize that *successful* early childhood inclusion is a positive and rewarding experience for young children, both with and without disabilities, and for their teachers and families. However, achievement of real success often presents surprisingly complex challenges. Success lies in *administrative leadership, individualized configurations of supports*, and in *creative and collaborative problem solving*.

This book takes a comprehensive and multidimensional approach—ranging from the conceptual/philosophical considerations of common challenges to everyday evidence-based strategies and solutions. A primary focus is on the ways key players can creatively configure and deliver *support service to meet the unique needs of each child*.

Challenges and solutions related to service delivery and teaching strategies are reflected in chapter topics that consider a range of dimensions that contribute uniquely to successful inclusion. Legal foundations for inclusive early childhood education are reviewed. These foundations encourage support teams to take a bold, problem-solving approach to designing the individualized educational program (IEP). Strategies are presented for supporting families as key players in both the IEP process and in the ongoing decision making on behalf of their children. Also foundational to inclusion success is an appreciation for the possible configurations of "models of inclusion support service *delivery*," which are as important to inclusion success as are the specific services and instructional adaptations. A chapter on administrative challenges helps the reader understand both the perspective of the school administrator and the importance of administrative leadership. The authors provide many practical suggestions and checklists to assist an administrator in the development and oversight of inclusive early education programs and classrooms. A chapter on collaborative communication and problem solving reflects the authors' belief that the lack of such skills can easily undermine inclusion success and team building.

Disability-specific considerations for children with hearing loss, visual disabilities, physical and health disabilities, and autism spectrum disorders are addressed in a chapter with contributions from specialists in those areas. An invited chapter on positive behavior support presents guidelines for creating inclusive environments that support the positive behaviors of all learners. Finally, two chapters review evidence-based general-classroom teaching strategies and curriculum issues related to preschool to kindergarten transition.

These chapters, whether considered together as an overview of challenges and solutions in successful early childhood inclusion support or as individual resources for early childhood teachers and special educators, administrators, parents and disability specialists, will uniquely contribute to planning and implementing effective inclusive early childhood classrooms.

Marci J. Hanson
Professor of Special Education
San Francisco State University

Acknowledgments

We must first acknowledge that without the patient, skillful support of Johanna Cantler this book would have never been possible. The expertise of all the Brookes editorial and production "key players," especially Sarah Zerofsky, was very much needed and appreciated. We also thank the early project reviewers who provided critiques and suggestions.

The many chapter contributions and real-life practical solutions described in the book were provided or inspired by parents, administrators, and many dedicated and brilliant students and colleagues. These include the preschool inclusion team at El Monte City School District as well as students and faculty at California State University, Los Angeles. We thank the following individuals:

- The El Monte City School District child development program personnel, including Lisa Dunbar and Olga Vasquez, and the many Head Start teachers and assistants who have consistently welcomed young children with disabilities into their classrooms and have always been willing to collaborate and work with us to determine how best to serve each child's individual needs

- The El Monte City School District Special Education Department, whose past administrator, Carol Williams, realized and promoted establishment of "formal" inclusion specialist positions and whose present administrator, Toni Kopilec, continues to support these positions in spite of often overwhelming budget crises

- The inclusion "team" of specialists who continue to be inspirational both personally and professionally, especially Estelle Charlebois and Janice Baroff; their daily energy, enthusiasm, and unwavering belief in the ability of children with disabilities to succeed with the appropriate supports in regular education settings inspire an ongoing commitment to inclusive practice

- The early childhood inclusion assistants, especially Juana Mejorado and Marisela Hernandez, who, on a daily basis, have provided "just enough" support for so many children to encourage their independence while learning to be true members of their inclusive classrooms

- Bonnie Karlin, Sharon Kilpatrick, Hannah Rodriguez, Mariela Avila, Rose Jenkins, Carol Dale, Tracy Eagle, Bernice Gonzalez de Torres, and June Szabo-Kifer for sharing their real-life stories of inclusion support

For their excellent chapter contributions we thank Drs. Kathleen C. Harris, Kathryn Peckham-Hardin, Jennifer Symon, Sherwood Best, Janice Myck-Wayne, Beth Moore, Sue Parker-Strafaci, Michele Dean, and Sarah Chen Ling.

Finally, we must thank the many families of children with disabilities who inspire us and keep us focused on the vision of inclusive possibilities for all children. Their commitment to their children and their willingness to campaign for inclusive educational services, often against great odds, fills us with a sense of awe at the inner strength they find, year after year. Many sincere thanks to the Welflin, Spinelli, and Daffron families, and to the members of Club 21 in Pasadena, California.

*To the many "key players" who
care about high-quality learning opportunities for all
young children, including parents and their children, early
childhood education teachers, early childhood special educators,
paraprofessionals, specialists, administrators, and the young men
and women who are beginning their training for careers in the field
of early childhood education and early childhood special education.
We hope the ideas, stories, and strategies in this text provide you with
the confidence that there are as many ways to create successful inclusive
programs as there are collaborative, creative, solution-oriented teams.*

An Introduction to Preschool Inclusion Support Practices

Inclusive schools begin with a philosophy and vision that all children belong and can learn in the mainstream of school and community life. The classroom is seen as a community where diversity is valued and celebrated and all children work, talk, cooperate and share.

—Winzer and Mazurek (1998, p. 103)

There is no better time or place to begin accessing inclusive communities than in preschool. This book is about preschool inclusion *support*. It is the intent of this book to describe the practices that support early childhood inclusion. The concept of "inclusion" has evolved from the 1975 legal mandate in federal education law that children who have disabilities must be placed in the "least restrictive environment" (LRE). This provision, reauthorized in the Individuals with Disabilities Act Amendments (IDEA) of 1997 (PL 105-17), requires that, to the maximum extent appropriate, children with disabilities are educated with children who do not have disabilities (IDEA Part B, 34 CFR §§300.550).

"Inclusion" is not a legal term. Rather, inclusion, and the phrase "full inclusion," are often described as a philosophy or a value related to fully belonging to a classroom or a community. (See the 2009 Division for Early Childhood [DEC] and the National Association for the Education of Young Children [NAEYC] joint position statement later in this chapter.)

Unlike in K–12 education, one of the challenges of preschool inclusion is the need to find, or create, an appropriate *general education program for placement.* However, placement is only the first step. As is often noted, inclusive education is not just about place. Simply placing a child in a setting with typical, same-age peers, without support and collaboration of key players, not only fails to meet the mandates for and expectations of an LRE but also can be very stressful for the child, family, and staff. Early childhood staff may feel overwhelmed and unsupported. Typical peers may feel threatened or confused by certain behaviors or characteristics of the included child. Families may suffer the feeling that their child is being rejected or not reaching his or her potential. This book is intended to offer readers strategies for mitigating these challenges by offering guidance on how to make *successful* preschool inclusion a reality.

We know what great inclusive preschool classrooms should look like, and we know that children with—and without—disabilities can thrive in those environments. The field of early childhood special education (ECSE)—the only field devoted exclusively to the developmental and educational well-being of young children who have disabilities—has produced volumes of evidence describing effective programs and practices. A well-established organization, the Early Childhood Technical Assistance (ECTA) Center (previously National Early Childhood Training and Assistance Center [NECTAC]), serves as a clearinghouse and provides technical assistance related to teaching strategies, adaptations, and classroom quality for early childhood inclusion. However, despite these resources and evidence-based recommended practices, challenges related to the quality of inclusion support—and the imperative of collaboration among key players—often threaten the sustainability of inclusive programs.

Effective inclusion support must be a careful, collaborative process that creatively plans and delivers the specialized services, accommodations, curriculum modifications, and differentiated instructional strategies appropriate to the specific needs and the unique strengths and interests of each child. Just as important, if not more important, administrative and organizational structures must be designed not just to support the child with a disability but also to maintain a creative, collaborative work environment for staff. It is the children's—as well as their teachers'—sense of belonging, accomplishment, and the joy of learning that is the real focus of this book.

One of the most significant achievements in U.S. education and civil rights law was passage of the Education for All Handicapped Children Act of 1975 (PL 94-142). Two of the most far-reaching provisions of PL 94-142 were mandates that ensured a "free and appropriate education" (FAPE) and guaranteed placement of students with disabilities in the "least restrictive environment." FAPE ensures that the educational program and services provided are paid for by the government (i.e., free) and appropriate to the individual learning characteristics and needs of the student. The LRE provision ensures that these services are provided in the same setting in which children without disabilities receive educational instruction or in a setting that is as close to that environment as is appropriate given the individual special challenges of the child. In addition, states must offer a *continuum of services* and settings in order to guarantee the child's access to appropriate education in the least restrictive environment. This federal law was reauthorized as the Education of the Handicapped Act Amendments of 1986 (PL 99-457) to ensure these same entitlements for *preschool* children and to encourage states to extend early intervention services to infants. In 1990 the law was again reauthorized, this time as the Individuals with Disabilities Education Act (IDEA) of 1990 (PL 101-476). The right of preschool-age children with disabilities to receive public education services under Part B (Section 619) of IDEA is the law of the land. The law automatically requires that these services be provided in the least restrictive environment, just as they are in K–12 education. (See the text box on page 3 for a summary of IDEA.)

IDEA: Least Restrictive Environment

300.114(a)(2) GENERAL LRE REQUIREMENTS

(2) Each public agency must ensure that—

(i) to the maximum extent appropriate, children with disabilities … are educated with children who are nondisabled; and

(ii) special classes, separate schooling or other removal of children with disabilities from the regular educational environment occur only if the nature or severity of the disability is such that education in regular classes with the use of supplementary aids and services cannot be achieved satisfactorily.

300.116 PLACEMENT

In determining the educational placement of a child with a disability, including a preschool child with a disability, each public agency must ensure that—

(a) The placement decision—

(1) Is made by a group of persons, including the parents, and other persons knowledgeable about the child, the meaning of the evaluation data and the placement options: and

(2) Is made in conformity with the LRE provisions.

Source: Individuals with Disabilities Education Act (IDEA) of 1990 (PL 101-476).

These provisions, when combined with a commitment to creative problem solving and to the *individualization* component in the individualized education program (IEP), can be used with confidence by members of a child's team to design supportive program plans to guarantee success in an inclusive setting. The law provides significant opportunity for creativity and flexibility in its insistence that each educational program be specifically designed to meet the individual needs of a young child eligible for services. IDEA is widely viewed as the strongest special education law in the world. Early childhood special educators should become very familiar not only with its provisions and protections but also with the way in which it can be used to create successful, inclusive early education for young children with special needs.

As described by Lipsky and Gartner (2001), the 1997 reauthorization of IDEA (PL 105-17) presumed that the *first* placement option the IEP team considers for a child should be the school the child would attend if the child did not have a disability. The team must give serious consideration to what supplementary aids and services would be needed to meet the child's educational needs in that placement. Gartner and Lipsky further commented that "these requirements clearly apply to preschool-age children and also the birth-to-three group" (2001, p. 43).

Despite the requirement by U.S. federal law that developmental and educational services be provided in the least restrictive environment, and the law's unequivocal support for providing those services in classrooms with same-age peers without disabilities, realization of widespread inclusive education in the United States continues to present challenges. For example, Sindelar et al. (2006) described difficulties with sustainability of even high quality inclusive programs, often due to changes in administrative personnel. Even within preschool populations—where full inclusion is often assumed to be more easily attainable because of less challenging academic demands than those required for K–12 students—successful inclusion can present many challenges.

An inclusive classroom is not the ideal placement for every child with special needs at every moment in his or her educational life. IDEA does not guarantee inclusive placement for every child. It does require good faith consideration of how to create a meaningful, effective plan designed specifically for that child. The IEP must also consider what supports and services the child needs and how these supports and services can be accommodated in the general education classroom. The IEP must be delivered in a manner and place that is *as similar as possible* to the classroom and instructional practices experienced by students without disabilities, that is, the least restrictive environment. In some cases a child's educational needs cannot be reasonably accommodated in a typical setting (e.g., because of significant health or behavioral needs). Placement in the general education classroom may not be feasible, and therefore it is not the least restrictive environment *at that time*. For most preschool children with disabilities, however, placement and learning in a general early childhood education (ECE) classroom can be both reasonable and feasible.

STATUS OF INCLUSIVE EARLY CHILDHOOD EDUCATION IN THE UNITED STATES

A 2011 U.S. Department of Education report provides statistics on the numbers of children ages 3 through 5 in each state receiving special education services through Part B of IDEA in inclusive or "other" settings (U.S. Dept. of Education, 2012). These data also describe the numbers of students in inclusive settings who received special education services in those settings or received them elsewhere. Using these data it is possible to calculate the percentage of preschool children with disabilities who received special education services within regular early childhood settings. For all special education preschoolers eligible for Part B services (745,954 children), approximately 62% spent some time in a regular education setting, but only 42% receive special education *services* in those settings.

Closer examination of these data reveals great variations across states. The percentage of preschoolers with special needs in each state who receive services in their inclusive setting ranges from as low as 9% to as high as nearly 90%. Reasons are not provided for why 42% of children do not attend a regular education setting or, if they do attend a regular education setting, why there is such variability in whether they receive special education services in those settings or receive them elsewhere (e.g., clinics, home, segregated special education classroom). However, one might speculate that it is due to the kinds of challenges discussed in this book. It is surely also related to the choices and commitments of state and local education decision makers to not only make inclusive placement options available but also to provide *appropriate services and supports* in those environments.

More than a decade ago, Bricker (2000) was one of the first to identify several challenges of inclusive preschool education, particularly related to the lack of teacher skills in collaboration and the importance of providing appropriate and effective supports. Those challenges continue.

The following essay is written by Karen Spinelli, mother of Luke Spinelli, an independent young man who has Down syndrome. Luke has his own YouTube channel and currently attends college. Karen recalls the many fears and questions she had when Luke was a baby. She worried about what Luke's disability would mean for his future. She reflects on how one teacher's early encouragement about inclusive education influenced the trajectory of Luke's life.

I Believe in Inclusion: A Lifelong Pursuit!

My name is Karen Spinelli, better known as "Luke's mom." My son Luke has Down syndrome. At age 22 Luke is fully included in most every aspect of his life. Full inclusion for me is a lifelong pursuit; it has been my guiding light in raising Luke. Currently, Luke is living at home, attending college, doing his chores, riding his bike, working out at the YMCA, visiting his girlfriend, pursuing his acting career, and applying for a volunteer position at the YMCA. He is working on his independent living skills, because he wants to have his own apartment, with an office, and his own refrigerator. At this very moment, all of his support system is working in harmony (amazing!). Luke is surrounded by people who believe he is capable.

When Luke was a baby, his early intervention teacher Brenda came to our home once a week. While Brenda sat on the rug, working with Luke to help him reach his first developmental milestones, she educated me on *inclusion* and *advocacy*. I learned that part of the philosophy of inclusion is the belief that all children must be valued equally and that advocacy entails being the voice for someone who does not have a voice.

Before I had Luke, I had never interacted with a person with disabilities. I grew up in a community that segregated people with disabilities. The philosophy of inclusion and valuing the "disabled" was a slow awakening for me.

Week after week Brenda would sit with Luke, working and playing with him, while I bombarded her with questions about "people with disabilities." The following is my recollection of that conversation:

Karen: "Do people with Down syndrome ever get married?"

Brenda: *"Yes, they do. They have all the hopes and dreams for their lives as we do for our lives."*

Karen: "Where do children with disabilities go when typical kids are in school?"

Brenda: *"The Individuals with Disabilities Education Act requires public schools to make available to all eligible children with disabilities a free appropriate public education in the least restrictive environment, appropriate to their individual needs. All children, regardless of their disabilities, should be able to go to their neighborhood school, and be educated with their neighbors, siblings, and friends.*

(continued)

(continued)

Karen: "What good does it do someone with a disability to be in a classroom if he can't do the assignments?"

Brenda: *"A lot is learned in a classroom. How to behave, how to interact with your peers, as well as school work. Just because a child learns differently does not justify segregation from his or her peers. Children can be taught with a modified curriculum and specific adaptations that address their individual learning needs and strengths. Typical students learn from their peers who have disabilities too. It is a win-win environment."*

Karen: "What will Luke do when he is an adult?"

Brenda: *"Well, what do adults do? Most likely, Luke will work; he'll go to the gym, to the movies, out to dinner, on vacations; he'll live with roommates or his wife; he'll go to family functions; and he will be a contributing member to his community."*

As I processed Brenda's answers, inclusion not only made sense to me, it gave me hope and direction. I knew I wanted it for Luke! When Luke started preschool I was surprised when I discovered that many teachers and administrators did not seem to understand the concept of inclusion. I was shocked to realize how much time and money and energy was spent on trying to keep Luke segregated. In preschool, kindergarten, and first grade we fought legal battles for Luke to be fully included. While we won those battles, I was not prepared for the hostility of the administration and school staff. It was frightening and confusing to me to witness how angry and threatened grown typical people can become when asked to include a child with a disability. I wanted to be a voice for inclusion in education. I passionately believed in it, but it felt like I was offering up my son as a sacrifice.

Facing another guaranteed legal battle as Luke was entering second grade made me reconsider my approach. I was heartbroken when I realized Luke's school district would not implement an inclusion support plan without a battle every year. So Luke was placed in a special education classroom, and I turned my efforts and energies for inclusion outside of the school environment. After meeting with the owners of an afterschool program, and the pastor of a Sunday "kids church," I found daily non-school environments where Luke would be fully included with his typical peers. I was thankful to discover adults in our community who believed that everyone would benefit from Luke being a part of their programs. How great it would have been if Luke's teachers and administrators felt the same way.

As I look back, I am eternally grateful for the people who mentored me when Luke was a baby and a toddler. They were the visionaries who set Luke and me on our path. My lifetime goal for Luke is to become a tax-paying citizen. I believe the way to achieve that goal is with the support of inclusive communities and schools.

—Karen Spinelli
November 30, 2011

Luke's story began in the 1990s. Many of the challenges described by his mother are still common. It is our hope that this book can provide helpful information and strategies for meeting those challenges. While the focus here is on preschool education, it sets the stage for lifelong advocacy and success for individuals of any age to pursue opportunities for inclusive schools and communities. Karen Spinelli's essay personalizes the great possibilities supported by a law enacted nearly 40 years ago. The essay also describes challenges and barriers that continue to be encountered by many families who request inclusive placement.

The concept of an inclusive life and community is not defined by school classroom placement. Many families find that at various points in their children's lives, a specialized placement is the best choice. As Karen pointed out, despite her disappointments regarding early educational placement, the concept of *inclusion* gave her hope and direction. An inclusive life *is* a lifelong pursuit.

THE EARLY EDUCATION MOVEMENT AND INCLUSION

During nearly three decades of legal and philosophical support for preschool inclusion, there has simultaneously been a renewed nationwide emphasis on the importance of ECE for young children who are at risk for school failure. Concerns regarding school readiness date back to the 1960s with the Economic Opportunity Act of 1964 (PL 88-452) and the beginning of the Head Start movement in the United States.

The achievement gap for low-income students in the United States continues to increase (Murane & Duncan, 2011). There is overwhelming evidence that the experiences of the first five years of life greatly influence a child's educational achievement trajectory. The achievement gap, which already exists at entry to kindergarten, does not decrease with years of formal schooling, and it may actually increase (Reardon, 2011). This makes a compelling argument for high quality early educational experiences for all young children, not just for children with disabilities. Lipsky and Gartner (2001) pointed out that early childhood educational practices provide unique opportunities to influence the learning and development of all children, with and without disabilities. It is also the case that many "generic" teaching strategies that are very effective for young children with disabilities (described later in this text) are equally effective for preschool children without disabilities, thus meeting the standard for universal design for learning (UDL).

In 2009, a joint position statement in support of early childhood inclusion was published by the Council for Exceptional Children, Division for Early Childhood, and the National Association of Education of Young Children (DEC/NAEYC, 2009). This statement defines early childhood inclusion as follows:

> Early childhood inclusion embodies the values, policies, and practices that support the right of every infant and young child and his or her family, regardless of ability, to participate in a broad range of activities and contexts as full members of families, communities, and society. The desired results of inclusive experiences for children with and without disabilities and their families include a sense of belonging and membership, positive social relationships and friendships, and development and learning to reach their full potential. The defining features of inclusion that can be used to identify high quality early childhood programs and services are access, participation, and supports. (p. 2)

This statement reflects a strong commitment, on the part of both early childhood educators and early childhood special educators, to collaborate and advocate for high quality and inclusive early education.

The following excerpt stands in contrast to Luke's experience described earlier. Lisa's mother Christina tells a very different story of her first experiences with preschool inclusion.

Christina and Lisa

The one practice that I felt was central to making this experience a positive one for Lisa (and for our family) was the focus on the progress Lisa was making rather than comparing her skills to the skills of peers. The staff that worked with her (classroom staff, special education consultant, speech-language therapist) praised Lisa's efforts even if they fell short compared to her peers. Their focus was what she could do, not what she could not do. Equally important, they shared those triumphs, no matter how small, with me. Those triumphs and successes were what carried our family through the challenges and difficult times.

Even though we are years past this preschool inclusion experience, it is still the most significant in my memory. We felt like it was a make or break year in regard to inclusion. In our minds it seemed that if inclusion was not possible this particular year, it would have been next to impossible to attempt it the following years on an elementary school campus. (I am not sure if this was a valid assumption, but it was how we felt at the time.) I believe it also stands out in my mind because of the remarkable way the team came together to support Lisa and help her succeed in the general education classroom. At the end of the school year at the final parent-teacher conference, the general education teacher told me that the year had been an important learning experience for her, too, and in the end she felt that she wasn't teaching a child with a disability. She was teaching a child who had a different learning style. How profound!

INCLUSIVE SETTINGS AND SERVICES

One of the most striking observations about preschool inclusion from program to program is the variability in whether and how supports are provided in various settings. A study by Odom et al. (1999) described the characteristics of 10 inclusive early childhood programs. Descriptions of these programs revealed that they varied significantly on many characteristics. This qualitative study described the programs in terms of two dimensions: organizational contexts and service delivery characteristics. These descriptions, summarized as follows, are still relevant and useful today.

Organizational context (settings):

1. Community-based child care: private or publicly funded

2. Head Start program: funds administered by Head Start agency

3. Public school: school district ECE and/or ECSE program; public school–Head Start collaborative or public school child care

4. Dual enrollment: ECE program during part of the day and specialized program for other parts of the day

Service delivery models for inclusion support:

While the terminology (in italics) used in that early study was somewhat different from the labels used today, they describe familiar models, including the following:

1. Itinerant–direct service: *pull-out* or *push-in.*

2. Itinerant-collaborative: *collaborative consultation.*

3. Team teaching: *co-teaching.*

4. ECE: Early childhood teacher has responsibility for the class; there is no special education support (*dump and hope*).

5. ECSE: Early childhood special education teacher has primary responsibility for a special education class; children without disabilities are brought into the class (*reverse mainstreaming*).

6. Integrative or inclusive activities: Children with disabilities and children without disabilities join together for specific activities, such as recess (*social mainstreaming*).

   Chapters 2 and 3 consider in more detail many of these service delivery and organizational components of preschool inclusion described by Odom et al. (1999). One of the challenges to the discussion of preschool inclusion is a lack of consistency in terminology. It is important that ECE and ECSE communities be able to have meaningful conversations about the possible and most effective administrative and organizational structures, curricula, and support strategy models. In order to describe actual programs and practices and study their effectiveness, it will be important to agree upon concepts, terminology, and definitions that can be used by ECE and ECSE practitioners as well as by researchers to move the field forward and to help ensure inclusive and effective early education practices for all young children.

UNIQUE CHALLENGES IN CREATING EFFECTIVE INCLUSIVE EARLY CHILDHOOD PROGRAMS

The field of special education policy and practices has a well-established history and literature describing and encouraging school-age (K–12) inclusion for students with IEPs. Certainly this literature is also applicable to preschool inclusion. However, the endeavor of including children under the age of 5 years with typically developing peers presents several unique challenges not faced in K–12 programs. The challenges included the following:

1. *Lack of access to general education early childhood settings:* State and local education agencies (LEAs) do not typically offer preschool services for 3- and

4-year-olds who do *not* have disabilities. As a result, ensuring a preschool LRE presents the unique challenge of finding an appropriate general education setting.

2. *Lack of parity between ECE and ECSE teachers:* While ECSE teachers must be trained and certified, in the United States, ECE teachers may have less training and no certification.

3. *Differences in core knowledge and philosophy between ECE and ECSE:* While individuals trained in special education have substantial knowledge of disabilities, they may be less experienced with general ECE curricula. Conversely, early childhood educators may have little knowledge and experience with children with disabilities and may be unaccustomed to the intense focus on the needs of individual children.

KEYS TO SUCCESSFUL INCLUSION

It comes as no surprise that the research regarding the keys to successful inclusion are related to finding ways to deal successfully with many of the challenges described earlier. Well over a decade ago, the factors that contribute to successful inclusive education for K–12 education were well documented. For example, Lipsky and Gartner (2001) summarized research related to both educational *practices* and *structures* that characterized effective inclusive schooling.

1. Responsive Instructional Practices

One of the frequently mentioned key elements of effective instructional practices in ECSE is the teacher's ability to read the child's cues to determine interest and motivation. Accurately reading the child's cues enables the teacher to provide teaching support within the child's "zone of proximal development" (Vygotsky, 1986) to determine appropriate language input, and to follow the child's lead (Cook, Klein, & Chen, 2012). Responsive instructional practices employ careful use of ongoing progress monitoring to determine each child's level of understanding and the effectiveness of teaching strategies, activities, and materials. Also important is the teacher's willingness to adapt and individualize curricular approaches. The concept of *integrated curriculum* increases responsiveness to student needs. For older students, Drake and Burns (2004) described integrated curricula as making connections among different areas of subject matter and making connections to real life: understanding that what children learn in school is connected to their daily lives.

This approach is particularly appropriate in early childhood education in that it creates meaningful interesting contexts in which hands-on projects help young children learn language, reading and writing, social skills, math, and scientific inquiry as functional, relevant problem-solving skills. Examples would be studying science by planning and maintaining a fish tank or planting a garden. Biology, reading, drawing, writing, math and measurement, and social collaboration can all be readily incorporated in an interesting, ongoing project. In early childhood education, these are often referred to as *theme-based* or *project* approaches.

(The current trend toward the use of scripted, fixed sequence, prescriptive curricula, which are aggressively marketed by textbook publishers, seems antithetical to the integrated approach and may present challenges to effective individualization of instruction for students with disabilities.)

2. Strategies to Accommodate Specific Barriers to Learning

The use of principles of UDL make it possible to plan for the full range of learners at the beginning of instructional planning, "at the design point ... rather than retrofitting" and modifying instruction and activities after the fact (Lipsky & Gartner, 2001, p. 46). In a perfect world, the planning and processes of providing supports in inclusive settings could be made less labor intensive via the application of principles of UDL. This approach includes several basic principles, which are described in Chapter 6.

3. Creating Supportive Learning Communities

Successful inclusive environments create a climate of interpersonal cooperation and caring and one that values the processes of problem solving and learning together. These values must be explicitly taught and modeled (for both children and adults). Concepts learned are extended and connected to the broader community, furthering the notion of true inclusion.

4. Organizational Structures that Support Heterogeneous Groupings of Students and Create Opportunities for Teaming and Collaboration

According to Lipsky and Gartner (2001, p. 46), such structures support time for teaming and reflection that foster "collaborative approaches to instruction, role-release activities that enable adults to work in a mutually supportive and collaborative manner, and building-based strategies and resource allocations."

Many investigations of the factors related to successful inclusion of preschool children with disabilities have since affirmed Lipsky and Gartner's 2001 findings. For example, Dinnebeil, Pretti-Frontczak, and McInerney (2009) discussed the effectiveness of a collaborative consultation model (as opposed to a direct service itinerant pull-out model) of inclusion support (see also Ruble, Dalrymple, & McGrew, 2010). Several factors were related to successful early childhood consultation:

- A thorough understanding of early childhood development and developmentally appropriate practice

- Availability of joint planning time

- Ability of the consultant to engage in role release, that is, sharing responsibilities across disciplines and key players

- Use of effective coaching and feedback strategies

- Use of distributed practice and embedded learning opportunities in the early childhood classroom

- High level of knowledge and skill regarding disabilities

- Clear specification of the roles and responsibilities of each stakeholder: Typical stakeholders that may have important roles in supporting young children with disabilities include the following:

  - Administrators

  - ECE teachers

  - ECSE teachers/consultants

  - Families

  - Disability service providers:

    - Speech-language pathologist

    - Assistive technology specialist (e.g., augmentative and alternative communication [AAC])

    - Behavior specialist

    - Occupational therapist

    - Physical therapist

    - Disability-specific specialists in:

      - Hearing impairment

      - Visual impairment

      - Autism

The importance of working collaboratively with all key players, including families and service providers, in order to meet the needs of learners is a repeated theme. The key to this, as found in Lipsky and Gartner's 2001 review, is the availability of joint planning time. This is an example of the kind of factor that can be influenced by the willingness of an administrator or director to set policy guidelines that are supportive of successful inclusion practices.

OUTCOMES OF INCLUSIVE EDUCATION

Reviews of the effectiveness of inclusive education across ages and disabilities consistently suggest that students learn equally well or better in inclusive settings. (See, for example, a recent review by Bui et al., 2010.) In addition, there is no evidence for a negative effect on students *without* disabilities. Several studies have found that young children without disabilities who have had positive experiences in inclusive settings develop more positive attitudes toward persons with disabilities. (See Diamond & Innes, 2001, for review.) More often than not, the challenges of inclusive classrooms are not the students with disabilities but the adults who must work together on their behalf.

Outcomes for Students with Severe Disabilities

Many assumptions are made regarding the inclusion of children with complex and intensive needs in typical early childhood settings. For example, it may seem logical to assume that children with severe disabilities will be less successful in inclusive settings than children with less severe needs and that their learning needs can be better met in segregated, small group settings. Many assume that their presence in a typical ECE setting will be very disruptive, and very expensive. A qualitative study by Cross, Traub, Hutter-Pishgahi, and Shelton (2004) used in-depth interviews of teachers, parents, ECSE personnel, and therapists to examine factors related to successful inclusion of young children with severe and complex disabilities. The results of this study emphasized the importance of the following:

- Positive attitudes and willingness to build on a child's strengths.

- The challenge and importance of communication among all key players, including the therapist's communication with the team, and finding effective ways to ensure parents are always in the loop.

- Parents' opportunities for shared participation and active partnerships with classroom staff and service providers (Study authors pointed out that this partnership was actually easier and more likely to occur when the child had more complex needs. Teachers and therapists readily acknowledge that the parents' knowledge of their child's specific strengths, needs, and unique characteristics is essential to their own expertise to provide support for learning and development.)

- Therapists' willingness and ability to provide services within daily routines rather than using a pull-out model.

- Specification of individual and team responsibility for determining IEP goals, with a focus on functional goals—identifying each person's role in planning, training key staff, and implementing specific classroom adaptations.

Rafferty, Piscitelli, and Boettcher (2003) examined outcomes for children with severe and "not severe" disabilities who received services in inclusive ECE settings compared with segregated ECSE programs. (While both groups of children had disabilities, those children categorized as "severe" performed more than two standard deviations below the mean on developmental assessments.) The findings are thought provoking: Children with *more* severe disabilities achieved higher language and social post-test achievement scores in the inclusive setting. Children with less severe disabilities achieved comparable gains in both settings. The researchers concluded the following regarding the keys to successful inclusion: "For inclusion to be successful, program quality must be high, and appropriate services must be provided. A lack of needed supports and services deprive not only the student with special needs but also the rest of the class" (p. 478).

Purcell, Horn, and Palmer (2007) examined the factors that supported the initiation and continuation of inclusive preschool programs. Key factors related to initiation of programs were often pressure provided by parents for inclusive opportunities for their child or impetus from special projects, external supports, and specialized staff training. Other important factors were federal, state, and local policy guidelines, such as those inspired by LRE legal mandates and Head Start policies.

Several factors were related to the successful continuation of inclusive programs. Especially important were collaborative relationships. True collaboration arose partly from a program's shared vision. Such a vision was found to evolve over time as programs adapted to include the views of all participants. Another important observation was that certain kinds of organizational structures were needed to support collaborations. These included clear interagency agreements, opportunities to share resources, and adequate time to engage in team communication.

The Role of Administrators in Inclusion

Another critical factor in the success of inclusion programs is administrator support and leadership, including administrators' willingness to think outside the box. It is clear that administrators play a critical role in determining the success or failure of inclusive programs (Praisner, 2003). The most commonly litigated area of education is related to violation of FAPE and LRE mandates within special education (Katsiyannis & Herbst, 2004). McLaughlin (2009, p. 4) described several things that every principal needs to know about special education. Several of these points are relevant to the topics in this book:

- The intent of LRE as described in IDEA is not about "cookie cutter programs and performance compliance."

- Effective special education must be truly individualized and match instruction to each student's learning characteristics and needs.

- Special education is "neither a place nor a program" but services and supports "tailored to the needs of individual students so they can make progress in the general education curriculum."

- Principals must know how to "create the conditions within schools ... that integrate special education into all aspects of school improvement. ... Times have changed. Principals are responsible for improvement of all students."

Chapter 3 discusses these important administrator roles and strategies in more detail.

Finally, it should be pointed out that many of the factors identified as critical to the success of inclusive education have been often reported as critical to success for all children and are not uniquely important only for students with disabilities. See Hattie (2009) for a synthesis of meta-analyses examining the influences of inclusion on educational achievement.

WHAT *IS* INCLUSION SUPPORT?

The research and practice literature in early childhood special education offers much information and discussion related to 1) the social value of inclusion in ECE, 2) the legal mandates, 3) children's relative performance in segregated versus inclusive sites, and 4) the factors related to effective inclusive education. Several of these topics have been considered previously. What is less available, however, are discussions and resources that address the array of specific strategies, creative problem-solving approaches, and configurations of key stakeholder relationships. How can these be used on a day-to-day basis to actually support children in inclusive early childhood settings? How can individualized inclusive services and supports, critical to the developmental and academic progress of young children who have disabilities, be provided in ways that are programmatically feasible, effective, and efficient?

Experts in the field of special education inclusion make the point that inclusive education can be effective only when appropriate supports are available. However, there is no single right way to create inclusive environments and provide inclusion supports and services. A review by Etscheidt (2006) of litigation related to preschool FAPE and LRE challenges is a testament to this point. One of the conclusions drawn was that a full continuum of options must be available and considered in each case and that administrators and IEP teams need to be flexible in ways that create truly individualized services for students.

As described earlier in this chapter, Odom and colleagues (1999) examined several inclusive ECE programs. Among those programs were many different organizational structures and service delivery models. No two were exactly alike. It is safe to say that there may be as many different designs for inclusive early childhood education as there are programs. There is no one "right" inclusive program design: one size does not fit all. This should encourage teams working in inclusive early childhood settings to create the "just right" organizational configurations and service delivery models to meet the unique needs of children and adults in their program.

Early Childhood Research Institute on Inclusion: Synthesis Points

In the late 1990s, a major longitudinal study was funded by the U.S. Department of Education to investigate the challenges and characteristics of preschool inclusion. A comprehensive study conducted throughout the United States was undertaken by researchers from five universities: San Francisco State University, the University of Maryland, the University of North Carolina, the University of Washington, and Vanderbilt University. These researchers formed the Early Childhood Research Institute on Inclusion. Their research and experiences with 16 inclusive preschool programs over the course of several years (Wolery & Odom, 2000) created an administrator's guide to inclusive preschool programs and included the following "synthesis points" describing inclusion at the preschool level. As communities consider implementing inclusive programs at the preschool level, these eight points are critical considerations as a vision is created and action planning proceeds.

ECRII synthesis point 1: Inclusion is about belonging and participating in a diverse society.

- Inclusion is not just a school issue; it extends to the communities in which children and their families live.

- Inclusion is not only a disability issue; all children and families have a right to participate and to be supported in the schools and community.

ECRII synthesis point 2: Individuals define inclusion differently.

- Definitions of inclusion are influenced by the varied priorities, responsibilities, and natures of the ecological systems.

- People within the same system (e.g., one school, school district) may have extremely different views of inclusion.

ECRII synthesis point 3: Beliefs about inclusion influence its implementation.

- The beliefs about schooling that families and professionals bring with them to the classroom influence how inclusive practices are planned and implemented; these beliefs are influenced by many complex factors.

- Beliefs about human diversity, that is, culture, race, language, class, and ability, influence how inclusion is implemented in schools and communities.

ECRII synthesis point 4: Programs, not children, have to be ready for inclusion.

- The staff of most of the successful inclusive programs observed view inclusion as the starting point for all children.

- Inclusion can be appropriate for all children; making it work depends on planning, training, and support.

ECRII synthesis point 5: Collaboration is the cornerstone of effective inclusive programs.

- Collaboration among adults, including professionals and parents, within and across systems and programs, is essential to inclusive programs.

- Collaboration among adults, from different disciplines and often with different philosophies, is one of the greatest challenges to successful implementation of inclusive programs.

ECRII synthesis point 6: Specialized instruction is an important component of inclusion.

- Participation in a community-based or general education setting is not enough; the individual needs of children with disabilities must be addressed in an inclusive program.

- Specialized instruction can be delivered through a variety of effective strategies, many of which can be embedded in the ongoing classroom activities.

ECRII synthesis point 7: Adequate support is necessary to make inclusive environments work.

- Support includes training, personnel, materials, planning time, and ongoing consultation.

- Support can be delivered in different ways, and each person involved in inclusion may have unique needs.

ECRII synthesis point 8: Inclusion can benefit children with and without disabilities.

- The parents of children without disabilities whose children participate in inclusive programs often report beneficial changes in their children's confidence, self-esteem, and understanding of diversity.

- High-quality early childhood programs form the necessary structural base for high-quality inclusive programs; thus, all benefit from them.

These key points generated by the extensive body of research and syntheses described so clearly by Odom and his colleagues in the Early Childhood Research Institute on Inclusion (ECRII) project more than a decade ago continue to provide a road map that points the way to designing *successful* inclusive preschool classrooms and systems of support.

PHILOSOPHY OF THIS TEXT

The perspective and philosophy of this text center around the following assumptions:

- A child placed in an inclusive setting must receive appropriate, effective supports.

- Successful inclusion can be challenging and complex, sometimes because of the characteristics of the child but more often because of the characteristics of adults.

- Successful inclusion requires good-faith engagement and problem solving.

- There are many ways to plan and implement effective early childhood inclusive education.

- When a serious, informed collaborative effort is made to find effective and feasible individual solutions, everyone wins.

- Whether a young child can be successfully included is greatly determined by the adults' collaborative creativity and problem solving.

Preschool inclusion, with the right ingredients and a true spirit of inclusivity for all, can be a highly rewarding endeavor for children and adults alike. The schematic in Figure 1.1 attempts to represent the various components of successful inclusion, including the following:

- *IEP process* to ensure LRE and FAPE

- *Organizational structure* of the inclusive program and *support service delivery models*, for example, consultation, co-teaching, and so forth

- *Classroom organization* and assignment or deployment of personnel

- *Key players*, including families and their roles and *mechanisms for problem solving (e.g., key player communication and collaboration) and specialized service provider roles and interfaces*

- *Curriculum modifications and adaptations* (academic and developmental), including simple and practical embedded instruction

The goal of this text is to serve as a comprehensive resource related to the challenges and solutions commonly associated with each of these components.

The chapters in this book present evidence-based, experience-based, practical ideas and ways of approaching each of these important components. Chapters 2–4 look at the basic components of inclusion support: models of inclusion support, the important role of administrators, and the IEP team and the family perspective. Chapter 5 analyzes the barriers as well as the effective practices associated with

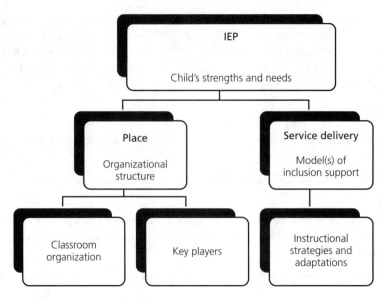

Figure 1.1.   Key components of planning for inclusive preschool education. *Key:* IEP, individualized education program.

collaborative communication, conflict resolution, and problem solving. Chapters 6–9 consider a wide range of specific teaching and support strategies. Chapter 6 presents a review of well-established general (generic) strategies that work with all learners. Chapter 7 presents disability-specific interventions and support strategies for success in inclusive settings (for students with visual impairments, physical disabilities, autism, and deafness). Chapter 8 presents an overview of positive behavior support approaches and implementation. Finally, Chapter 9 considers the important challenges to preschool teachers as they prepare children with disabilities for the critical transition to kindergarten.

While well aware of the challenges of preschool inclusion, the authors of this text can attest to something very magical that happens in those classrooms where skilled and caring adults, who celebrate diversity, are committed to truly inclusive teaching and learning for all children.

REFERENCES

Americans with Disabilities Act (ADA) of 1990, PL 101-336, 42 U.S.C. §§ 12101 *et seq.*

Bricker, D. (2000). Inclusion: How the scene has changed. *Topics in Early Childhood Special Education, 20,* 14–19.

Bui, X., Quirk, C., Almazan, S., & Valenti, M. (2010). *Inclusive education research and practice: Inclusion works.* Hanover, MD: Maryland Coalition for Inclusive Education. Retrieved from http://www.mcie.org

Cook, R., Klein, M.D., & Chen, D. (2012). *Adapting early childhood curricula for children with special needs* (8th ed.). Upper Saddle River, NJ: Pearson.

Cross, A.F., Traub, E.K., Hutter-Pishgahi, L., & Shelton, G. (2004). Elements of successful inclusion for children with significant disabilities. *Topics in Early Childhood Special Education, 24*(3), 169–183.

DEC/NAEYC. (2009). *Early childhood inclusion: A joint position statement of the Division for Early Childhood (DEC) and the National Association for the Education of*

Young Children (NAEYC). University of North Carolina at Chapel Hill. FPG Child Development Institute.

Diamond, K.E., & Innes, F.K. (2001). The origins of young children's attitudes toward peers with disabilities. In M. Guralnick (Ed.), *Early childhood inclusion: Focus on change* (pp. 159–177). Baltimore, MD: Paul H. Brookes Publishing Co.

Dinnebeil, L., Pretti-Frontczak, K., & McInerney, W. (2009). A consultative itinerant approach to service delivery: Considerations for the early childhood community. *Language-Speech Hearing Services in Schools, 40*, 435–445.

Drake, S.M., & Burns, R.C. (2004). *Meeting standards through integrated curriculum.* Alexandria, VA: Association for Supervision and Curriculum Development.

Duncan, G.J., & Murnane, R.J. (2011). *Whither opportunity? Rising inequality, schools, and children's life chances.* New York, NY: Russell Sage.

Economic Opportunity Act of 1964, PL 88-452, 42 U.S.C. §§ 2701 *et seq.*

Education for All Handicapped Children Act of 1975, PL 94-142, 20 U.S.C. §§ 1400 *et seq.*

Education of the Handicapped Act Amendments of 1986, PL 99-457, 20 U.S.C. §§ 1400 *et seq.*

Etscheidt, S. (2006). Least restrictive and natural environments for young children with disabilities: A legal analysis of issues. *Topics in Early Childhood Special Education, 26*(3), 167–178.

Hattie, J. (2009). *Visible learning: A synthesis of over 800 meta-analyses relating to achievement.* London: Routledge.

Individuals with Disabilities Education Act (IDEA) of 1990, PL 101-476, 20 U.S.C. §§ 1400 *et seq.*

Individuals with Disabilities Education Act Amendments (IDEA) of 1997, PL 105-17, 20 U.S.C. §§ 1400 *et seq.*

Katsiyannis, A., & Herbst, M. (2004). Minimize litigation in special education. *Intervention in School and Clinic, 40*, 106–110.

Lipsky, D.K., & Gartner, A. (2001). Education reform and early childhood inclusion. In M.J. Guralnick (Ed.), *Early childhood inclusion: Focus on change* (pp. 39–48). Baltimore, MD: Paul H. Brookes Publishing Co.

McLaughlin, M.J. (Ed.). (2009). *What every principal needs to know about special education.* Thousand Oaks, CA: Corwin Press.

Odom, S., Horn, E.M., Marquart, J.M., Hanson, M.J., Wolfberg, P., Beckman, P., … Sandall, S. (1999). On the forms of inclusion: Organizational context and individualized service models. *Journal of Early Intervention, 22*(3), 185–199.

Praisner, C.L. (2003). Attitudes of elementary school principals toward the inclusion of students with disabilities. *Exceptional Children, 69*(2), 135–145.

Purcell, M.L., Horn, E.H., & Palmer, S. (2007). A qualitative study of the initiation and continuation of preschool inclusion programs. *Exceptional Children, 74*(1), 85–99.

Rafferty, Y., Piscitelli, V., & Boettcher, C. (2003). Impact of inclusion on language development and social competence among preschoolers with disabilities. *Exceptional Children, 69*(4), 467–479.

Reardon. S.F. (2011). The widening academic achievement gap between the rich and the poor: New evidence and possible explanations. In G. Duncan, & R.J. Murnane, (Eds), *Rising inequality, schools, and children's life chances* (pp. 91–116). New York, NY: Russell Sage.

Ruble, L.A., Dalrymple, N.J., & McGrew, J.H. (2010). The effects of consultation on individualized education program outcomes for young children with autism: The collaborative model for promoting competence and success. *Journal of Early Intervention, 32*(4), 286–301.

Sindelar, P.T., Shearer, D.K., Yendol-Hoppey, D., & Liebrt, T.W. (2006). The sustainability of inclusive school reform. *Exceptional Children, 72*, 317–331

U.S. Dept. of Education, Office of Special Education Programs. (2012). *Part B, Individuals with Disabilities Education Act, implementation of FAPE requirements, 2008.* Retrieved from http://www.ideadata.org

Winzer, M.A., & Mazurek, K. (1998). *Special education in multicultural contexts.* Upper Saddle River, NJ: Prentice Hall.

Wolery, R.A., & Odom, S.L. (2000). *An administrator's guide to preschool inclusion.* Chapel Hill, NC: FPG Child Development Institute.

Models of Inclusion Support

Kathleen C. Harris, Ph.D.

This chapter defines various components and types of **inclusion** support and provides examples of common inclusion support service delivery models. (The definitions of bolded terms may be found in the glossary at the end of this chapter) A basic premise of this chapter is that developmentally appropriate preschool and child care center activities and practices can produce effective instruction for many children with disabilities if the activities are appropriately adapted and delivered by collaborative teams of early childhood and special educators.

Early in the discussion of inclusive education, Winzer and Mazurek (1998, p. 103) offered this description: "Inclusive schools begin with a philosophy and vision that all children belong and learn in the mainstream of school and community life. The classroom is seen as a community where diversity is valued and celebrated and all children work, talk, cooperate and share." If one accepts this premise, that children with disabilities belong in the mainstream of school and community life, then the inescapable responsibility of educators and policy makers is to identify and carefully plan effective individualized supports to increase the likelihood of each child's success, and then determine an effective system or model for delivering that support. How children with disabilities get the support they need through collaborative teams of educators is the subject of this chapter.

Trying to identify and describe the various models of inclusion support for very young children with special needs is a challenging and complex task. This is related primarily to some of the unique factors discussed in Chapter 1. Public schools do not typically house educational programs for preschool children who do *not* have disabilities. Often there are no readily available general education programs with which to create the inclusive education partnership within the public school district. As a result, a variety of creative administrative models and district–community partnerships has emerged. Examples of general education preschool partners include community-based Head Start programs, family day care, private preschools, and state and local early education and care programs. There are also examples of public-school-district-sponsored inclusive early education programs.

Beyond the search for partners—hopefully, once partners are found—a particularly important dimension of preschool inclusion, and the focus of this chapter, is the *model of service delivery*. How are the support services configured and delivered? This chapter will describe examples of common configurations. However, the reader should keep in mind that there are potentially as many different "models" of inclusion support service delivery as there are creative individualized education program (IEP) teams. Variable features of these service delivery configurations include the following:

- Number of key players

- Number of adults in the room on behalf of target child

- Whether they interact directly with the child

- Whether they use a pull-out model or push-in model of service delivery

- How and whether they interact with nontarget children

- How and whether they interact directly with the classroom teacher

- How and whether service providers interact and communicate with each other

Grisham-Brown, Hemmeter, and Pretti-Frontczak (2005) reported that the most common inclusive configurations in the United States for preschool children with disabilities are blended inclusive programs, in which children's individual learning needs are met within a preschool curriculum used for all the children in the inclusive program. The term *blended* often (though not always) refers to some version of a program in which two groups of preschool children—those with special needs and typically developing children—are combined in one classroom. However, the administrative responsibilities, staffing, and the particular ways in which support services are provided vary greatly. This chapter aims to provide terminology and examples that describe these different kinds of support models.

WHAT IS INCLUSION SUPPORT?

The primary topic of this book is "preschool inclusion support." As described in Chapter 1, much has been written about the importance and effectiveness of inclusion of young children with their typical same-age peers. The research has consistently demonstrated that students—with and without disabilities—generally do as well, or better, both academically and socially, in inclusive settings (ECTAC, 2010) The federally mandated **least restrictive environment** for teaching children with disabilities does not refer to a building or a particular classroom. Rather, it refers to the whole package of educational and social supports and teaching strategies, which are used to ensure access to the core curriculum as well as students' participation in schooling with their same-age peers. Equally important for preschoolers is the support for important developmental and social-emotional goals. The key to successful inclusion is adequate and competent support.

What are the various kinds of supports used in inclusive classrooms to ensure that each student with an IEP is making appropriate progress in that setting? According to the joint position statement on preschool inclusion by the Division for Early Childhood (DEC) and the National Association for the Education of Young Children (NAEYC) (2009), *supports* can refer not only to the instructional strategies, environmental accommodations, and curricular adaptations but also to systemic resources such as professional development, incentives for inclusion, and opportunities for communication and collaboration among families and professionals. Particularly important in this text are models of delivery of support provided through collaboration among educational service providers. Regardless of the type of inclusive program or the setting in which the inclusive program exists, we define inclusion support as the following:

> The service or services, teaching strategies and adaptations, and service delivery system used on behalf of a child with disabilities (referred to as the *target child*) to meet his or her educational and developmental goals while effectively maintaining that child as a full participant in an inclusive environment with same-age peers who do not have disabilities.

This chapter focuses on how support services are configured and delivered, that is, on inclusion support service delivery models. (Chapters 6 through 9 will describe specific examples of teaching strategies, curriculum modifications, disability-specific interventions, and positive behaviors supports that can be used to ensure successful individualized support for each child.)

Defining and Describing Inclusion Support
Service Delivery Models: The Inclusion Tower of Babel

One of the challenges in describing models of inclusion support *service delivery* in early childhood is the lack of a common language or terminology with which to describe variations in kinds of support structures and services. For example the term **co-teaching** typically refers to a general educator (an early childhood education, or ECE, teacher) and a special educator (an early childhood special education, or ECSE, teacher) who share classroom teaching responsibilities equally but who report to different supervisors. However, such an arrangement may also be referred to as a *blended classroom* or a *partner teacher* model. The terms *co-teaching* and *team teaching* are sometimes used to refer to a model in which a special education consultant occasionally teaches a lesson jointly with the classroom general education teacher but does not share equally in classroom responsibilities. **Consultation** models may be referred to as *itinerant* support, *push-in* or *pull-out* services, or *direct* versus *indirect* services. Therapies and other specialized services (typically provided no more than once or twice per week) are sometimes referred to as *designated instructional support* (DIS) services. How DIS service providers actually deliver their services (e.g., direct service, consultation) is also an important variable. For example, in the delivery of speech-language services, one speech-language pathologist (SLP) may use a direct pull-out model, with little communication with the classroom staff. Another SLP may combine a brief pull-out therapy session with in-class observation of the child and a brief consultation with the teacher. A third SLP may use a push-in model providing small group therapy activities to a selected group of children, including children with disabilities, or to the entire classroom.

It is not possible to have a meaningful conversation about possible models and configurations of early childhood inclusion support without a common terminology. Communication among administrators, practitioners, families, and researchers requires definition and precision as we think and talk about the range of possibilities for effective inclusion support.

One of the most thorough and widely used texts on educational consultation and inclusion (Heron & Harris, 2001) has provided helpful definitions of many of the terms used in this text. These can be found in the glossary at the end of this chapter.

Conceptualizing Inclusion Support Service Delivery

One way to differentiate various types of inclusion support is as either **direct** or **indirect.** Direct support involves direct contact and interaction with the child. The following are examples of common *direct* support in ECSE inclusive settings:

- Use of a one-to-one paraeducator assigned to the target child

- Direct teaching by the classroom ECE teacher

- A pull-out speech therapy session provided by the SLP

- Daily discrete trial training provided by a behavior specialist or trained assistant

- Implementation of sensory integration techniques by the occupational therapist within the classroom routine

- Direct assessment of the target child by the ECSE co-teacher for progress monitoring and documentation

In each of these examples, the adult is directly interacting with the child. Often an included child may have many individuals providing direct inclusion support, as represented in Figure 2.1.

    Indirect supports are those provided by one individual (e.g., an ECSE consultant) to a second individual (e.g., the ECE teacher, a parent) who then uses that information or skill to provide direct service to the target child (see Figure 2.2). A consultant may observe a child, read the child's file, obtain information from classroom staff or parents, and provide demonstration or in-service training to the ECE teacher and staff but never directly provide intervention or support to the child.

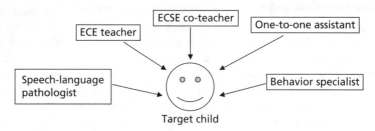

Figure 2.1. Many individuals provide direct inclusion support. *Key:* ECE, early childhood education; ECSE, early childhood special education.

Using Consultation

One common example of indirect support is the provider who works as a collaborative consultant. A consultant is an itinerant, that is, he or she is not permanently housed in the classroom but rather visits the classroom and impacts the target child primarily by providing information and modeling strategies to and engaging

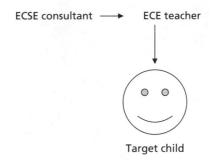

Figure 2.2. Indirect inclusion support. *Key:* ECE, early childhood education; ECSE, early childhood special education.

in problem solving with classroom staff. It is the classroom staff who directly affect the child, but the consultant's knowledge and skill may impact the child indirectly via the classroom staff members' direct efforts.

Consultation may be delivered using either an *expert* approach or a *collaborative* approach. In an expert approach, the consultant assumes the role of an expert who performs evaluation, imparts information, or demonstrates specific strategies for the classroom staff. In expert consultation, communication is fairly one sided. A familiar example of an expert consultant would be a cardiologist. Patients, who usually have limited expertise in heart disease, go to the doctor to receive expert consultation. Rarely is there parity (i.e., equality or mutuality) in the doctor–patient relationship, and there is little true collaboration. The medical specialist provides the information, and the patient receives the information.

In educational settings, however, effective consultation must be reciprocal and collaborative (Heron & Harris, 2001). The consultant has knowledge and expertise that the teacher does not have (for example, disability-specific knowledge or skills related to behavior analysis and management). The teacher similarly has knowledge not immediately available to the consultant. The teacher has knowledge of the classroom routines, the target child's preferences and behaviors in different learning activities, classroom rules, curricular goals, and so on. Both parties have information and expertise that will be critical to the success of the other and to the effectiveness of the consultation in delivering support to the child. They must share this information as co-equals. They must express concerns and opinions honestly, learn from each other, and work together to solve the child's educational challenges. This is referred to as **collaborative consultation.**

Collaborative consultation in education is described as "triadic" (Dettmer, Knackendoffel, & Thurston, 2012) in the sense that two people must collaborate on behalf of the third—the child, who is the recipient of the effects of the collaboration. Figure 2.3 reflects triadic nature, as well as the collaborative, reciprocal nature of *collaborative consultation*. Both adults bring important skills, information, and observations to the teaching effort. Typically the consultant's support of the child is mostly indirect, (i.e., via the teacher), while the teacher's is direct.

Realistically, in ECSE consultation there are elements of both collaborative and expert consultation (Klein, Richardson-Gibbs, Kilpatrick, & Harris, 2001). When an ECSE practitioner provides consultative support, the early childhood or Head Start teacher may have very little expertise in disabilities and relatively less

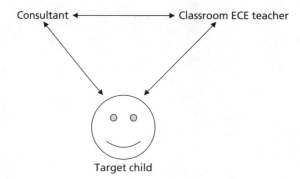

Figure 2.3. Triadic collaborative consultation. *Key:* ECE, early childhood education.

formal training than the ECSE credentialed teacher. Thus, the ECE teacher is often expecting the ECSE consultant to have expertise and solutions related to young children with disabilities and may be disappointed if the ECSE consultant cannot deliver the "expert" support needed. On the other hand, the ECE teacher is the expert on the classroom, the curriculum, and how the target child actually functions across the curriculum and the daily routines. So in this way successful ECSE consultation has elements of both expert and collaborative approaches.

Consultative approaches to inclusion support can have many advantages. As an itinerant service delivery model, they can be used with great flexibility and cost-effectiveness. A co-teacher is typically assigned to one classroom throughout the day. However, it might be the case that the co-teacher is really only needed during certain parts of the day, depending on the specific characteristics of the child, the experience and skill of the ECE teacher, and so forth. Using an itinerant model makes it possible to deploy support personnel when and where they are needed. It has the potential to serve many children and to provide the "just right" amount of support as needed, thus increasing cost-effectiveness. A truly collaborative consultant also enhances the skills and confidence of the consultees. Via the mutual **collaborative relationship,** the skillful consultant increases the skill sets of the ECE teacher and staff. Over time, the intensity of consultant support can be decreased, as classroom staff become more proficient at including students with a wide range of disabilities and learning characteristics.

Table 2.1 lists common ECSE consultation activities, such as carefully observing and assessing child skills and behaviors, training paraeducators, providing information and materials to the ECE teacher, debriefing with the teacher after observing the target child, modifying curriculum, listening to observations and concerns of staff, and so on. These are not direct supports for the child. Rather, they indirectly impact the child via the classroom staff. However, there are also opportunities for direct intervention with the child, for example, when demonstrating (modeling) a particular teaching technique with the target child, assisting the staff with general classroom support if they are short handed, managing a child's temper tantrum, and so forth.

Scenario 1 Let's consider a possible scenario for moving from an *itinerant direct service* model, with an SLP, to an *indirect collaborative consultation*

Table 2.1.   ECSE inclusion consultative support: Common support activities

Consultation activity[a]	Example
Sharing information	Provide written materials describing Down syndrome or give a 15-minute overview of simple communication techniques.
Problem solving	Briefly meet with the teacher and behavior specialist to exchange views and possible solutions to a child's biting.
Observing	Carefully observe the child at different times of the day; provide data recording for ABC analysis as part of a positive behavior support assessment.
Modeling	Demonstrate a successive approximation strategy to encourage the child to gradually tolerate longer time in circle.
Coaching staff	With the paraeducator's permission, observe his or her working with the target child and make ongoing suggestions as well as positive evaluations of the adult's teaching strategies.
Providing direct instruction	For assessment purposes, or to assist staff, teach the target child a new skill, for example, recognizing his or her own name or reducing anxiety about change in classroom location.
Adapting curriculum, materials	Provide examples of more developmentally appropriate ways for the child to access the curriculum; create simple picture choices for choosing a song at circle time.
Adapting the environment	Provide more supportive seating for tabletop activities; arrange classroom activity centers so they are more clearly marked; decrease clutter.
Coaching child peers	Teach peers to use the child's picture communication book to choose a play area; teach peers to use visual script to remind the child to wait for his or her turn.
Assisting classroom staff	Help prepare a snack or lead a small group activity if a regular staff member is absent.
Collaborating with specialists	Make referral to VI specialist for functional vision assessment; obtain information for working with a child who has a cochlear implant.
Involving parents	On behalf of a busy ECE teacher with 20 children in an inclusive classroom, share information with the parent about his or her child's successes and challenges.
Coordinating team meetings	Offer to bring lunch to encourage a problem-solving discussion or encourage group cohesion.

Key: ECE, early childhood education; ECSE, early childhood special education; VI, vision impairment.
[a]See Cook, Klein, and Chen (2012) for more detail related to these activities.

model (Figure 2.4). An ECE teacher is very concerned about the limited language development of Elsie, a 4-year-old included in her preschool class. Elsie has moderate developmental delay and has been receiving 30 minutes per week of pull-out speech therapy services. While the SLP has found her to be uncooperative in the sessions and has recommended discontinuing services, the ECE teacher has found Elsie to be very social in the classroom, though she sometimes becomes frustrated when she cannot make her needs known.

The SLP is busy serving several preschools in the area and has a large caseload, so the ECE teacher and SLP rarely communicate. The ECE teacher arranges a phone conference with the itinerant SLP and describes Elsie's communication in the classroom, her typical activities and routines, and what strategies she has tried to increase Elsie's language skills. The SLP listens carefully and then describes a few other strategies that might be effective. The ECE teacher and the SLP decide on one or two strategies that the ECE teacher will try over the next two weeks.

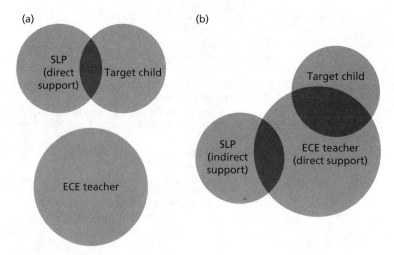

Figure 2.4. Scenario 1: Moving from direct to indirect support. (a) Direct services model; (b) collaborative consultation model. In the direct services model, the SLP provides direct support to the child with no consultation with the ECE teacher. In the collaborative consultation model, the SLP provides consultation support to the ECE teacher, and the teacher works directly with the child. *Key:* ECE, early childhood education; SLP, speech-language pathologist.

The SLP provides the ECE teacher with some materials, shows the teacher how to use them, and offers to meet with him or her in a couple of weeks to see how things are going. The ECE teacher agrees to implement the strategies and observe the effect on Elsie's language.

In this scenario, via some brief problem solving, the SLP and ECE teacher are moving toward a collaborative consultation model of service delivery. The SLP is now providing indirect inclusion support services to the target child through the ECE teacher, using **collaborative problem solving.** The ECE teacher could not provide the service without the support of the SLP, and the SLP could not provide the service without the teacher's information about the day-to-day interactions with the target child. This is a collaborative consultative relationship between the SLP and the ECE teacher.

The activities in scenario 1 also reflect the kinds of activities that are characteristic of a *transdisciplinary team.* Such a team has several characteristics, including a high degree of collaboration and joint decision making among team members and a commitment from members to teach the skills traditionally associated with their own discipline to other team members (Heron & Harris, 2001). In this scenario, the ECE teacher and the SLP collaborated in jointly designing the intervention. The SLP taught language development strategies to the teacher, who provided direct service to the target child. For this interaction to be successful, the ECE teacher and the SLP had to share a common goal and deal with differences in their respective training and orientations.

Collaborative versus Expert Consultation

There are two different ways the consultation between the ECE teacher and SLP in scenario 1 could have occurred: using an expert model or a collaborative model. As mentioned earlier in this chapter, expert consultation is the type of consultation that often occurs between a medical doctor and a patient.

For example, the doctor solicits information from the patient, then, as the expert, writes a prescription for the patient. Using the typical expert model, the patient, who will be responsible for "implementing" the prescription, is not involved in the development of the prescription. The patient may or may not actually comply with the prescription. In contrast, with a collaborative model, after basic information is shared, the parties responsible for implementing any plan of action are active *creators* of that plan of action. If the exchange between the doctor and the patient were collaborative in nature, the doctor might identify several different interventions, and talk with the patient about the possible consequences of each intervention, the patient's lifestyle, and which interventions have the greatest likelihood of success given the patient's lifestyle. The patient would then select the intervention to try and work out a plan of action with the doctor to implement the intervention.

The collaborative model usually results in better compliance in implementing the plan of action because the skills and perspectives of all key players are valued and solicited. A collaborative approach in educational environments has become the desired process over the past several decades. A collaborative approach acknowledges and values different perspectives and establishes buy-in by the implementers of the plan (Heron & Harris, 2001).

In scenario 1, the SLP and the ECE teacher collaborated with one another during the consultation process. If the **indirect service** provider (the SLP) did not get information from the ECE teacher about the target child and the classroom environment, the SLP might not have been able to identify strategies that would work for the target child and that could be implemented by the teacher. If the ECE teacher did not meet with the indirect service provider (SLP) and share information, the direct service provider (ECE teacher) would not have been able to identify and implement possible effective instructional strategies for Elsie. This demonstrates the importance of using a collaborative rather than an expert model of consultation in preschool inclusion support.

Scenario 2 This scenario provides an example of an ECSE consultant and an ECE teacher providing indirect support through a paraeducator who is providing direct support to the target child, Jessie (see Figure 2.5). The paraeducator provides one-on-one assistance to Jessie during activities conducted by the ECE teacher in the inclusive preschool class.

However, the paraeducator has noticed that Jessie has started exhibiting behavior problems during some of the activities in the inclusive preschool class. The paraeducator requests a meeting with the ECSE consultant. The paraeducator describes the problems Jessie is experiencing with cutting and pasting materials. She asks the ECSE consultant for suggestions for what she can do to reduce Jessie's frustration with this activity. The ECSE consultant shares possible strategies that the paraeducator could use to help Jessie have greater success with the task by adapting for sensory issues with the paste and making the cutting task easier. This, in turn, can decrease Jessie's resistance and prevent escalating behavior problems. The ECSE has a brief interaction with both the ECE teacher and the paraeducator in which they decide which of the suggested strategies would be easiest to implement. Jessie will use cotton swabs to spread glue rather than using the squeeze bottles, which he cannot control. Also, the paraeducator will draw thick black lines to help Jessie see where to cut.

The ECE teacher and paraeducator agree to try the new strategies for two weeks. At that point, all three key players (ECE teacher, ECSE consultant, and

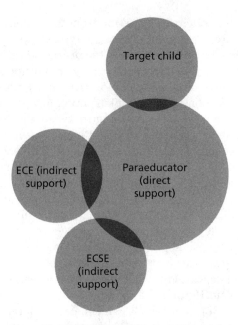

Figure 2.5. Scenario 2: Consultation with paraeducator providing direct support to child. *Key:* ECE,
early childhood education; ECSE, early childhood
special education.

paraeducator) will briefly touch base to check on the effectiveness of these interventions. In scenario 2, the direct service is being provided by the paraeducator,
while both the ECE teacher and ECSE consultant provide indirect support to
Jessie via consultation with the paraeducator.

The Roles of Paraeducators in Inclusion Support

It is clear from the relationships depicted in Figure 2.5 that the primary contact and
direct support for Jessie comes one-to-one from the paraprofessional. There are
obvious advantages with this scenario for those few children who are a danger to
themselves or others or whose disabilities present potential health and safety concerns. However, the use of a VELCRO® aide, as this practice is sometimes called,
can pose serious impediments to the child's true integration and interaction with
peers. It may in the long run interfere with the development of social skills and may
increase a strong dependence upon one individual, which creates its own set of serious challenges.

Even when the IEP team determines that a one-to-one interaction is needed,
the following considerations and guidelines are important:

- The method should be considered only a temporary support model.

- The goal should be for the one-to-one aide to gradually decrease his or her proximity to and direct interaction with the child, focusing on increasing the child's
interactions with peer play partners by using specific, carefully planned interventions toward that goal.

- Clear efforts should be made to increase the target child's comfort level with
other adults by rotating the one-to-one assignment.

In reality, the most common "model" of inclusion support is the use of a one-to-one paraeducator assigned to a particular child in the inclusive classroom. Many paraeducators assume primary responsibilities for assisting children in inclusive environments and sometimes also for data collection used to make decisions regarding the instruction of a child. It is important for the ECE teacher and ECSE co-teacher or consultant to include paraeducators as key members of the instructional team. With proper training and supervision, the use of paraeducator support can be both programmatically effective and cost effective. However, there are many challenges and cautions to consider when working with a one-on-one aide, including the following:

Training: It is not unusual for paraeducators to have little training in working with young children with disabilities. It is important to determine the training and experience of paraeducators working in the inclusive classroom and to provide additional training and information as needed.

Supervisory responsibility and communication: In some cases, the responsibility for supervision of the paraeducator may be unclear. For example, in some states behavior therapy agencies may provide personnel to collect data and implement behavior plans. Thus, the responsibility for supervision is assumed by the agency, rather than the district or the community-based program in which the inclusive classroom is housed (e.g., Head Start). In these situations, lines of communication can be problematic.

Team participation and role definition: The paraeducator can be a very important member of the educational team. Achieving success in this role requires clear communication, problem solving, planning, and developing common philosophies of instruction that include the active participation of the paraeducator. To develop an effective team with paraeducators, consider the following suggestions for teachers offered by Riggs (2004, pp. 8–12):

- Know the paraeducator's name, background, and interests.
- Be familiar with school/facility policies for paraeducators (e.g., can they be paid to attend after school meeting, can they "bank" hours if their child is absent).
- View the teacher(s) and paraeducators as a team.
- Share classroom expectations with paraeducators.
- Clearly define specific roles and responsibilities for paraeducators and teachers.
- Assume responsibility for directing the paraeducator.
- Help the paraeducator get to know all the children even if assigned to only one.
- Communicate clearly with the paraeducator.
- Show respect for the paraeducator's knowledge and experience.

Scenario 3   This scenario provides a complex example. An ECSE classroom co-teacher (who provides direct support in the classroom) will provide indirect in-home consultation to the mother of Dana, one of the target children in the inclusive classroom (Figure 2.6).

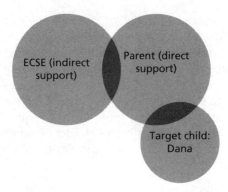

Figure 2.6. Scenario 3: ECSE provides indirect support to Dana via consultation with Dana's mother. *Key:* ECSE, early childhood special education.

The parent tells the ECSE co-teacher about behavior problems she is experiencing at home with Dana. Dana increasingly refuses to transition from activities she enjoys. She has begun to have tantrums at bedtime and sometimes resists leaving her toys when it is time for dinner.

The ECSE co-teacher shares information about Dana's behavior patterns in the classroom and the behavior interventions that have been successful there. She and Dana's mother design a simple positive behavior support plan that will be easy to implement in the home. The mother will increase predictability of certain routines by encouraging Dana's older brother (who Dana adores) to play with her just prior to dinner each evening; then he can provide a positive model to transition to the dinner table. Dana's mother will also create a predictable bedtime routine (which the family does not currently have). It will include Dana's favorite song, then putting pajamas on her bear, and then tucking her and her bear in for the night.

Dana's mother agrees to try it for two weeks and let the ECSE consultant know, via e-mail, how it is working: for example, what is easy or difficult about the intervention, what she has observed, changes she has made in the procedure, and so forth. In this scenario, the ECSE classroom co-teacher provides indirect consultation support to the parent. The parent, in turn, provides direct support to the child via implementation of the procedure at home.

Scenario 4 This scenario provides an example of several key players—an occupational therapist, the SLP, and the ECSE teacher—who provide indirect support to the ECE teacher of the target child (see Figure 2.7). Note that the spheres in Figure 2.7 do not intersect with the target child, but each intersects with the ECE teacher. This suggests that for the most part these individuals observe the child (and may interact briefly with him or her), but the teacher carries out the recommended interventions by embedding certain strategies and practices into the ongoing daily routines and staff interactions with the child.

While many therapists have traditionally preferred a direct pull-out model of service delivery, the scenario depicted here reflects an indirect (consultative) model. Increasingly in preschool settings, therapists are expanding their service delivery models to embrace more collaborative models and a combination of both

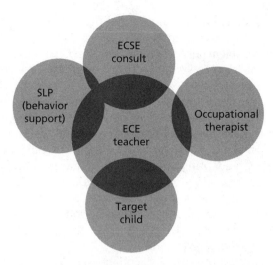

Figure 2.7. Scenario 4: Multidisciplinary collaborative consultation with ECE teacher providing indirect support to child. *Key:* ECE, early childhood education; ECSE, early childhood special education; SLP, speech-language pathologist.

direct (direct therapy) and indirect (teacher consultation) support. Many therapists make sure to use consultation with the classroom teacher to exchange observations regarding the target child. Many have also moved toward more ecologically relevant in-class therapy, a push-in model of service delivery. The ECSE itinerant in this scenario provides primarily indirect consultative support for the child by communicating on a regular basis with the classroom ECE teacher.

All four scenarios depicted in this chapter show how the level of collaboration can become more complex as more adults become involved. In scenario 2, the ECE teacher, ECSE teacher, and paraeducator all work together to identify an effective strategy to implement in the inclusive classroom. This complexity also evolves in scenario 3. Initially the ECSE teacher provides indirect support to the parent. As a result of the collaborative process the parent then provides direct support to the target child at home. Regardless of the nature of the inclusion support, the process used by all adults is the same, that is, collaboration.

COLLABORATION: THE KEY TO MAKING INCLUSION SUPPORT WORK

Regardless of the people, the setting, or the types of inclusion support involved, collaboration is essential. In fact, a synthesis of research on preschool inclusion states that "collaboration is the cornerstone of effective inclusive programs" (Odom, Schwartz, & ECRII, 2002, p. 162). This book defines collaboration as *two or more individuals who jointly develop a program of inclusion support*. The program of inclusion support can involve indirect as well as direct support and should be tailored to meet the needs of the target child.

How does one set the stage for effective collaboration among inclusion support providers? Whether indirect or direct support is being provided to the target child, the providers must have the skills and the opportunity to develop a common philosophy, communicate, problem solve, and plan with one another. Resolution requires more than what just one individual can provide. Applications of effective communication and problem solving are provided in Chapter 5.

It is obvious that inclusion support providers must have the opportunity to communicate. However, time to collaborate is not always incorporated into the daily activities of inclusion support providers. If itinerant professionals such as SLPs schedule time only for direct support of target children in pull-out situations, it is quite possible that they will not have the time and therefore the opportunity to consult with other inclusion support providers who could assist them or who need their assistance in adapting the program for a target child. Similarly, if ECE teachers, ECSE teachers, and paraeducators schedule only direct support time in their daily activities, they may not have the opportunity to collaborate with one another to adapt the program of a target child or collaborate with one another to plan instruction using the most effective support models and teaching strategies for the desired outcomes of a given activity.

It is critically important to establish collaborative relationships and communication that support ongoing problem solving and solutions related to teaching and learning in inclusive settings. Equally important, an ongoing collaborative climate can mitigate potential conflict.

Co-teaching: Joint Instruction Provided by Early Childhood Education and Early Childhood Special Education

A common model of *direct* support for children in inclusive settings is often referred to as *co-teaching*. A variety of terms have been used to refer to the joint instruction provided by a general (ECE) and special educator (ECSE). Examples of these terms include *team teaching* (Friend, Reising, & Cook, 1993; Salend, 2008), cooperative teaching (Hourcade & Bauwens, 2003; Idol, 2006), collaborative teaching (Harris, 1998), and co-teaching (Austin, 2001; Fennick & Liddy, 2001; Scruggs, Mastropieri, & McDuffie, 2007). This chapter uses the term *co-teaching* to refer to the direct service that is provided by the ECE teacher and an inclusion support provider when they instruct the target child together. Co-teaching is defined as two or more adults planning and instructing the same group of students at the same time and in the same place. Co-teaching is often said to have many of the same challenges as marriage!

Planning Co-teaching Structures   There are many components to successful co-teaching, including planning how to arrange the physical environment, the curriculum, and activities. The following sections of this chapter focus on the classroom *structures* that co-teachers can use to instruct jointly. The use of **co-teaching structures** changes as the co-teaching partnership matures. A mature co-teaching relationship is reflected in structures that involve both co-teachers engaged in instruction. With true co-teaching, children perceive the co-teachers as a team, each member of which is equally in charge (Gately & Gately, 2001). The examples of co-teaching structures discussed in the following sections are derived from the following: Hourcade and Bauwens (2003), Friend and Cook (2003), and Walther-Thomas, Korinek, McLaughlin, and Williams (2000).

One Teaching, One Supporting   In this structure, one teacher designs and delivers the activities for all the children. The second teacher (usually the ECSE co-teacher) supports the lead teacher, providing assistance as needed. This is a simple approach used by many new co-teaching partners. It requires that both teachers know the children and the activities, but it does not take a lot of planning by the co-teachers. If this structure is used indiscriminately or exclusively, it often results in the ECSE co-teacher functioning as a "floating" assistant. With this arrangement, typical children in the class are well aware that the ECSE teacher works primarily with certain children who "need help" and is not the "real" teacher. It is not recommended that co-teachers use this structure exclusively.

Station Teaching   This is a common arrangement in early childhood environments. Students move among subject stations set up by the teachers. The co-teachers divide responsibility for monitoring the stations. This method reduces the teacher-child ratio and ensures that the teacher with specific ECSE expertise can lead the station activity that will pose the greatest challenges to certain students. For example, several students will need careful scaffolding or adaptations for the fine motor activity of making fruit loop necklaces; the ECSE co-teacher therefore takes responsibility for that station.

Alternative Teaching   In alternative teaching, one child or a small group of children receive preteaching or reteaching of skills necessary to participate in a specific activity. All co-teachers need to be familiar with the activity and the skills needed to participate in the activity. Together they determine which students will need alternative support for skill development. Alternative teaching can provide the opportunity for children to receive one-to-one or small-group support. However, if the same children (i.e., children with disabilities) consistently receive the one-to-one or small-group support from a special educator (i.e., ECSE or paraeducator), then the co-teaching structure will segregate the target child from his or her peers and will not support real inclusion of children with disabilities. For example, in preparation for "picture day," the co-teachers agree that several of the children with special needs in the class will benefit from some "priming" for the photography experience. The ECSE co-teacher implements this alternative teaching via creation of a new dramatic play center in which all of the children role-play the photography experience.

Complementary Teaching   This co-teaching structure implements a child's specific adaptations during the actual activity. In complementary teaching, the ECE teacher might maintain primary responsibility for implementing the activity and the ECSE teacher or the paraeducator might assume responsibility for addressing the target child's specific goals. For example, a child with quadriplegia seated in a wheelchair has little or no access to prewriting activities such as painting as they are set up in the room. After consultation with the child's physical therapist, several complex adaptations are implemented: the angle and height of the easel, the type of paint brush, a newly designed splint, and a support to elevate the child's arm position. The ECSE co-teacher uses complementary teaching during the art activity for several weeks to work out any bugs in these adaptations and to task analyze the appropriate teaching steps and strategies.

In complementary teaching, all classroom staff are made aware of the activity and the goals, but the special educator takes responsibility to determine how best to support the target child. The adaptations required for the target child are incorporated into the activities done by the whole group of children. Over time, peers may assume some of the responsibility for these more complex supports, and the target child moves toward greater independence.

Supportive Learning Activities   These are educator-developed activities that supplement the primary learning activities. Typically, the early childhood teacher designs the lesson and the ECSE teacher identifies, develops, and leads the additional supportive activities designed to reinforce, enrich, and augment learning a new skill. For example, the ECE teacher might design a science experiment and the ECSE teacher might design specific prompts, materials, and adaptations so that all children, including the target children, can successfully engage in the exploration process. This co-teaching structure does require joint planning by co-teachers. Usually, both the ECE and the ECSE teachers are present and monitor all activities.

Parallel Teaching   In this structure the co-teachers jointly plan instruction, but each delivers it to a heterogeneous group composed of approximately half the children in the class. This approach reduces the teacher-child ratio. However, since parallel teaching requires the co-teachers to implement the same activities, the co-teachers must have comparable skills and must carefully coordinate their efforts. The ECE teacher must feel comfortable and competent in individualizing instruction, and the ECSE teacher must be knowledgeable and effective in teaching the core curriculum. This co-teaching structure is probably best used by ECE and ECSE co-teachers who have developed a strong co-teaching relationship and have the time to plan.

Team Teaching   In this co-teaching structure, both co-teachers jointly plan and present the activities using appropriate instructional strategies for all the children in the class. The two teachers, together, teach the lesson to the whole class. This co-teaching duet involves considerable planning and is particularly effective when the co-teachers possess similar areas of expertise. Team teaching is also best used by co-teachers who have developed a strong co-teaching relationship.

There are many possible co-teaching structures. It is important to realize that these are *instructional tools*. The co-teaching structure that matches the needs of the children and the skills of the co-teachers should be selected for each activity. Therefore, ECE teachers, ECSE teachers, and paraeducators should be familiar with a variety of models. They should also realize that some co-teaching structures require more planning time than do others and that, as their collaboration matures, they will be able to design and use many models effectively to best meet the needs of the students and the particular learning goals. One structure does not fit all!

THE MULTIPLE DIMENSIONS OF INCLUSION SUPPORT

It should be clear from this discussion that effective models of inclusion support are multidimensional. They can be elegantly simple or extremely complex. They can involve just two or three key players or a large entourage of specialists. There is no one best model of inclusion support service delivery. *Effective inclusion support plans are like snowflakes: no two are alike.* Each is unique and designed to meet the needs and strengths of children, communities, and key players.

Each plan must address and consider the following important dimensions of inclusive service delivery:

- Setting

- Costs

- Configuration of support service delivery (e.g., consultation, co-teaching, para-educator, multidisciplinary)

- Total number of key players and their areas of expertise:

  - number of persons interacting with classroom teacher

  - number of persons interacting with target child

- Coordination of services

- Indirect versus direct service delivery and their related lines of communication

- Degree of child access to peers; use of pull-out or push-in services

Figure 2.8 reflects four different examples of these many possibilities.

---

a. District and Head Start partnership

Model: Co-teaching

Setting: Head Start classroom

District cost: ECSE teacher + paraeducator

Structure: SLP and OT intinerant direct in-class support (push-in)

Program coordination: Head Start director and district special education program specialist

---

b. District reverse mainstreaming

Model: ECSE lead teacher

Setting: District specialized class

District cost: Teacher and staff

Structure: Typical peers attend special education class

1 ECSE paraprofessional; 1 ECE paraprofessional

---

c. District provides services (as designated in the IEP) for children attending private preschool programs

Model: Itinerant collaborative consultation

Setting: Wherever child is enrolled, with support requested by parent

District cost: ECSE teacher (serves 20 students)

Program coordination: None—ECSE teacher reports to district special education coordinator

Other services determined by each family's IEP or funded by family (e.g., one-to-one aide from private agency)

---

d. Hybrid examples

Model: ECSE serves as either consultant or co-teacher as necessary (depends on classroom student needs)

Setting: Classrooms, single site, multiple classrooms, morning or afternoon

District cost: ECSE teacher

Program coordination: Contingent on model

Figure 2.8. Administrative configurations and inclusion support service delivery models. *Key:* ECE, early childhood education; ECSE, early childhoold special education; IEP, individualized educational program; OT, occupational therapist; SLP, speech-language pathologist.

Figure 2.9. *Adventures in Zipping* cartoon.

Finally, it is also important to acknowledge one more powerful source of inclusion support: the children in the classroom. One must not underestimate the positive effects of becoming valued, active participants in the classroom community. These positive effects occur for all children—with and without disabilities. (See Diamond and Innes, 2001, for a review.) The design of inclusion support models should enhance rather than impede the target child's opportunities for interactions with peers. The reason for this is delightfully represented in Figure 2.9. Ultimately, as will be discussed in Chapter 5, collaborative communication and problem solving will be the glue that holds the support plan together.

This chapter has set the stage for detailing the ways in which educational personnel in early childhood settings can combine various dimensions to provide direct and indirect inclusion support services. The following vignette is a true story of the journey of two co-teachers, one general education early childhood teacher and one early childhood special educator, toward a truly collaborative relationship. It reflects many of these dimensions.

The Road from Me to We: A Co-Teaching Essay

By Tracy L. Eagle and Babi Gonzalez De Torres

THE BACK STORY

Before *We*

In September 2008, our urban elementary school site housed two preschool "collaborative" inclusion classes. Each combined a pre-K readiness general early childhood class and a preschool special education class. Both classes were short staffed. With only one special education teacher and one special education assistant, the classes were missing a general education co-teacher and a general education assistant. Then the school administrator, beset by budget cuts, determined that much of the special education assistant's time would have to be spent in upper-grade classrooms. To partially compensate for this loss, the administrator hired a substitute teacher to help until a permanent general education preschool teacher could be found. The substitute teacher, Babi, was an early primary grade teacher and did not have preschool experience.

Tracy, the special education teacher, had just interviewed 30 general education students and their parents: 15 students in the morning class and 15 in the afternoon class. The students with special needs would be divided between the earlier and the later classes, creating two inclusive preschool classes with 19 students each. Tracy realized careful planning would be critical with limited personnel. Tracy and the substitute co-teacher would have to lead the learning centers alone, with only occasional help from the special education assistant.

In this district, typically a general education preschool classroom is comprised of one early childhood general education teacher, one general education assistant, and fifteen students. Because programs vary, students may attend preschool from two to six hours each day. The general education preschool classroom had worked well when the student-teacher ratio remains at 15 students to 2 adults. Formerly, this was the norm, and the two-person teaching team taught both a morning and an afternoon class. The smaller class size allowed for individualized attention; the team had time to meet each student's differing needs.

Tracy and Babi: How *We* Got There

We believe that the successful inclusive programming that characterizes our classroom today grew out of our determination and commitment to moving, as teachers, from a *me* to a *we* point of view. It was a risky move, requiring scrupulous honesty, continuous communication, and mutual support, but the rewards for our students and ourselves have been considerable. We learned to practice parity and to treat each other as equals. We discovered the joy of sharing our gloriously teachable moments with each other. We developed the confidence to try innovative ideas, certain of the other's feedback and support. We saw our students thrive in a well-supervised classroom with two nurturing teachers. We experienced the satisfaction of exposing our students, at an early age, to an environment as diverse as the world outside, a world in which they could learn to interact with and respect children from different backgrounds as well as

(continued)

children with special needs. Implementing the concept of *we* allowed us to teach caring and promote empathy among all our students—and the adults who interact with us as well. But getting there wasn't easy.

Tracy's Experience

Tracy has a doctorate in education and a credential in early childhood special education. She is a patient, caring perfectionist whose perfectionism is mitigated by a good sense of humor. She had taught long enough to have serious concerns about whether the particular curriculum adopted by the district was appropriate for use with students with IEPs. She also had strong reservations about using the pull-out method for delivering special services like adapted physical education, occupational therapy, and physical therapy. She believed this created a distinction between the general education and special education students that elicited myriad questions from all the students.

Very soon, however, those concerns were superseded by others when the school administrator hired a general education teacher to be Tracy's co-teacher. Tracy had many uncomfortable questions.

Tracy's Perspective: Don't Rock the Boat, Babi!

Who is this new teacher? What is she like? Would she agree or disagree with the way I've had organized the classes? Would she share my educational philosophy? Why hadn't she come to the preschool classroom to meet me when she met with the administrator? Babi's program at her previous school had closed, due to low enrollment. By the time she transferred to my site, classes had been in session for six weeks.

One week later, I met Babi. Babi had a bachelor's degree in elementary education and was working on her master's degree in educational administration. She had high energy, arriving every morning ready to greet each student individually. She could bond with a frightened child in minutes, reassuring a little boy experiencing separation anxiety until he felt secure enough to wave goodbye to his parents with a smile. So far so good!

Babi's Perspective: What Have I Gotten Myself Into?

On my first day of work, the assistant principal gave me these ominous words of advice: "Watch your back!" What did she mean? Who was this dangerous person I was supposed to collaborate with? What terrible act had Tracy committed to elicit such enmity from the administrator? And why didn't she mention it before I accepted the position! I would just have to wait and see.

Tracy's Concerns

Tracy and her assistant observed Babi for a week, watching her classroom behaviors closely. Babi seemed nice and supportive; she did not criticize them, but she gave them no clue about what she was thinking. Tracy sensed her apprehension but didn't understand its source, so she gave her space and stayed out of her way. They noticed that Babi liked to rearrange the classroom furniture—a lot! But she was supportive of Tracy's creative center ideas. Was it possible that they could have similar educational philosophies? How could Tracy break the ice so that they could get to know each other? Would it be possible to start building a relationship that they both could trust?

(continued)

Tracy's Suspicion

Our first day together was very awkward. Although we went through the routine I had established, the classroom air was really oppressive and there was little conversation among the classroom staff for nearly a full week. Babi had said some nice things to me, assuring me that she considered all the students to be our students and suggesting that we should work together. This proposal sounded great, but remembering my experience with other co-teachers, I refused to get my hopes up. I'd heard those same words last year, but the teacher hadn't meant them at all. Could I really be lucky enough to have found a kindred spirit? It was hard to believe.

Babi's Impressions

Despite the administrator's warning, I was filled with excitement on that first day, beaming and confident. After all, I'd already had some successful team-teaching experiences and so was looking forward to the assignment.

There were two women in the classroom when I arrived. The blonde woman seemed to be in charge. I guessed that she was Tracy, and my first thoughts were, "Hey, Blondie, come on out and play! We're going to be creative and do wonderful things for these students." Instead, I simply said hello and introduced myself.

My new partner wasn't nearly as excited as I was, but she was polite and introduced herself and her assistant. She next informed me that there was no general education assistant assigned to the class, then carried on with what she had been doing and seemed to ignore me.

"Hmm," I thought, "this is going to be tough, but somehow it will all work out. . . . I hope!"

THE AWAKENING

The Parent Meeting

The inclusive preschool program model requires monthly parent meetings. These are particularly important because of the many family members who do not speak English. Tracy and Babi held their first joint meeting in the classroom on a Friday morning. Both teachers would speak and the special education assistant would translate. Tracy would open the meeting by introducing Babi, and the meeting would conclude with a question-and-answer period, allowing parents to ask any questions they might have about the preschool program.

That Friday, the classroom filled with parents and children of all ages, and Tracy and Babi worked their way through the agenda. By the end of the meeting, when they asked if the parents had questions, lots of hands went up. The first question seemed to express what was on everyone's mind: *Who's in charge?* The rest of the questions followed in the same vein: *Who's my child's teacher, Babi or Tracy? Which of you is responsible for my child's education?* The questions seemed to be easy ones, but the answers were unexpectedly complicated. Tracy and Babi hadn't worked that out yet! They had a lot of decisions to make, but they were barely communicating at all!

When Babi Met Harry: Babi's Perspective

In the days that followed the parent meeting, Tracy and I were still not really working things out. While the students were at their learning centers, I observed 4-year-old

(continued)

(continued)

Harry working diligently at connecting interlocking LEGO blocks. Though he tried many different combinations, none of the combinations worked. Despite this, Harry never gave up. At the end of center time, Harry asked me if I would save his work so that he could continue the next day. I agreed, and together we carefully placed his blocks on the shelf behind my desk. When Harry returned the next day, he took the blocks back to the carpet and continued working with them. This went on for nearly a week until, at last, Harry called out to me proudly, saying, "Look teacher, I did it!" He had finally snapped all the blocks together to form a beautiful cohesive structure.

Watching Harry work so conscientiously that week had made me think about the power of perseverance. If Harry could succeed at what had to seem to him like a Herculean task, I should be able to succeed in forging a connection with my aloof partner. I wanted to share this with Tracy. Before I lost my courage, I asked Tracy to have lunch with me. She accepted.

We went to a quaint little cafe near school and began our conversation with a brief chat about Harry's achievement. Having broken the ice, I took a risk and told Tracy what was really on my mind: neither the classroom setup nor the classroom schedule was working for me. To my surprise, Tracy felt exactly the same way! She had been reluctant to approach me with her concerns because of her negative experience with last year's teacher. That teacher had invalidated Tracy's learning and experience and left her feeling silenced. The habit of silence had continued because, unwittingly, I had been hired under similar circumstances.

After confessing our misgivings about each other, we began to talk about our educational philosophies and discovered that, although we differed in a few areas, we agreed on almost every key issue. What an unexpected and welcome meeting of minds that was!

The Epiphany: Tracy Speaks

After my lunch with Babi, I began to reflect on our purpose as teachers, reviewing the questions we had raised and the barrage of questions we had encountered at the parent meeting. I was especially focused on "Who's in charge?" That crucial question made me think about the purpose of inclusion. I began to wonder how Babi and I might change the culture and climate in and around our school.

Then I had an epiphany. One word resounded as the answer to every question that the parents had asked; one word clarified every idea I'd been mulling over. That word was *we*. Who's in charge? We are in charge! Who's my child's teacher, Babi or Tracy?
We are your child's teachers, Babi and Tracy. Who's responsible for my child's education? We are all responsible—parents, teachers, students, assistants, support services providers, administrators, the entire community—and we must all accept responsibility for every child's education.

I dubbed my insight "The Concept of We," knowing that it must begin with a transformation at the roots that are Babi and Tracy—no longer I, me, or you, but we.

GLOSSARY

Selected terms excerpted from Heron and Harris (2001, pp. 565–576)

collaborative consultation   An interactive process that enables people with diverse expertise to generate creative solutions to mutually defined problems; it often produces solutions that are different from those that individual team members would produce independently.

collaborative problem solving   A strategy for dealing with conflict that preserves the goals and relationships of group members faced with solving a problem.

collaborative relationship   An interactive relationship between the consultant and consultee that connotes parity, reciprocity, mutual problem solving, shared resources, responsibility, and accountability.

conflict management techniques   A general class of problem-solving strategies that includes majority vote, third-party arbitration, and authoritative rule; collaborative problem solving is the preferred strategy for conflict management because it preserves goals and relationships.

consultation   Has several definitions, varying in substance and context, depending upon the setting, target, or intervention; in the main, consultation should be voluntary, reciprocal, and mutual, and it should lead to the prevention and/or resolutions of identified problems.

co-teaching   Two or more teachers planning and instructing the same group of students at the same time and in the same place.

co-teaching structures   The mechanisms by which co-taught instruction is delivered; co-teaching structures change as the co-teaching partnership matures.

direct services   Training or assistance provided by a teacher, therapist, specialist, etc., directly to the child with special needs. In some cases, direct services may also be provided to adults, as when a therapist provides direct training to teachers, who then implement the procedures with the child.

inclusion   Like other terms related to integrating students with disabilities in general education settings (e.g., mainstreaming, least restrictive environment), inclusion has multiple definitions, connotations, and meanings; no single meaning exists in the literature.

indirect service   Service provided by a consultant who works with a mediator (e.g., teacher, parent), who in turn works to change a student's behavior. Indirect services to students are accomplished by providing direct service to the mediator.

least restrictive environment   By federal rule, the environment where the student with disabilities is to receive instruction with his or her general education peers to the maximum extent possible, to be removed only when he or she cannot achieve, even with supplemental learning aids; it may also be that educational setting that maximizes a student's opportunity to respond and achieve, permits proportional interaction with the teacher, and fosters acceptable social relationships between students with and students without disabilities.

REFERENCES

Austin, V. (2001). Teachers' beliefs about co-teaching. *Remedial and Special Education*, *22*, 245–255.

Cook, R., Klein, M.D. & Chen, D. (2012). *Adapting early childhood curricula for children with special needs*. Upper Saddle River, NJ: Pearson.

DEC/NAEYC. (2009). *Early childhood inclusion: A summary*. Chapel Hill: University of North Carolina at Chapel Hill, FPG Child Development Institute.

Dettmer, P., Knackendoffel, A., & Thurston, L.P. (2012). *Collaboration, consultation and teamwork for students with special needs* (7th ed.). Upper Saddle River, NJ: Pearson.

Diamond, K.E., & Innes, F.K. (2001). The origins of young children's attitudes toward peers. In M. Guralnick (Ed.), *Early childhood inclusion: Focus on change* (pp. 159–178). Baltimore, MD: Paul H. Brookes Publishing Co.

ECTAC. (2010). *Quality indicators of inclusive early childhood programs/practices: A compilation of selected resources*. Retrieved from http://www.ectacenter.org/topics/inclusion/research.asp

Fennick, E., & Liddy, D. (2001). Responsibilities and preparation for collaborative teaching: Co-teachers' perspectives. *Teacher Education and Special Education*, *24*, 229–240.

Friend, M., & Cook, L. (2003). *Interactions: Collaboration skills for school professionals* (4th ed.). New York, NY: Longman.

Friend, M., Reising, M., & Cook, L. (1993). Co-teaching: An overview of the past, a glimpse at the present, and considerations for the future. *Preventing School Failure*, *37*(4), 6–10.

Gately, S.E., & Gately, F.J. Jr. (2001). Understanding co-teaching components. *Teaching Exceptional Children*, *33*(4), 40–47.

Grisham-Brown, J., Hemmeter, M.L., & Pretti-Frontczak, K. (2005). *Blended practices for teaching young children in inclusive settings*. Baltimore, MD: Paul H. Brookes Publishing Co.

Harris, K.C. (1998). *Collaborative elementary teaching: A casebook for elementary special and general educators*. Austin, TX: PRO-ED.

Hattie, J. (2009). *Visible learning: A synthesis of over 800 meta-analyses relating to achievement*. New York, NY: Routledge.

Heron, T.E., & Harris, K.C. (2001). *The educational consultant: Helping professionals, parents, and students in inclusive classrooms* (4th ed.). Austin, TX: PRO-ED.

Hourcade, J.J., & Bauwens, J. (2003). *Cooperative teaching: Rebuilding and sharing the schoolhouse* (2nd ed.). Austin, TX: PRO-ED.

Idol, L. (2006). Toward inclusion of special education students in general education. *Remedial and Special Education*, *27*, 77–94.

Klein, M.D., Richardson-Gibbs, A.R., Kilpatrick, S. & Harris, K.C. (2001). *Project support. A practical guide for early childhood inclusion support specialists*. Los Angeles, CA: Division of Special Education, California State University Los Angeles.

Odom, S.L., Schwartz, I.S., & ECRII Investigators. (2002). So what do we know from all this? Synthesis points of research on preschool inclusion. In S. L. Odom (Ed.), *Widening the circle: Including children with disabilities in preschool programs* (pp. 154–174). New York, NY: Teachers College Press.

Riggs, C.G. (2004). To teachers: What paraeducators want you to know. *Teaching Exceptional Children*, *36*(5).

Salend, S.J. (2008). *Creating inclusive classrooms* (6th ed.). Columbus, OH: Pearson.

Scruggs, T.E., Mastropieri, M.A., & McDuffie, K.A. (2007). Co-teaching in inclusive classrooms: A metasynthesis of qualitative research. *Exceptional Children*, *73*, 392–416.

Walther-Thomas, C., Korinek, L., McLaughlin, V.L., & Williams, B.T. (2000). *Collaboration for inclusive education: Developing successful programs*. Needham Heights, MA: Allyn & Bacon.

Winzer, M.A., & Mazurek, K. (1998). *Special education in multicultural contexts*. Upper Saddle River, NJ: Prentice-Hall.

Getting Started

Administrative and Leadership Strategies for Building Inclusive Preschool Programs

As discussed in Chapter 1, administrators must respond to mandates to provide inclusive preschool education as part of their least restrictive environment (LRE) continuum of services. This chapter offers a plan of action for school administrators who are considering expanding existing preschool special education services from segregated classrooms to more inclusive education options. It provides a blueprint for effective inclusion support at the preschool level and addresses several components of program design:

- Partnering with general education preschools

- Designing inclusion support service delivery models that are programmatically effective and cost effective

- Preparing and training personnel

- Understanding that there is no single "best" model of inclusion support service delivery

There are a variety of approaches and models designed to meet the individual needs of each child, and some may fit one school district more effectively than others. Heron and Harris (2001, p. 184) make this point very clearly:

> In our view, whether a student receives instruction as part of a full-inclusion program (participates totally in the general education classroom) or is selectively included (receives instruction along a continuum of services, some of which may occur in general education settings) rests with the student's individualized education program [IEP]. By keeping our educational focus on the student, we are less likely to adopt methods based on well-intended but misguided considerations of what is best. . . . In short, despite the increase in the number of students who are being placed in "inclusive classrooms," we do not find that one size can possibly fit all.

DESIGNING AN INCLUSIVE PROGRAM

Establishing inclusive preschool programs presents many unique challenges, including the following:

- Finding appropriate settings: Where will classrooms be located?

45

- Creating effective administrative/organizational structures: Who will organize and supervise the programs?

- Planning models of service delivery: What will the program look like?

- Managing funding and personnel challenges: How do we find the best teachers and staff? How will we fund the program?

The decision to create an inclusive early childhood program can be difficult for school administrators for several reasons. Early childhood special education (ECSE) services are a small percentage of the overall special education program in most school districts. Providing special education services for 3- and 4-year-olds in preschool programs is a minor line item in a comprehensive budget that must also cover services for children in kindergarten through eighth grade or high school. The amount of time and energy an administrator may be able to spend on preschool programs is miniscule when compared to the intense time demands of K–12 administration.

Despite these challenges there are many incentives for administrators to creatively support inclusive preschool programs.

- Section 612(a)(5) of the Individuals with Disabilities Education Act (IDEA) of 2004 (PL 108-446) requires that education for preschool children with disabilities must be provided in the least restrictive environment.

- By definition, possible LREs cover a continuum of placement options, including fully inclusive programs with typical preschool children.

- The Americans with Disabilities Act (ADA) of 1990 (PL 101-336) specifies that children whose parents wish to enroll them in programs receiving federal funds (e.g., child care centers, Head Start) cannot be excluded from services because of their disability.

- Head Start federal guidelines require that 10% of children enrolled have disabilities.

These laws and national policies create a healthy climate and opportunities for state and local educational agencies to support inclusive preschool education.

However, a significant challenge faced by administrators is the difficulty of finding general education partners with whom to create inclusive preschool programs. As discussed in Chapter 1, public school districts do not typically house early education programs for preschool children who do not have disabilities. Thus, unlike K–12, there is usually no readily available general education classroom in which to include preschool children with disabilities. The most common settings within which to create inclusive preschool programs are summarized in Table 3.1.

WHERE: DEFINING SETTINGS AND PROGRAMS FOR INCLUSION

Two major components address the creation of an inclusive preschool program: *where* and *how*. In this section we discuss several examples of where inclusive preschools might be housed—and what types of programs might be housed there. More information on settings appears later in this chapter, under "First Steps."

Table 3.1. Early childhood programs with possible access for children with disabilities

Program	Funding/fees	Possible support service delivery model
Head Start	Free for families meeting eligibility criteria; waivers for a small percentage of families	Interagency agreement with local school district or dual enrollment in special education class, or family brings child to local school for therapies
State preschools	Free for families meeting eligibility criteria; waivers for a small percentage of families	Interagency agreement with local school district or dual enrollment in special education class or family brings child to local school for therapies
Private preschools	Tuition	School district provides itinerant consultation or dual enrollment in special education class, or family brings child to local school for therapies
Licensed family childcare	Tuition	School district provides itinerant consultation or dual enrollment in special education class, or family brings child to local school for therapies
Community early childhood programs (e.g., parks and recreation departments)	Local funding; modest tuition costs	School district provides itinerant consultation or dual enrollment in special education class, or family brings child to local school for therapies
District-sponsored early childhood education (ECE) programs, with ECE and early childhood special education (ECSE) teachers or with ECSE teacher as lead teacher	Children without disabilities: private pay Children with disabilities: special education funding	Co-teaching or blended program or itinerant consultant; therapies delivered to children at program site

As illustrated in Table 3.1, there are many ways to support preschool inclusion. The range of possibilities begins with a simple mainstreaming approach between special education and regular education classrooms and expands to designing and supporting a district-managed inclusive early care and education program. The following sections define and describe different types of preschool settings and programs that offer a range of inclusive experiences for young children with disabilities.

Mainstreaming

Mainstreaming is not synonymous with *inclusion*. Mainstreaming involves creating opportunities for preschoolers with disabilities to leave their special education classroom to spend brief periods of time visiting an early childhood education (ECE) classroom. The goal is to provide opportunities for students with disabilities for social integration—and, hopefully, interaction—with their typical peers, preferably on a daily basis and with enough time for children to participate fully in a variety of appropriate activities and get to know their peers. Obviously this requires that there be an early childhood center or classroom within easy walking distance of the special education classroom and school personnel available to accompany students for both supervision and support. Consider the following scenario.

The ABC District coordinator of special education would like to create a program where ECE and ECSE teachers co-teach children. However, he needs to build the relationship with the child development director in the district and knows it will take time to try to organize a formal inclusive program. Meanwhile, three school sites in the district have Head Start classes and preschool special day classes (SDCs) co-located on the same campuses. Some of the ECE and ECSE teachers have begun discussing how to mainstream preschoolers as the school year begins. The ECSE teachers propose sending four children and an assistant teacher from the SDC to the Head Start classroom during rug time and work time (about 60 minutes) on a daily basis. They have arranged to meet Head Start teachers during their lunch breaks one time each week to share information about the childrens' IEP goals, plan modifications, or accommodations based on the Head Start lesson plan for the coming week and write brief notes to share with the assistant teacher. The child development director agrees to the plan and suggests that, if it is successful, perhaps another group of students from each SDC can join Head Start peers during small group and outside play periods on a daily basis, also accompanied by an assistant. Teachers find this model runs smoothly during the year and feel confident that this plan works well for their students when discussing and suggesting daily mainstreaming opportunities with parents during IEP meetings.

Reverse Mainstreaming

Reverse mainstreaming involves bringing typically developing children into the special education classroom for a portion of the day and having them spend regularly scheduled time there for activities that will enhance the opportunities for all children to learn together. A related strategy is the use of *peer tutors*, who are usually older, general education students from a classroom at the same school site. Although it may seem easier to plan for mainstreaming or reverse mainstreaming activities rather than for an all-day inclusion program, ideally these models should include planning time for teachers to meet and to choose and modify activities so that all children can be actively engaged in learning.

Early Childhood Special Education Teacher Leading a Blended Classroom

An ECSE classroom teacher acting as the lead teacher for a blended special education/ECE classroom is another variation of the reverse mainstreaming theme. In this model, a district creates a traditional preschool special education class, with a credentialed early childhood special educator as the lead teacher. Additional slots in the classroom are offered to children of employees of the district or to families in the community at a reasonable private pay rate, creating a mix of typical children and children with disabilities. Given the extreme shortage of early childhood education for typically developing children, this can be a very successful and cost-effective program. (It is important to ensure that the ECSE teacher assigned to this classroom not only be highly qualified in preschool special education methodology but also have knowledge and experience working with typically developing preschool children.) Another advantage of this organizational structure is that potential conflicts between two co-equal administrative authorities (e.g., school district and Head Start) would be avoided.

District D's director of special education is committed to building an inclusive preschool program for the approximately 50 preschoolers with IEPs who receive services each year. There are no publicly funded state preschool programs in the district. The director speaks to the four ECSE teachers on staff about this idea; two volunteer to try the new approach. A flyer is sent home to all families of the elementary school students, offering a 4-day-per-week inclusive preschool program from 8:00–11:00 a.m. at two school campuses. The fee is $15.00 per day or $60.00 per week. Each class will be limited to 20 children, half with IEPs. One assistant will help in each class, so the ratio will be 10:1. The district receives more applications than there is room for typical children and needs to establish a waiting list. Children of district staff are given priority for acceptance into the program. Parents of paying children are asked to sign a waiver stating an understanding that the program is not licensed by the state department of child development but does meet the criteria for education programs. Over the course of three years, the classes are expanded to four afternoons per week. Teachers use Fridays as planning, assessment, and IEP days. The district opts to keep two ECSE classes of 10–12 students (with IEPs) who may need smaller classrooms and more intensive services.

Districts Sponsoring Early Childhood Education Programs

Increasingly, districts are establishing their own community early care and education centers, becoming Head Start grantees, or creating private-pay early childhood programs. These programs offer much-needed ECE services to district employees and families in the community while simultaneously creating inclusive special education settings for preschoolers with disabilities. However, they often present a new set of challenges: learning about licensing requirements, establishing fee-based services, hiring staff, advertising a new program, and so on.

The Alta District assigned two credentialed teachers (one kindergarten general education teacher and one ECSE teacher) as co-teachers in an ECE classroom in which there was one group of 15 children in the morning class and a different group of 15 children in the afternoon class. In each class, 8–10 students had active IEPs, and the remaining 5–7 students were typically developing with no IEPs. As a district program, licensing and fees were no issue (unlike a private, nonpublic program), and both teachers were under district contracts as credentialed teachers. The teachers shared responsibility for both classes, with one acting as lead teacher in the morning and the other in the afternoon, each maintaining a support role in the classroom when not the lead teacher. One day each week was designated as an early dismissal day, when all 30 children (both morning and afternoon) attended for the morning only, leaving the afternoon free for teachers to plan together. Classroom paraprofessionals were assigned and funded through both special education and general education funds, as they would have been if the classes were separate.

Partnering with Head Start Programs and State Preschools

Collaborative arrangements between organizations are used widely throughout the United States. They have been very successful in lower-income communities. The programs provide high-quality early childhood education at no cost. Head Start programs are mandated to allocate a minimum of 10% of their enrollment to preschool-age children with disabilities. There is a wide range of inclusion support service delivery models (described in Chapter 2) that can be used in these partnerships. Examples include the following:

*   *Co-teaching*, in which the district funds its own credentialed preschool special education teacher to work with the Head Start teacher

*   *Contracting with a district-funded ECSE consultant* who serves preschool children with disabilities in several Head Start classrooms

*   *Using paraprofessionals* employed, trained, and supervised by the district and assigned to individual children with IEPs

*   *Using specialized service providers* who provide either direct, designated instructional *itinerant* services to individual children on weekly basis or who work at a multiclassroom site as permanent employees of the district (These providers could be occupational therapists, speech-language pathologists, physical therapists, behavior therapists, and so on.)

It is important to consider that any combination of the elements in these examples can be used creatively to design the right inclusion support service delivery model for a given program, community, or child.

Partnering with Private Preschools

Private ECE programs may be difficult to access as inclusive partners. However, for families who have to send their child with disabilities to a private preschool, districts can easily use an *itinerant consultation* model to provide appropriate support to that child. District administrators should keep in mind that a well-trained early childhood special educator can carry a consultation caseload of 20 or more preschool students with disabilities (depending on students' needs) and provide support in their neighborhood preschool programs.

HOW: CREATING AND DESIGNING
SERVICE DELIVERY MODELS FOR INCLUSION SUPPORT

Because of the unique characteristics of early childhood inclusion, it will be helpful to create a *written vision and mission statement* for the desired program. There are two reasons: first, to provide a roadmap as school personnel, parents, and students plan and adapt to changes in existing service delivery and program options; and second, to ensure sustainability of the inclusive program. Without a clear idea of what the goals and values are, programs can be implemented but not sustained over time, especially if key personnel leave or are shifted to other positions (Sindelar, Shearer, Yendol-Hoppey, & Liebert, 2006).

As noted, the two major components to address in the creation of an inclusive preschool education program are *where* and *how*. We have already discussed several examples of where inclusive preschools might be housed, and more information on settings appears later in this chapter, under "First Steps." Here we address the *how*. Once the inclusive setting has been identified, the next component is how students' educational needs will be met in that setting. Administrators will need to become familiar with the various models of inclusive support service delivery, including both the advantages and possible drawbacks of these models. *Placement of children with disabilities in inclusive programs with same-age peers will not be successful without adequate inclusion supports.* Some support models may be implemented easily in specific districts due to the availability of personnel, the ease of access to community-based programs, the geography and size of the district, the attitudes and philosophies of special education teams, and the collegiality of partner personnel and other key players. There is no evidence that there is one best model of inclusion support.

The two models of support most commonly used for young children with special needs in inclusive preschool programs are some version of co-teaching and itinerant consultation. Each of these was introduced in Chapter 2. Some of the administrative advantages and disadvantages of the two approaches follow.

Co-teaching Model

The co-teaching approach is a team design utilizing an ECE teacher and an ECSE teacher working together in one classroom setting comprised of children with and without disabilities. Sometimes these classroom arrangements are referred to as *blended* classrooms. Both teachers ideally share all aspects of planning and teach all students in the classroom. The co-teaching inclusion model assumes that an early childhood classroom is available and administrators are open to sharing resources, personnel, and educational philosophies. Co-teaching programs are much like a marriage: mutual respect, a shared vision, and open communication must exist in order for the program to work effectively. Ideally, administrators will ensure that teachers have time to plan together and closely monitor blended programs to ensure that all children's needs are being met. An administrator's support *and expectation* that teams will collaborate is very important. It can be challenging, especially when staff in partner community-based programs are paid only for the time they are with children. Strategies such as rotating paraeducator staff who take responsibility for monitoring free play while remaining staff meet in the corner of the room (and so remain available) or meet during lunch breaks between morning and afternoon sessions are examples of creative (though less than perfect) ways of maintaining communication, at least every other week. Even e-mails phone conferences, or happy hour, though they infringe on off-work time, have been used effectively.

Challenges of Two Administrative Authorities One of the common challenges of co-teaching models is that often each co-teacher is supervised and employed by a different agency. For example, the early childhood teacher is supervised by the Head Start agency while the ECSE teacher is supervised by the school district. When administrators and teachers come from diverse agencies, both entities need to learn about each other. Funding sources, legal requirements such as licensing, and a host of rules and regulations vary significantly from agency to agency. The ability of administration and staff to consider each other's perspective can be challenging. However, with appropriate planning and adequate time for both parties to learn about each other and establish a working relationship, the co-teaching approach to supporting the inclusion of young children with disabilities can be exciting.

- A co-teaching model can provide opportunities for all children from the same community to attend school together.

- The on-site special education teacher may help with early identification and referral of children enrolled in the program.

- When teachers work together in an early childhood environment, special education teachers are reminded of curricular and developmental expectations for typically developing peers, while the early childhood teacher may learn effective strategies for helping struggling learners.

- Sharing resources from both programs can result in a more comprehensive and creative program for all involved.

In a survey of 7 communities throughout the United States offering programs with co-teaching models, 13 strategies for setting up and operating successful programs were suggested by the participants (Rosenkoetter, 1998). Although the study was published in 1998, we find all points made to be as relevant today as they were over a decade ago.

1. *Language matters:* Program-specific jargon and acronyms and the words used by staff to refer to *all* children ("our children" versus "your" and "mine") need to be addressed so all involved are on the same page.

2. *Facilities matter:* Be aware of how it feels to be absorbed by one program versus sharing a new or renovated site together (everyone needs to "own" their space).

3. *Leadership is essential:* Administrators committed to blending programs together are the key to successful partnerships. Additionally, administrators must be able to work with their agencies to clarify and resolve financial issues.

4. *Choices build ownership:* All staff, not just those in charge, need to have some voice in program planning.

5. *Personalities matter:* Some staff members will be eager to take on new roles, while others cannot easily shift roles and responsibilities until they observe children's progress and the positive benefits of the program.

6. *Shared in-services and other trainings are critical:* Funding and allotted time for personnel to train together create opportunities to gain needed skills in collaborative teaming, special education methodology, and early childhood development.

7. *Staff need time to confer:* Daily and weekly planning time is a necessity both for formal planning together and for informal opportunities to build trusting relationships.

8. *Families are the heart of the blended program:* Keeping families involved and informed is imperative.

9. *Despite possible salary, benefits, and education disparity among staff, share job responsibilities:* All staff monitoring and teaching *all* children, sharing documentation and paperwork, and sharing home visits are extremely important.

10. *Resolve thorny issues:* Administrators have many issues that need to be resolved when coordinating a shared program. These should be addressed head on; the ability to work together and resolve issues is challenging but can, in the end, support long-term stability.

11. *Manage stress:* Working in blended programs with families that have their own levels of stress and with new partners in new programs can be overwhelming at times. Administrators should be aware of the need for staff members to engage in stress relief (e.g., through fun staff activities, group mental health training).

12. *Careful consideration of class composition:* Teachers were adamant that not just adult-child ratios should be considered but also the special needs and personalities of specific children due to disabilities or behavior.

13. *Patience! Patience! Patience!:* The study reported that most participants stressed the need for patience with themselves and others and to remember that new programs are not created in the space of one year. They take time.

Consultation Model

Another common model of inclusion support service delivery is the *itinerant consultation approach,* introduced in Chapter 2. Typical features of this model are as follows:

- An ECSE teacher (or another special education service provider) works as an *itinerant,* that is, he or she travels from place to place and is not permanently housed in one classroom.

- The itinerant usually maintains a caseload of up to 25 or 30 children with disabilities.

- The children are located in several early childhood classrooms throughout the district.

- The itinerant uses a consultative model in which she provides mostly *indirect services* to teachers and other team members. Best practice requires a *collaborative consultation* approach, in which the consultant and the teacher engage in mutual respect and exchange of ideas and use a collaborative communication style and problem solving to ensure children's learning. On occasion, the itinerant may also provide *direct services* to specific children as needed.

- The frequency of contact (e.g., daily, weekly, monthly) is based on the provision in the child's IEP as well as changes in child and teacher needs.

- There is less need for planning and coordination between two or more agencies other than obtaining an agreement with the early childhood agency to allow personnel to provide special education consultative services in their classrooms.

- There is less need for administrators to work out sharing resources and develop an understanding of each other's rules and regulations than in a co-teaching program.

- Different types of early childhood sites can be involved (e.g., private schools, state-funded centers, community-based early childhood programs).

While there are several advantages of consultation models of service delivery, it must be pointed out that, in order to be effective, *the itinerant inclusion specialists must be very well trained.* They must be knowledgeable specialists with expertise and experience in early childhood education and know a range of disabilities and appropriate resources. They must be able to balance a caseload of children at a variety of different sites. Itinerant teachers need to be able to establish a collaborative relationship with several adults at multiple sites, not just one group of adults at one site. See Klein and Harris (2004) and Richardson-Gibbs (2004) for a discussion of the skills and training needs in ECSE collaborative consultation. In addition, Dinnebeil and McInerney's *A Guide to Itinerant Early Childhood Special Education Services* (2011) offers an in-depth discussion about the role of the itinerant consultant.

The itinerant model is potentially less administratively complex than the co-teaching model. However, much of its success lies in the ability to find independent and experienced personnel who are willing to spend much of their day traveling from place to place and engaging in collaborative problem solving as needed by the children and staff in each program.

Horn and Sandall (2000) described the itinerant consultant as an experienced ECSE teacher skilled in managing collaboration with many partners and the content of the consultation. Communication occurs among several players for each child: family members, the ECE teacher, other service providers, and paraprofessionals. The content of the consultation will look different from child to child, site to site. Knowing about physical access, social inclusion, active engagement, and meeting IEP goals and then being able to communicate this information and provide support at each visit is extremely challenging. Good communication skills are required as the itinerant consultant moves among multiple sites, families, and professionals on a daily basis. With these skills in hand, the experienced itinerant consultant begins to create and build collaborative partnerships.

Variations and Hybrid Support Models

In addition to these common models of co-teaching and consultation, there are variations and hybrid approaches to providing inclusion support. Creative approaches are often the most successful. These will depend upon specific factors such as number of children, severity of special needs, service delivery options, classroom designs and locations, available community partners, and so on. Given the multifaceted designs of districts and their communities, the inclusion models just described may not meet the needs of a particular district. Hybrid designs, such as those described in the following examples, may be more adaptable.

1. *Employing early childhood special education teachers in dual roles:* For example, an ECSE teacher may co-teach in a blended morning Head Start program with four children with significant disabilities, then spend afternoons providing itinerant consultative support to eight children with more mild disabilities attending local Head Start afternoon classes. This model may work best in smaller districts where the numbers of young children identified with disabilities fluctuates from year to year. It can fail if administrators do not allow planning time for both the ECE teacher and ECSE teacher, or if they overload a teacher with too many students to serve adequately during the second half of the day.

2. *Using paraeducators as inclusion support providers:* It is not unusual for districts to use one-to-one paraeducators (also referred to as *assistant teachers* or *paraprofessionals*) as their service delivery model for preschool inclusion support. Also, paraprofessionals increasingly are being used to deliver specialized services—for example, as health aides and as behavioral intervention, occupational therapy (OT), physical therapy (PT), and speech-language pathology (SLP) assistants—and *must* be supervised by their respective specialists. There is much discussion and concern throughout the special education literature about the challenges associated with using paraprofessionals as the primary support providers for students in inclusive settings. (See, for example, Giangreco, 2003.) Despite these challenges, districts often view the assignment of paraprofessionals as a simple and cost-effective solution. While this can be true in some cases, all too often effectiveness is compromised because of the following common challenges:

   • Lack of training

   • Inadequate or unclear responsibility for supervision

   • Lack of clear delineation of paraeducator's role

   • Increasing use of subcontracted nonpublic agency personnel who may rely heavily on the use of minimally trained personnel

Possible solutions to these concerns include:

• Providing trainings for paraprofessionals, both before and while on the job, giving them a base of knowledge and a sense of what the job entails

• Clearly defining roles and responsibilities for both paraprofessionals and classroom teachers from day one so all team members understand their roles both in the classroom and with specific students

• Providing regular, ongoing supervision of the paraprofessional; encouraging his or her observations and feedback about the environment and people offers the opportunity to expand on his or her base of knowledge, applying it appropriately and effectively in specific situations and with individual children.

- Avoid one-to-one assignment if possible (defining the job as an "extra classroom assistant" emphasizes less shadowing of a child and more general classroom support, especially when other adults in the classroom, such as the teacher, are working with or supervising the child with disabilities).
- Prioritize safety (in some cases, an assistant may need to function as a one-to-one for health or safety reasons, such as medical conditions or dangerous behaviors).
- Gradually decrease paraprofessional's proximity to child. Help the paraprofessional view the child in the context of being part of the whole classroom instead of a one-to-one basis. (The goal, in most cases, is to reduce adult support as much as possible to encourage a sense of independence in young children.)
- Avoid exclusivity (too much support for a child may result in that child seeking out the assigned adult rather than peers for interactions and assistance during the course of the school day).
- Encourage paraprofessional input—based on observations and data collection—about the child and/or environment, including classroom adults and students, and provide feedback to support specific questions or concerns.
- Clarify roles, responsibilities, and supervision for ABA paraprofessionals (especially if they are funded and supervised by outside agencies).

Figure 3.1.   Recommendations for use of paraprofessionals in preschool inclusion support.

Figure 3.1 offers simple guidelines to help paraeducators effectively provide support for children in inclusive settings. Table 3.2 provides a summary of the preschool inclusion support service delivery models that have been described.

Table 3.2.   Preschool inclusion support service delivery models

Model	Definition
Co-teaching (blended)	One early childhood education (ECE) teacher and one early childhood special education (ECSE) teacher work together as co-equals in one classroom setting combining typical children and children with disabilities.
Itinerant consultant	ECSE teacher (or another identified special education service provider) maintains a caseload of several children in early childhood classrooms throughout the district or community, providing consultative services to teachers and other team members, as needed, on a daily, weekly, or monthly basis depending on child and teacher needs.
Itinerant direct service (pull-out/push-in)	Specialist pulls child from classroom to deliver services in another setting or classroom (e.g., the speech therapist takes child out of the preschool classroom and into the therapy room for speech therapy). Specialist works with child within classroom (e.g., the occupational therapist delivers or "pushes in" his services in the classroom, assisting the child as he or she participates in the daily preschool activities).
One-to-one paraprofessional	Assistant is assigned as "extra classroom assistant" to assist teacher with child(ren) with disabilities or as a one-to-one to provide specific support for one child due to needs related to the disability.

FIRST STEPS: DEVELOPING
PARTNERSHIPS AND CREATING PROGRAMS

When a district decides to begin an inclusive program, the primary question is "Where do we find the typically developing children?" In larger districts, there are often district-sponsored child development programs. Administrators may find it easier to begin a dialogue with district personnel in different departments but under the same administrative roof. In districts with fewer resources due to size or location, community-based programs may need to be approached by district personnel and a conversation initiated about serving young children with disabilities.

Early childhood education programs typically serve families in the surrounding community. These programs are usually sustained by state or federal funds and some, like Head Start, have a mandate to show that at least 10% of all enrolled students have some type of disability. Students with disabilities enrolled in these programs may receive district therapy services in pull-out models (most commonly speech and language therapy). If there is no formal service delivery model embedded in the district child development programs, most children will have mild, rather than moderate to severe, disabilities. It is likely that these districts have separate special day classes for children with moderate to severe special needs requiring more intensive special education services. Administrators wishing to expand to a more inclusive model should seriously consider both itinerant and co-teaching inclusion support approaches (or combination hybrid designs) if their districts have established child development programs. Co-teaching programs, as discussed, require more administrative support and planning, but, with special education staff present in the classrooms on a daily basis, children with moderate to severe special needs can be included. The itinerant model, while easier to establish, may not offer enough support for children with severe disabilities without additional paraprofessional support.

Establishing Relations with Potential Preschool Education Partners

Once tentative approval from the school board or administrative counsel is determined (in most school districts, new programs, proposals, or budgets must be presented to and approved by the school board before action is taken), arranging to meet with potential partners begins. Partners may be administrators within a district, such as the director of special education and the coordinator of Head Start or community child development programs. Somewhat more challenging may be partnering with community-based programs that do not share the same administrative oversight and run under completely different guidelines and requirements (e.g., nonprofit early childhood programs with governing boards versus early childhood special education programs under the direction of pupil personnel services). Arranging these first meetings can be daunting, as all players have priorities and responsibilities for their own jobs, and making time to discuss possible additional responsibilities in the form of a new project is one more task to add to the to-do list. Establishing regular meeting times and keeping planning meetings on target with organized agendas help to establish a concise action plan without taking too much time from already overburdened participants.

One important issue to address is that of income qualifications for the ECE program. While districts serve all school-age children who qualify and live within the district boundaries, early childhood federal and state programs have strict rules governing family income and eligibility. Some school districts may serve a majority of families who do qualify for such programs (these districts probably have state-funded ECE programs operating within their boundaries). However, districts serving neighborhoods that are predominately middle or upper-middle class may not have access to such programs or find that there are few families who qualify for co-enrollment based on income. In these districts, partnerships may need to be developed with private preschools.

In a study of 52 directors of early care and education programs, Craig, Haggart, Gold, and Hull (2000) found that child care directors are an underused resource for possible inclusive settings. Following 24 hours of training on providing inclusive child care and reviewing their centers' policies and procedures, the interviewed directors proposed a list of considerations for other child care directors that might also be applied to special education early childhood administrators. The list of ideas includes the following:

- Invite trained special education service providers into child development programs not only to serve the child with disabilities but also to provide input on other children during their time in the center.

- Invite special education agencies to provide training to child care staff.

- Review and revise program policies that might discriminate against children with particular disabilities.

- Actively recruit children with special needs from the community into the child care program.

Funding Inclusive Preschool Programs

Administrators are trained to understand funding streams and balance the fiscal demands of a variety of programs. Moving from a segregated special day class model to an inclusive model should not cost more—at least on paper. A teacher and one or two assistants leave the special day class and join the Head Start program. Twelve students from the special day class are co-enrolled in Head Start. The special education department no longer funds materials and furniture needed in the special day class. Transportation costs are reduced because children with disabilities are not bussed to one central site; they attend the Head Start located at their school of residence, close to home. What could be simpler and more cost-effective?

Administrators who have established a vision, created a plan, and begun the process of collaboration with early childhood programs need to gain approval from district superintendents and school boards for these changes. Creating a clearly stated action plan with a concise summary of costs and a comparison of costs from the "old" program design may help with gaining approval. Unfortunately, experience has shown that, in spite of savings on costs such as busing, *initial* expenditures for some inclusive preschool models may be higher. This is usually temporary and related to the following: 1) the need to provide more para-professional assistance for some students, 2) more planning and training time for all teachers, 3) more administrator time devoted to meeting with personnel, and 4) problem solving and providing administrative oversight to establish a smoothly running program.

Odom, Parrish, and Hikido (2001) found that comparing costs of traditional noninclusive classes with the variety of available inclusive preschool classes yielded data that can be confusing and inconclusive at best. Based on an analysis of costs of 5 programs in 5 states, the authors found that inclusive education did appear to cost less than traditional special day classes. Additionally, Odom and Buysse (2005) found the costs related to an itinerant teacher model at Head Start sites tended to be less than special day class models or blended co-teaching programs. However, they also noted that blended or co-teaching programs may offer higher quality service, and overall program costs appear to be related to the severity of disabilities of children in attendance.

Odom et al. (2001) examined the costs of inclusive education versus traditional noninclusive education for preschoolers with disabilities in five local education agencies (LEAs) around the United States. While they found that instructional costs appeared to be slightly less for the inclusion programs, the noninstructional costs differed within programs. The study noted that varying inclusion programs were designed with various models, making it difficult to provide definitive answers common to all. The researchers examined the following components of nine different inclusive programs:

- *Salaries:* These were the largest cost, but differences were noted between models (itinerant versus co-teaching models), which agencies funded regular education teachers, and which funded instructional assistants (most often LEAs).

- *Child care tuition:* When tuition was required for private child care settings, LEAs occasionally paid the tuition; otherwise, parents often funded the tuition.

- *Equipment:* Costs for setting up classrooms with furniture, toys, and so on often depended on where the inclusive program was located. If they were within LEA buildings, the LEA paid, but typically the LEA did not pay if the program was located outside of its facilities. The LEA usually paid for specialized equipment for specific children.

- *Materials and supplies:* Costs were similar to equipment costs. LEAs paid for ongoing consumable supplies such as paper, paint, and snacks if the program was within the LEA but not if the program was run by a separate agency (such as Head Start).

- *Busing for children:* In community-based models, parents often transported their children to programs; in LEA-funded programs or special education classrooms, the LEA funded transportation.

- *Itinerant teacher transportation:* LEAs funded driving costs for itinerant teachers or other service providers.

- *Building costs:* These costs included depreciation, maintenance, and utilities and were funded as described earlier: LEA buildings paid for by LEA and community-based buildings paid by the relevant owner/leasee agency or covered by tuition costs.

- *Administrative costs:* A percentage of total cost was assigned to administrative expense based on numbers of children being served. Each agency, LEA or community based, covered its own administrative charges.

Overall, the study revealed several issues that need to be addressed by administrators of inclusive preschool programs. For example, co-teaching in a blended program may cost more than itinerant consultation, but the severity of needs of individual children may require more services (or teacher hours) than those children with less intense needs. Caseloads for special education teachers will affect the overall cost of a program; an itinerant teacher may be able to carry more children on his or her caseload if the amount of driving time between programs is not too great and if the children on the caseload are balanced between those with mild and those with severe disabilities. Also, if a school district elects to pay tuition for some preschoolers at a private preschool, costs will increase, but there may subsequently be less need for additional services, again, depending on the needs of individual children.

Establishing and overseeing appropriately sized caseloads for teaching staff is imperative, but this is often more difficult to establish for itinerant models of service compared to the typical model of the special day class with 12 students, one teacher, and one assistant. (Matching the number of children on a caseload effectively with the number of hours of service provided includes many variables and is often not a straightforward task.) Carefully determining levels of appropriate services needed for preschoolers to show progress on their goals and being willing to provide a variety of service delivery models within inclusive settings is key to managing the cost of preschool special education programs. An older resource that continues to be useful to administrators today is *An Administrator's Guide to Preschool Inclusion* (Wolery & Odom, 2000).

A Final Note on Costs Administrators are pulled in many directions. The active involvement of families, as well as the increasing use of legal advocates, often contribute to adversarial relationships. In addition, special education funding may be a source of tension. Two recent policy reports (Levenson, 2011; Levenson, 2012) addressed the great challenges of serious budget shortfalls faced by school boards and administrators. The author of the reports suggested that the unique challenges of special education funding are particularly perplexing. U.S. special education expenditures continue to increase, both in terms of the proportion of total school budget and per student spending. Yet despite decreasing dollars in district budgets, several factors tend to take attempts to increase efficiency and reduce special education costs off the table. There is a common assumption that the Individuals with Disability Education Act (IDEA) does not allow costs to be considered when planning IEP services or that districts are never allowed to reduce special education spending levels. According to Levenson (2012), these are misconceptions.

Also, special education constituencies (i.e., parents, educators, and service providers) often believe that more is always better and are strong advocates for more specialized services and support personnel. General educators, on the other hand, may feel resentment toward increasing special education budgets, which, compared to general education funding, may seem quite ample. This can set the stage for antipathy between general education and special education administrators. Special education administrators are caught between a rock and a hard place, as depicted in Figure 3.2

Interestingly, Levenson's (2011, 2012) studies suggest that special education student outcomes are not closely related to expenditures. These reports also examined inclusive classrooms, although they did not specifically address preschool. They suggest that skills of personnel and *configurations of supports* are the key to increasing both efficiency and effectiveness, and they decried the overuse of paraprofessionals. These conclusions support one of the key points in this chapter: successful inclusive classroom environments depend on creative, "just right" supports, which do not necessarily cost more money.

Figure 3.2. School administrations often find themselves between a rock and a hard place.

IMPLEMENTING THE INCLUSIVE PRESCHOOL PROGRAM

As administrators review existing programs and begin planning for change, taking stock of what's already in place is helpful so that the wheel isn't reinvented. Looking at existing structures of service delivery can determine personnel, environmental, and material needs. Consider the following scenario.

District Z has run three preschool special day classes each year for the past 10 years. Each class begins in September with 5 to 7 students. By January, all three classes have an enrollment of 8 to 12 students and will be completely full by May (that is, at least 12 students in each class). The classes serve 3- and 4-year-olds, and approximately two thirds of all students transition to kindergarten the following year. Each classroom has one early childhood special education teacher and one paraprofessional. Sometimes extra assistants are assigned to a class due to numbers (more than 12 students) or the needs of specific children (e.g., behavioral challenges, health impairments). The classes are located on three different campuses in the district, and buses deliver the students each day. Speech therapy services are delivered by the speech therapist assigned to the elementary school campus. Other therapies such as OT therapy are provided at a clinic in the community that contracts with the district. The special education director wants to implement a more inclusive model.

In this example, administrators take stock of teachers, assistants, classrooms, furniture and materials, busing, and therapies to determine how each will be practically affected by the philosophical change. Will changes happen in stages? Should the new model be fully implemented immediately or over the course of the school year? What is the appropriate time line given the details of the transition plan? The case study of three administrators who worked together to implement an inclusive program—as presented in the vignette "Administrator Interview: Putting Ideas into Action"—describes some of the challenges and solutions from their perspectives.

Administrator Interview: Putting Ideas into Action

Three administrators sat down to discuss the inclusive preschool co-teaching programs in their school district. Carol was the Director of Special Education when the district began trying different types of inclusive special education more than 10 years ago. Lisa is currently the Director of Child Development programs (including Head Start), and Olga is the Disabilities Coordinator for the Head Start programs.

First Attempts

Carol remembers beginning to think about inclusion for young children with disabilities in the mid-1990s as she became more aware of the federal mandates to provide services for children in least restrictive settings. Following school board approval, she hired an early childhood special education (ECSE) teacher and spoke to the Head Start director about co-enrolling children with special needs in Head Start classes. With no planning and little training, the ECSE teacher and two Head Start teachers were thrown together and tried to initiate a co-teaching program. A consultant was hired

(continued)

during the school year to work with the teaching team by bringing both Head Start and special education programs together to share and understand differences in the two agencies and develop mutually acceptable goals for continuing this program. Unfortunately, the teachers had difficulty understanding their roles and working with each other, and, at the end of the school year, the program was abandoned.

Finding Key Players

Carol was busy coordinating all of the district's special education programs (preschool through 8th grade) and had not revisited the idea of blended programs since the first failed attempt. However, she realized that having inclusive classrooms for preschoolers would be beneficial and began looking for personnel who could take her ideas and operationalize them. Carol also mentioned that she wanted someone who could "educate her and had a passion for including children." She hired an ECSE teacher with experience running inclusive programs. Carol remembers that she was willing to go to her district administrators and the school board and ask for personnel, services, and budget allowances, but she needed people working for her who would put her ideas into action. The ECSE teacher began providing itinerant consultation services to preschoolers with disabilities enrolled in the Head Start programs.

At the same time, Olga was hired as Disabilities Coordinator, and during a 2-year period she began working with Lisa, Director of Child Development Programs, to explore models of inclusion in Head Start programs in other districts. They observed a co-teaching program in one district and felt this could be an effective model to implement in their district. They began a dialogue with Carol.

Implementing the Plan

Carol and Lisa remember proposing the co-teaching idea to their administrators and receiving approval to implement the planned changes. For Lisa, there was no issue with budgeting for this; Head Start was funding classrooms and teachers, but they did need to meet the mandate of providing services to 10% of children with disabilities from their total preschool population.

Carol received approval to advertise a position for an ECSE teacher specifically for the co-teaching assignment. She also requested and received funding for an extra assistant for each Head Start class and based the request on the fact that, in past years, teachers had requested extra assistants to work in their special day classes based on individual child needs. Funding was also granted for extra hourly pay for teachers, because Carol fully supported the idea that, for this program to work, teachers needed time to meet.

At this point, these two busy administrators asked Olga and the ECSE teacher to continue with the details of actually putting the program together. Olga and the ECSE teacher held a series of meetings with interested Head Start teachers. The meetings included information about how a co-teaching program would look, and training videos and information from a federal grant through Cal State Los Angeles were used to illustrate teamwork, problem solving, and early intervention teaching strategies in co-teaching programs.

(continued)

Both Head Start and special education administrators worked together to determine the best (i.e., most central, easily accessible) Head Start sites. Special education accepted the responsibility for busing and most designated instructional services, such as occupational therapy. Special education and Head Start shared the funding of speech therapists, with special education providing supervision and oversight. Head Start agreed to fund all classroom materials and other equipment. Head Start also sponsored several staff trainings throughout the school year, and special education agreed to pay for the special education teacher and assistants to attend. Calendar issues surfaced when it was noted that district and child development calendars had different start and end dates and different pupil-free staff training days. Rather than change calendars, both agencies agreed to follow the child development programs' calendar, and special education funded the extra school and training days for special education staff.

Olga worked with Carol and the preschool assessment team to determine which children should be co-enrolled in the Head Start classes. Individualized education program meetings were held to become acquainted with families, explain the program and team recommendations for the preschoolers, and note the change of placement for these young students.

The Program Begins

When school began in September, personnel and classes were ready to go. Unfortunately, Carol retired as the program began, but with her encouragement and endorsement the program grew from one site to three sites during the next four years. Both Lisa and Olga advocated strongly for expanding the program and continued to provide the Head Start classrooms and teachers in addition to all materials and equipment (including adapted equipment for children with disabilities, such as special chairs, writing utensils, and weighted lap pads). Head Start funded and hosted several disabilities-related trainings for both staff and parents throughout the school year and a "thank you" lunch at the end of each year for all co-teaching staff and supervisors. Special education continued to provide funding for extra hours for staff to attend trainings and additional school days on the child development programs calendar.

Communication: A Key to Success

As the administrators discussed the program and looked back on the beginning of the project, they all agreed that communication was a key to success. Lisa expressed the need for "blending philosophies" and wanted to ensure that all people involved in the process would be kept "informed and updated, as information is crucial." Carol agreed, adding that "the staff [just] wants someone to listen to them." Both administrators agreed that when people are shut out or not asked for input resentment or misunderstanding occurs. Olga concurred, adding that sometimes "teachers can't [always] solve problems on their own but they need to talk to each other first then seek more support."

All agreed that ongoing communication with parents was a critical part of a successful inclusive program. Olga remembered that at times she has been labeled an

(continued)

(continued)

"advocate" for parents, and the implication was negatively implied. She did not like the implications but said this was her job for parents in Head Start programs.

A Successful Partnership: Key Points

1. Legal requirements

   - Special education administrator recognized the need for more inclusive environments for preschoolers based on federal law: specifically, the mandates in Education of the Handicapped Act Amendments of 1986 (PL 99-457).

   - Head Start administrators recognized the need to expand services to children with disabilities and began observing models in neighboring districts.

2. Agency collaboration

   - Special education administrator first tried a co-teaching model with minimal planning and collaborative effort and could not sustain it after one year.

   - Two years later, administrators from both agencies began a conversation and recognized the need to plan cooperatively.

   - Administrators jointly approached superintendents and pushed for board approval to move forward with vision.

3. Implementing action plans

   - Administrators recognized the need to assign co-workers with knowledge of programming details and a passion to see the project move forward by implementing an action plan.

   - Head Start did not write a formal action plan but acknowledged that one could, and probably should, be included in the required annual memorandum of understanding with the school district.

4. Supporting program needs

   - As needs were identified and discussed, administrators supported solutions and backed assignment of responsibilities (e.g., classroom materials, busing) and funding needs (e.g., extra hourly pay for staff to attend trainings).

5. Communication

   - Administrators recognized and supported the need for people to be informed of what was happening with the process and that teachers needed time to meet on a regular basis to develop relationships and plan together.

Establishing a Time Line

Allowing time for staff to prepare is most important when the new program incorporates the co-teaching model, which involves teachers teaming together and sharing one classroom and responsibilities. Given the need for teachers to work together on a daily basis, administrators may want to consider carefully which

- Personnel should be assigned and preliminary meetings scheduled for staff to meet together and begin to establish relationships and responsibilities. (This is especially critical in co-teaching models.)
- Initial training and mentoring should occur as necessary for some staff, depending on experience.
- Individualized education programs (IEPs) may need to be amended for children going to the new program.
- Administrative input will be needed to write appropriate services into the IEP (for example, the number of actual minutes of special education support per month).
- Classrooms must be selected.
- Busing needs must be identified and addressed.

Figure 3.3. What should be in place before beginning a new program. (Adapted from Sexton et al., 1996.)

teachers will be involved in this model. (Sometimes asking for volunteers reveals those who are willing to embrace change and are willing to try.) Due to the complexity of the blended (co-teaching) approach, the time line for discussion and planning should begin several months prior to the start of the new school year. In an itinerant approach, less time is needed for planning and preparation with personnel. However, depending on the severity of disabilities of children enrolled in regular early childhood programs, staffing, training of ECE staff, and consideration of necessary modifications to the ECE environment may be factors that affect for establishing a reasonable time line for preparing. By the beginning of the summer, the planning actions presented in Figure 3.3 should be in place.

Shifting Teacher Roles: Segregated to Inclusive Service Delivery

As early childhood special educators begin moving from segregated classrooms to inclusive models of service, there may or may not be strong resistance to such changes. In taking on an itinerant model of inclusion support, the ECSE teacher will need to understand the differences between the segregated special day class teaching model and the itinerant model. For some teachers, this is a huge shift: rather than being the primary teacher the itinerant now becomes a support person providing consultative services to several ECE teachers. Additionally, the need for careful scheduling is imperative in order to meet the needs of both children and their teachers throughout the week. Driving from school to school and essentially working independently is a very different job when teachers have typically had one room, one desk, and one staff member to work with.

The co-teaching model presents a different set of challenges: Early childhood and special education agencies with different rules, expectations, salaries, and paperwork must be acknowledged and respected. Administrators need to be cognizant of the disparity in education and salaries between ECE and ECSE personnel, which can lead to difficulties working together in some cases.

Whenever feasible, the administrators should consider asking personnel to volunteer to work in these different models, or more specifically a *willing* volunteer—not an unwilling educator forced to change. The case study in the vignette on pages 67–70 illustrates a positive partnership based on teachers who volunteered to try out the new program model, resulting in the "Dream Team."

The "Dream Team"

Sylvia, Maria, and Paige call themselves the "Dream Team." Sylvia and Maria are Head Start teachers with 27 years of teaching experience between them. Paige is an early childhood special education (ECSE) teacher with 8 years of experience. The Dream Team has worked together for a total of 4 years in a blended preschool classroom.

The blended model for these teachers encompasses two Head Start classrooms side-by-side in one building. Each classroom has 20 students. Of the 20, 6–7 students have special needs. During the past school year the students were identified with disabilities including moderate to severe autism, physical handicaps, intellectual disabilities, and moderate to severe expressive/receptive language and speech disorders.

Paige's caseload is a total of 12–14 students, all of whom met district qualifications for a segregated special day preschool class if the inclusive option was not available. Two assistants funded by the district special education program provide support in each classroom. Paige splits her time between both classes each day. Maria and Sylvia are responsible for all 20 students in their classrooms and collaborate with Paige to provide appropriate supports to the children with disabilities. Both Head Start teachers also have an assistant in each classroom.

First Unsuccessful Try

When the district first implemented the program before Paige joined the team, another ECSE teacher had been hired. Sylvia and Maria had volunteered to participate in this new program. Unfortunately, the first half of the school year was extremely difficult for that team. They remember the year starting with the new ECSE teacher: she informed them that she wouldn't come in early to plan before the school year began, as her contract did not begin until the first school day. When she did sit down to meet with them she didn't ask any questions about the Head Start program. The Head Start teachers felt that the weekly meetings weren't productive; there was little sharing or planning. This ECSE teacher often said she was too busy to meet with the Head Start staff or join them for home visits.

In the classroom, the ECSE teacher often pulled "her" students aside to work on individualized education program (IEP) goals on an individual basis and rarely worked with the "other" children. She was unable to make suggestions or follow through with strategies to control preschoolers' behavior in the classroom and seemed generally uncomfortable being in this setting. Based on her supervisor's observations, input, and review, this teacher was asked to leave the school district after four months. Paige was hired to replace her.

The "New" Teacher

The three teachers remember being a "little nervous" when Paige was introduced. Maria and Sylvia describe their feelings as cautious and observant. "How will *this* special education teacher be?" they wondered. Sylvia decided they would "concentrate on the job, not the personalities." When Paige came in on her first day, she remembers being overwhelmed by the number of adults in the classroom. "I came from a special day class with just me and one assistant. Here there were two teachers, more

(continued)

assistants, and parents. The rooms were full of people." Paige decided to observe for those first few days and let the Head Start teachers take the lead.

When they all met for the first time, Maria and Sylvia remember Paige asking them questions about the Head Start program. The meetings took on a very different character from the first experience. All three teachers agreed that they brought an open mindedness to the meetings, took turns, and brainstormed ideas. Paige felt that she had so much to learn about Head Start rules; there were many more than what she'd dealt with in her own special day class. She felt that the teachers rather than her administrators taught her how to work in the blended classroom setting because the teachers were there in the classroom on a daily basis.

Prioritizing Head Start Needs

Their second year together started off smoothly; they felt like they were already a team. All three teachers were more comfortable with each other and the program. They all agree that they respected each other; "we know we're a team."

Salaries and Work Hours

When asked about inequities in their jobs such as work hours and salaries, both Sylvia and Maria acknowledged that other teachers and Head Start employees assumed they were being paid more to work in the blended program and were quite surprised to find out that they were not. While acknowledging that it "would be nice if the teachers could get paid more," Sylvia said she chose to join the program because she welcomed the change and the challenge. Paige said that while she usually left at the end of her work day, which is contractually shorter than the Head Start teachers, she was always available for meetings and home visits (she also often took work home with her). All three agreed that Paige prioritizes Head Start needs. In fact, she attends all parent conferences and home visits, and the teachers attend all IEPs for the students in their classes.

Preplanning

The teachers agreed that their overall approach to the program is "how do we work to get things done?" Strategies that have worked well for them included Paige writing out her students' IEP goals and objectives prior to the beginning of the year. She also writes notes about the preschoolers with disabilities for both teachers and assistants. These notes help when the team sits down to plan because they can add in individual accommodations or modifications as needed, based on the objectives and teacher notes.

Schedules

The teachers ended up using a system of trial and error to decide on the most effective ways to schedule Paige's time between the two classes. They remember at least six or seven changes to the schedule before they felt like they had a workable routine. Both Maria and Sylvia acknowledged that they received administrative support to be more flexible than is sometimes allowed in the Head Start classrooms, because this was a new and different kind of collaborative model. Paige follows a planned schedule but will spend more time, at least temporarily, in one class or during particular activities depending on the needs of children and staff or if asked to by staff.

(continued)

Staff Assignments

The teachers agreed that organization and planning were absolutely essential to the smooth running of the program. Defining assignments for all adults, teachers, and assistants and assigning individuals to be responsible for specific activities or groups is always a part of the planning. Group leaders rotate monthly and a specific person is assigned to supervise small or large groups. The three colleagues also spoke about the need to carefully assign some chores to make sure no one carries an undue burden, such as when toilet training a child or when a child needs diapering. The tasks are equally split between assistants and teachers.

Meetings

Paige respects time lines required by Head Start and tries to help teachers by scheduling her IEPs at least a month in advance. While Sylvia sometimes forgets to let Paige know about a home visit until the last minute, the three show obvious respect and understanding for each other and their specific job demands. They could not think of any time during these past four years when conflicts arose. They did agree that they sometimes had to talk together to provide a thoughtful and united approach when occasionally dealing with parents who went from one teacher to another to make requests or demand change.

Adjusting to a Different Model

Paige said that one of her biggest challenges when she first began was working in a large group setting with all the children. She found this very different from the smaller special education setting, where much of the teaching took place in a one-to-one or small group setting. Figuring out appropriate accommodations or modifications for students in the large group setting was difficult for her at first. Maria found that the larger numbers of adults in the classroom took some getting used to. This included not just the adults assigned to work in the classrooms but also the number of supervisors or monitoring adults coming into the classroom. There were more visitors and observers of the program, too. Both Head Start teachers asked administration to be more aware of scheduling visits and observations so no more than one or two additional adults were in the classrooms at any one time.

Sylvia felt that it was most important to learn to share and "let it go" when it came to issues about time, materials, and "even your ego." She also talked about acknowledging differences in training and expertise and learning to know when to "step back and let someone else take over" (e.g., when a child is having a hard time). Most tellingly, all three teachers agreed that they looked forward to coming to work. Paige said, "I look forward to coming to work every Monday." To which Maria jokingly added, "I *always* look forward to coming to work, not just on Mondays!"

Keys to Successful Blended Programs

- Getting to know and understand the partner program (school district/Head Start)
- Having administrative support
- Using principles of good communication

(continued)

(continued)

- Knowing how to collaborate
- Having positive attitudes
- Letting go of egos and respecting each other
- Being flexible
- Prioritizing program needs over individual needs
- Respecting program demands and time lines
- Acknowledging differences in training and expertise
- Maintaining awareness and respect of individuals (especially for less desirable chores like toileting)
- Agreeing on ownership of all students (mine/yours/ours)
- Focusing on children and their needs
- Making time for meetings
- Being prepared for and participating in lesson planning
- Planning and scheduling
- Knowing and using positive behavioral strategies

Responsibilities of Early Childhood Educators and Special Educators

Both the early childhood teacher and the early childhood special educator will need to clarify job descriptions with their supervisors. Work hours may need to change and decisions made about classroom responsibilities. Typically, teachers working for school districts work under contracts with details specified by union and administration agreements. When working in an early childhood environment where teachers may not have union-negotiated contracts, there may be a disparity in daily hours and break periods, paid time off, and calendars of teaching days. Determining the legalities of work hours and breaks will need to be discussed by administrators from both agencies. If schedules cannot be matched equally, will extra hourly pay be available? How will the disparity be discussed between staff?

Table 3.3 illustrates examples of possible differing and shared responsibilities for assessment, planning, and home visits between ECSE and ECE teachers in a blended program.

Adjusting Designated Instructional Services in Inclusion Support Models

In some programs, the model of inclusion support service delivery might be referred to as the *multidisciplinary* approach. Children with disabilities are supported by itinerant therapists who provide the various services recommended in the child's IEP: S/L therapy, OT, PT, and behavioral intervention therapy or applied behavior analysis as well as specialist support for visual impairment (VI) and deaf and hard of hearing (DHH) services. This approach has several challenges. More

Table 3.3. Suggested teacher responsibilities in blended programs

ECSE teacher responsibilities	ECE teacher responsibilities	Suggested shared responsibilities
Complete annual IEPs with appropriate assessments.	Attend IEP meetings or Student Study Success Team meetings as needed for students.	ECSE teacher conducts IEP meeting with input from ECE teacher.
Assess child progress with two screenings per year per child.	Complete multiple developmental screenings and rescreenings for all children at least two times per year.	Teachers plan for one of them to take the lead in all screenings, assessments, and reporting. The ECE teacher provides input. Typically the ECSE teacher takes the lead for students with disabilities.
Provide weekly lesson plans and teaching assignments.	Provide weekly lesson plans and teaching assignments.	Teachers meet together each week to share planning. ECSE teacher provides accommodations to lessons for specific students per IEPs. Teachers plan specific staffing duties so teaching assignments are shared and rotated on a weekly or monthly basis.
Schedule one parent–teacher conference per year.	Schedule home visits and parent–teacher conferences two times per year.	Teachers combine conference and home-visit requirements and agree on mutually acceptable schedule.

Key: ECE, early childhood education; ECSE, early childhood special education; IEP, individualized education program.

often than not, therapists communicate very little, if at all, with one another due to different and busy schedules and, often, differing points of view on service delivery approaches. This lack of collaborative teaming among service providers fails to take advantage of possible transdisciplinary learning from one another, which can enhance the effectiveness of their interventions. In addition, it is not unusual for recommendations and strategies of multiple service providers to be at odds with one another. Finally, when service providers use a pull-out itinerant model rather than a collaborative consultation model, there are limited opportunities to communicate with and learn from the classroom teacher.

Therapists and other specialized service providers who have traditionally worked in segregated or clinical settings may express some discomfort providing interventions in inclusive settings. Another very practical concern is the fiscal challenge to specialists who travel to inclusive sites in which there may be only a single client. Administrators need to be ready and available to discuss these concerns and provide support in the transition to working within the ECE setting.

One of the issues commonly raised regarding the service delivery model of specialists is whether the provision of direct service (for example, small group pull-out speech therapy) is less or more effective than a more collaborative consultative model. According to McWilliam (2006), a consultant model in which the specialist provides demonstration and guidance to early childhood staff, who then embed the guidance within the daily routines, results in greater effectiveness for the child and a more collaborative team approach for staff. McWilliam makes the point that what happens *during* the visit is not as important as how designated instructional service interventions are reinforced in the classroom (and at home) on a daily basis *between* visits.

Specialized service providers require consideration and consultation from administrators as inclusive models are planned. Including specialists in planning and collaborative meetings with early childhood staff sets a precedent for true teaming and can help all personnel communicate more effectively with each other as the school year proceeds.

Resistance to Change and the Need for Training

Probably one of the more frustrating aspects of creating a new inclusive model in an ECSE program is resistance by well-meaning staff. Why change something that was working well? The need to address resistance is imperative but often quite difficult to do. Offering training in collaboration and problem-solving processes may help those involved gain in their ability to participate in discussions using a proactive, rather than a destructive, approach. (This topic is discussed at length in Chapter 5.) If training needs are not addressed formally as part of the time line for beginning a new program they might receive scant attention, because once the school year begins, schedules become impacted. Scheduling time for trainings, possibly based on a needs assessment completed by teachers and support staff, should be considered prior to the start of a school year when possible.

It is often very helpful to have educators and staff from other districts and schools share their positive experiences and describe the successful implementation of early childhood inclusion. The opportunity to voice concerns and fears and exchange ideas with colleagues and peers who have had success can be powerful.

Understanding adult learning styles is very important when planning trainings. Sexton et al. (1996) found that the most successful in-service trainings included active participation *and* follow-up support. More recent studies support that passive listening to in-service presentations are minimally effective (Sheridan, Edwards, Marvin, & Knoche, 2009). Ironically, the most common features of in-service training (e.g., lectures and handouts) were reported to be the least effective. The list in Figure 3.4 describes teacher perceptions of in-service activities.

One of the most important areas of need for professional development is collaborative teaming and problem solving. However, team members themselves may often fail to appreciate their importance until a major conflict arises. Providing training on collaboration may appear to be a waste of time, especially if there is initial camaraderie among the group members. There is often a general belief that if one has good intentions and really wants what is best for the children, collaboration will not be difficult. However, as discussed in Chapter 5, establishing a culture of collaborative problem solving is essential, but not simple. Providing training opportunities to teach personnel the basics of active-listening, perspective-taking, and problem-solving strategies can provide valuable tools as the program begins. Often, those working in inclusive programs will admit that it is the adults who cause the "problems," not the children. Having teams agree on a basic problem-solving process in advance of problems that may arise can be helpful.

Least likely to effect change:
- Handouts
- Lectures
- Videos or movies

Least likely to result in change of practices:
- Filling out self-revealing inventories
- Trainer-provided resources
- Follow-up reminders
- Back-home plans (writing what you will do as a result of training)
- Panel discussions

Most likely to result in change of practices:
- Live observations of practices being implemented
- Small-group discussions
- Demonstrations or modeling by trainer
- On-the-job follow-up assistance
- Microteaching (videotaping of trainee implementing a practice)

Figure 3.4. Teacher perception of in-service activities.

Staff development is critical. Ongoing training after a program is established is essential to ensure that all staff are offered opportunities for learning or polishing expertise. Wolery and Odom (2000) suggested several steps to effectively plan staff development opportunities, including formalizing a vision, identifying a planning team, using a needs assessment, defining training goals and desired outcomes, evaluating, and following up.

Ratio of Children with Disabilities to Typically Developing Children

An important part of planning a blended program is determining the mix or balance of children in the classroom. There is some controversy among supporters of inclusive education regarding the most effective ratio of children with special needs to typical children. Some suggest that there should be no more children with disabilities in a classroom than would be seen proportionally in the community at large. This figure is typically set at around 10%. However, currently there is no evidence base for a particular number.

There is no perfect formula for determining the right mix of children, whether one considers the ratio of children with disabilities to typical children or whether one considers the complexity or specific characteristics of each child's learning needs. Administrators often take into account the severity of disabilities and the total number of children with IEPs enrolled in the class. Placing too many children with moderate to severe needs in one classroom, especially children with severely disruptive behaviors, can overwhelm personnel and interfere with the feasibility of implementing a typical early childhood program. However, enrolling children with *a range* of special needs from mild to severe can create a truly blended program. The scenario presented in the vignette at the top of the following page illustrates this process.

Example of Program Flexibility

District A has 10–12 children with individualized education programs (IEPs) and disabilities ranging in intensity from mild to severe. Administrators and teachers agree that these students would do well in an inclusive co-teaching model. Following a district discussion on the best ratio of children with disabilities to typically developing students, administrators decide to split this group of students into two groups of 5–6 children and enroll them in adjoining Head Start classrooms. The early childhood special education teacher works with the two Head Start teachers and splits his time between both classrooms.

   The next year, administrators in District A note that there are more children with moderate to severe disabilities on a teacher's caseload. After observing the effects of several children with very intensive needs grouped in one early childhood education (ECE) setting, administrators decide that half of the students (with more severe disabilities) should be enrolled in two morning, blended programs, while the other half of the students (with more mild to moderate disabilities) will be enrolled in several afternoon Head Start classrooms throughout the district. They will be served on an itinerant basis in the afternoons by the early childhood special education (ECSE) teacher. His special education paraprofessionals will work in the morning blended programs and then be deployed, based on child needs, during the afternoon classes. Using this strategic creativity, a more efficient and effective model for support and service delivery can be implemented.

There is also an assumption that children who are higher functioning (i.e., a child with speech delays and normal cognition) or who have less complex disabilities (i.e., a child with a physical disability affecting her ability to walk but no speech, cognitive, or behavioral concerns) are easier to include. Some research suggests that higher functioning children tend to perform better in inclusive settings than in segregated preschool settings (Holahan & Costenbader, 2000), particularly children with speech and language disorders. This may seem obvious, and it is clearly supported by Vygotsky's (1980) tenet that children learn best in the presence of more capable peers. Interestingly, however, there are also studies that suggest that children with intellectual disabilities (i.e., a child with Down syndrome) make even greater gains from inclusive settings than do children with learning disabilities (Hattie, 2009). A study examining inclusion of preschool children with severe disabilities found very positive outcomes (Alquraini & Gut, 2012).

   Another common assumption is that the smaller the class size, or the smaller the student-to-teacher ratio, the better children learn (Barnett, Schulman, & Shore, 2004). However, in a synthesis of several meta-analyses described by Hattie (2009), the positive effect is very slight and related primarily to differences in teaching activities and strategies used in small versus large classrooms rather than directly to class size.

Checklist: Evaluating quality in the inclusive preschool program

Program philosophy supports inclusion

_____ Program has clear goals and objectives.

_____ Program promotes parent partnerships.

Staff management and training

_____ Staff has written job descriptions to define their roles.

_____ Staff has ongoing training and support to implement interventions.

_____ Staff has regular meeting times for staff development, planning, and lesson preparation.

_____ Staff feels supported by administration, which communicates clear expectations.

Adequate space, equipment, and materials

_____ Classroom areas are adaptable and accessible to all children.

_____ Functional signs and picture schedules facilitate transitions.

_____ A variety of developmentally appropriate and accessible materials are available.

_____ Equipment and material adaptations are made as needed for individual children.

_____ Outdoor equipment encourages children with disabilities to engage with typical peers.

Individualizing the curriculum and instruction

_____ Goals for children with disabilities are functional; instruction is embedded into daily routines and activities.

_____ Children have multiple times throughout the day to practice and learn individualized goals.

_____ Children with disabilities participate in the same activities, routines, and transitions as other children in the class.

_____ Planned cues and prompts for children with challenging behaviors are used consistently.

Staff planning and implementation

_____ Staff plans a daily schedule that includes predictable routines and activities.

_____ Staff facilitates child engagement and play using naturalistic techniques and systematic prompts.

_____ Staff consistently uses behavior management procedures.

_____ Staff adapts environment to promote participation, engagement, and learning.

_____ Staff modifies materials or equipment so children with disabilities can participate as independently as possible.

_____ Staff utilizes child preference to increase engagement and responds to child-initiated behaviors.

Staff monitoring and evaluation

_____ Ongoing monitoring of child performance on targeted goals is maintained; data are used to evaluate and revise intervention programs.

_____ Evaluation is conducted on a regular basis.

_____ Data are used to improve program.

Figure 3.5. Checklist: Evaluating quality in the inclusive preschool program. (Adapted from Jones & Rapport, 1997; Raab & Dunst, 1997; and Wolery et al., 1999.)

Evaluating Program Quality

Once preschool programs are established, the need to assess all aspects of the program for effective service delivery, safe environments, staff communication, and so on becomes important. A full discussion of program evaluations is beyond the scope of this book. However, the checklist in Figure 3.5 highlights the critical components of any inclusive preschool program and may be useful to administrators, providing initial information for building or maintaining a quality inclusion program.

CONCLUSION

The first years of implementing inclusive models can seem overwhelming as both ECE and ECSE staff settle into their new roles, families become more confident and familiar with how services and supports are provided, and administrators oversee the changes and ensure that problem-solving and collaborative processes are being implemented on a regular basis. As programs become more inclusive, administrators may need to consider changing or adapting existing inclusion models of support and shifting staff to address projected changes in student populations. In some programs, working with unions and teachers to redefine job descriptions to allow for flexibility in implementing the basic models of inclusion support or hybrid combinations may be necessary.

Administrators play a critical role in the success or failure of inclusive programs. Behind every effective and thriving inclusive early childhood program is an administrator who does the following:

- Understands how to use IDEA law to the fullest to ensure individualization, flexibility, and creativity on behalf of young children with special needs and their families

- Supports joint planning and collaboration among all key players

- Insists on a collegial, problem-solving approach

- Communicates effectively and frequently with administrators of partner programs

- Provides decision-making support for key personnel thinking outside the box

Flexibility and the need to think outside the box are keys to effective administration of inclusive early childhood programs. An established problem-solving approach ensures ongoing consideration of potential problems and possible solutions. In spite of the challenges presented earlier, or perhaps because of them, the positive outcomes observed in truly inclusive programs can be exciting. They inspire more creative changes to meet children's educational needs and create more truly inclusive communities over time.

REFERENCES

Alquraini, T., & Gut, D. (2012). Critical components of successful inclusion of students with severe disabilities: Literature review. *International Journal of Special Education, 27*(1), 42–59.
Americans with Disabilities Act (ADA) of 1990, PL 101-336, 42 U.S.C. §§ 12101 *et seq.*

Barnett, W.S., Schulman, K., & Shore, R. (2004). *Class size: What's the best fit?* National Institute for Early Educational Research: New Brunswick, NJ. Retrieved from http://nieer.org/resources/policybriefs/9.pdf

Craig, S., Haggart, A., Gold, S., & Hull, K. (2000). Expanding the circle of inclusion: The childcare director's role. *Young Exceptional Children Monograph, 2,* 7–36.

Dinnebeil, L., & McInerney, W. (2011). *A guide to itinerant early childhood special education services.* Baltimore, MD: Paul H. Brookes Publishing Co.

Education of the Handicapped Act Amendments of 1986, PL 99-457, 20 U.S.C. §§ 1400 *et seq.*

Giangreco, M.F. (2003). Working with paraprofessionals. *Educational Leadership, 61*(2), 50–53.

Hattie, J. (2009). *Visible learning.* New York: Routledge.

Holahan, A., & Costenbader, V. (2000). A comparison of developmental gains for preschool children with disabilities in inclusive and self-contained classrooms. *Topics in Early Childhood Special Education, 20*(4), 224–235.

Horn, E., & Sandall, S. (2000). The visiting teacher: A model of inclusive ECSE service delivery. *Young Exceptional Children Monograph, 2,* 49–58.

Individuals with Disabilities Education Act (IDEA) of 2004, PL 108-446, Section 612(a)(5), 20 U.S.C. §§ 1400 *et seq.*

Jones, H.A., & Rapport, M.J.K. (1997). Research-to-practice in inclusive early childhood education. *Teaching Exceptional Children, 29*(2), 57–61.

Klein, M.D., & Harris, K. (2004). Considerations in the personnel preparation of itinerant early childhood special education consultants. *Journal of Educational and Psychological Consultation, 15*(2), 151–165.

Levenson, N. (2011). *Something has got to change: Rethinking special education* (AEI Future of American Education Project Working Paper No. 2011-01). Retrieved from http://www.aei.org

Levenson, N. (2012). *Boosting the quality and efficiency of special education.* Washington, D.C.: Fordham Institute.

McWilliam, R. (2006). *Implementation manual* (2nd ed.). Nashville, TN: National Individualizing Preschool Inclusion Project, Center for Child Development, Vanderbilt University Medical Center. Retrieved from www.cde.state.co.us/early/downloads/PreSpEdOnline-Courses/IntegratedServicesNIPIP.pdf

Odom, S.L., & Buysse, V. (2005, August). *Preschool inclusion in the United States: Cost, quality, and outcomes.* Paper presented at the Inclusive and Supportive Education Congress International Special Education Conference, Glasgow, Scotland. Retrieved from http://www.isec2005.org.uk/isec/abstracts/papers_o/odom_s.shtml

Odom, S.L., Hanson, M.J., Lieber, J., Marquart, J., Sandall, S., Wolery, R., … Chambers, J. (2001). The costs of preschool inclusion. *Topics in Early Childhood Special Education, 21*(1), 46–55.

Odom, S.L., Parrish, T., & Hikido, C. (2001). The costs of inclusion and noninclusive special education preschool programs. *Journal of Special Education Leadership, 14,* 33–41.

Raab, M.M., & Dunst, C.J. (1997). *The preschool assessment of the classroom environment scale—revised (PACE-R).* Asheville, NC: Orelena Hawks Puckett Institute.

Richardson-Gibbs, A.M. (2004). Itinerant consultation in early childhood special education consultation: Personal reflections from a practitioner. *Journal of Educational and Psychological Consultation, 15*(2), 177–181.

Rosenkoetter, S.E. (1998). Together we can: Suggestions from the pioneers of classroom blending of multiple early childhood programs. *Young Exceptional Children, 1*(4), 7–16.

Sexton, D., Snyder, P., Wolfe, B., Lobman, M., Stricklin, S., & Akers, P. (1996). Early intervention in-service training strategies: Perceptions and suggestions from the field. *Exceptional Children, 62,* 486–495.

Sheridan, S.M., Edwards, C.P., Marvin, C.A., & Knoche, L.L. (2009). *Professional development in early childhood programs: Process issues and research needs.* Nebraska Center for Research on Children, Families and Schools. University of Nebraska-Lincoln. Retrieved from www.digitalcommons.unl.edu/cgi/viewcontent.cgi?article=content

Sindelar, P., Shearer, D., Yendol-Hoppey, D., & Liebert, T. (2006). The sustainability of inclusive school reform. *Exceptional Children, 72*(3), 317–331.

Vygotsky, L.S. (1980). *Mind in society: The development of higher psychological processes.* Cambridge, MA: Harvard University Press.

Wolery, R.A., & Odom, S. L. (2000). *An administrator's guide to preschool inclusion.* University of North Carolina at Chapel Hill, FPG Child Development Center, Early Childhood Research Institute on Inclusion. Retrieved from http://www.fpg.unc.edu/resources/administrators-guide-preschool-inclusion

Wolery, M., Paucca, T., Brashers, M.S., & Grant, S. (1999). *Quality of inclusive experiences measure.* University of North Carolina at Chapel Hill, FPG Child Development Center.

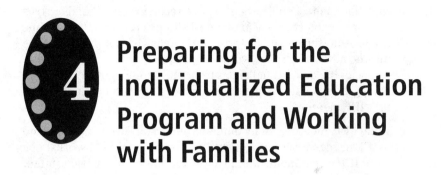

4 Preparing for the Individualized Education Program and Working with Families

There is perhaps no single event in the educational life of a young child with special needs more important than the initial development of the individualized education program (IEP), a carefully planned legal document for a child who has a disability. Too often, however, preparing the IEP is viewed as either a drain on busy professionals' time or a source of considerable stress by parents (Roe, 2008). Both regular education and special education teachers report feeling overwhelmed by the demands of IEP preparation and paperwork, while families report high levels of stress related to interactions with the professionals responsible for their children's education. According to Cheatham et al. (2012, p. 50), research on parents' reports of their IEP experiences suggest that "favorable perceptions are the exception rather than the norm".

The IEP should be viewed as an important legal contract that offers a vision of what a child with disabilities needs in order to progress in school. The IEP meeting is an opportunity to bring together a team of knowledgeable key players to carefully examine the child's strengths and needs and, in good faith, generate a plan that will address educational and developmental goals in the least restrictive environment (LRE). Professionals who understand the power of a well-written IEP can help parents understand the importance of this document. It can be the key to ensuring appropriate, effective educational services.

Unfortunately, because of the cost and complexity of difficult IEPs (for example, IEPs involving large teams of people, including advocates or lawyers, or meetings that last for many hours), both parents and educational personnel sometimes dread the IEP process. When IEP meetings are not approached by the team as an important or positive experience, the potential for exciting and creative educational planning can be jeopardized. When this occurs at the preschool level, the stage can be set for years of lack of trust, adversarial interactions, and sometimes costly litigation.

IEP planning for preschool age children—particularly the initial IEP meeting—is, for families, a very high-stakes experience, their first encounter with educational systems and regulations. While some families will have received early intervention services prior to transition to preschool, others may be receiving an initial diagnosis for their preschooler. Parents sometimes hear diagnostic information for the first time in the initial IEP. As a result, they may be starting an intensive grief process at the same time they enter the new and strange world of special education. (The vignette on p. 85 illustrates some of the unique challenges from one family's perspective.)

The following suggestions can mitigate some of the common challenges parents face at their first IEP meeting:

- Prior to the initial IEP meeting, help families understand the purpose and structure of the IEP process. Encourage family members to attend workshops or trainings on the IEP components and process and on families' legal rights.

- Also prior to the meeting, the team should agree on basic ground rules: for example, using common vocabulary and explaining all acronyms, allowing each person to have his or her say by taking turns, and encouraging members to listen to each other.

- Keep to a logical sequence during the IEP meeting by developing and following an agenda (more on the actual meeting below).

- Involve parents actively in the process of developing a strong IEP to help avoid future conflict or disagreement. Do not pressure parents to sign documents at the meeting. Parents of preschool children often need additional time to process the information presented in the initial IEP meeting.

- If conflicts do arise (ranging from disagreement over types and amount of service provided to a student to where a child will receive supports and services), encourage the use of conflict-resolution and problem-solving processes, as described in detail in Chapter 5, to help team members reach agreement.

It is important to realize that the best way to prevent conflict and litigation is with a carefully and collaboratively crafted individualized program. It is equally important to realize that disagreements, when managed effectively, can be harnessed to generate creativity and problem solving. Also important to families is the realization that nothing is "written in stone." The IEP document can and should be changed as needed. Parents or educators can request a meeting of the IEP team and can create an addendum as needed. While there is a natural inclination among busy administrators to resist the addendum process, understanding that it can be done can feel like an important fail-safe for families.

REVIEW OF THE COMPONENTS OF
THE INDIVIDUALIZED EDUCATION PROGRAM

The Individuals with Disabilities Education Act (IDEA) of 1990 (PL 101-476), Part B, provides special education services for students with disabilities ages 3–21. Families and educators alike should be mindful of the important ways the provisions of IDEA play out within the IEP process (Cheatham et al., 2012).

- All students with disabilities are entitled to a free and appropriate public education. Assessments of students must be fair. Families have the right to understand and question their child's assessments.

- Students with disabilities must receive *individualized* and *appropriate* education services, which are agreed upon and described in an IEP.

- Students with disabilities should be educated, to the greatest extent beneficial, in a typical setting with same-age peers who do not have disabilities, that is, in the LRE.

- Educators and families hold each other mutually accountable for these provisions via "procedural due process" or safeguards and dispute resolution procedures described in the law.

- Parents with disabilities work in partnership with educators in decision making related to students' education.

For more detailed information describing the provisions of IDEA, see Turnbull, Stowe, and Huerta (2007) and the web site of Wrightslaw (www.wrightslaw.com).

Transition from Part C to Part B: Individualized Family Service Plan to Individualized Education Program

In some intial IEPs, children will have received early intervention services prior to age 3 under Part C of IDEA. It is helpful for members of the IEP team to understand how these early intervention experiences can influence parents' perceptions and expectations of the IEP process. For example, the services change from being very *family* focused, as required by the individualized family service plan (IFSP), to being much more *child* focused, with the emphasis on the child's education, guided by the legal guarantee of free appropriate public education and the IEP. Also, services offered from birth to 3 may have been more frequent, offered in the family's home, and more focused on parent support. The heart of Part C, the IFSP, is a legal document for families of infants and toddlers who have or are considered at risk for disabilities. While similar to an IEP, as a legal contract between families and agencies responsible for coordinating and providing services, the IFSP is also very different from the IEP. The IFSP provides for appropriate services for infants and families in their natural environments.

Because IFSPs are written for children from birth to 3, if a child is found eligible for special education services at age 3 under Part B of IDEA, the legal document that defines appropriate services and supports shifts to an IEP. A very important component of Part C is the requirement that between approximately 2.6 and 2.9 years, preparation for the toddler's transition to preschool special education services (if eligible) must begin. How this transition is handled can often set the stage for success or failure in the extremely important, and often stressful, hand-off to Part B services via the child's initial IEP.

In some states, IFSPs may follow children through preschool if state policies and public agencies are in agreement. Table 4.1 summarizes the similarities and differences between Part C and Part B regulations regarding time lines, team members, and review periods.

Part B Time Line and Types of Individualized Education Program Meetings

In reality when families and educational personnel think of an IEP, they are often not thinking of a document or the details of a child's educational program.

Table 4.1. Comparing individualized family service plans, preschool individualized education programs, and elementary school individualized education programs

	Time lines	Reviews	Transitions	Team members
IFSP	Presented within 45 calendar days of referral	Every 6 months	Prior to child's 3rd birthday	Family, service coordinator, service providers
IEP (preschool)	Presented within 60 calendar days of receiving parental consent for evaluation (This is the federal time line; individual states may establish longer or shorter time lines.)	At least once annually	Prior to child entering kindergarten (or in some cases, first grade)	Parents, administrator, general and special education preschool teachers or service providers, and other service providers at parent or district discretion
IEP (K–21 years)	Presented within 60 calendar days of receiving parental consent for evaluation (This is the federal time line; individual states may establish longer or shorter time lines.)	At least once annually	Prior to student entering high school	Parents, administrator, general and special education teachers or service providers, and other service providers at parent or district discretion

Key: IEP, individualized education program; IFSP, individualized family service plan.

Rather, they think of the preparation for, and the interactions within, the many meetings that take place at regular intervals to address the details of the program described in the IEP document. The following summarizes those legally required meetings. See Table 4.2 for a brief outline of IEP meetings and time lines.

The Initial Individualized Education Program Meeting The initial IEP meeting is held following a period of time in which a child is evaluated in order to determine eligibility for special education services. If a child is found ineligible for services, an initial IEP meeting is still held to document these results. If a child is eligible for services, the initial IEP meeting will serve to document eligibility, strengths, areas of need, goals, services, and placement options. Team members mandated to attend IEP meetings include an administrator, general education teacher, special education teacher, parents, and any other service provider who has participated in the evaluation and needs to interpret results. Parents may give permission for specific team members to be absent, but an informed person must be available to deliver and interpret the absent member's report.

It is important to note that the services are not based on the child's disability category (e.g., intellectual disability, hearing loss, physical disability). Services must be based on the actual specific needs of the student, identified in the assessments conducted by a team of specialists with relevant expertise. Placement also cannot be based solely on the child's disability category. The LRE provision requires that once the team determines the child's individual learning needs, a case would have to be made that the necessary services and supports *cannot* feasibly be applied in a typical classroom with same-age peers.

Table 4.2. Types of Individualized Education Program meetings and time lines

	Time lines	Reasons	Team members
Initial IEP	Meets within 45 calendar days of referral	Child is evaluated in order to determine eligibility for special education services.	Administrator, psychologist general and special education teachers, parents, and any other service provider who has participated in the evaluation and needs to interpret results
Annual IEP	Meets annually or earlier, based on date of initial IEP	The child's progress during past year is reviewed; the team determines new goals, services, and supports based on present levels of performance.	Parents, administrator, general and special education teachers and/or service providers, and other service providers at parent or district discretion
Transition IEP	Generally meets prior to child going to kindergarten	This ensures a smooth transition into kindergarten.	Parents, psychologist, administrator, general and special education teachers and/or service providers, and other service providers at parent or district discretion
Triennials	Held every three years, usually in conjunction with the annual IEP	A child's eligibility for special education services is reviewed.	Parents, psychologist, administrator, general and special education teachers and/or service providers, and other service providers at parent or district discretion

Key: IEP, individualized education program.

The Annual Individualized Education Program Meeting   An annual IEP is held every year per legal mandate and includes a review of the past year's progress and assessments as well as a determination of new goals, services, and supports based on present levels of performance. A child's IEP must be reviewed at least annually.

The Transition Individualized Education Program Meeting   In early childhood, transition IEP meeting are held when a child transitions from Part C early intervention services to Part B preschool services (coinciding with his or her initial IEP meeting) and again when the child transitions from preschool to kindergarten. State regulations may differ on specific requirements for preschool and kindergarten transitions, but the intent is to ensure smooth transitions for families and school teams.

Preschool transition meetings must be convened before a child turns 3 years old to determine eligibility and special education services under Part B of IDEA. This transition meeting must be scheduled with enough time for teams to agree on appropriate services and placement so that a child is ready to start the program by his or her third birthday.

The Triennial Individualized Education Program Meeting   As the name implies, triennials are IEP meetings held every three years, usually in conjunction with the annual IEP meeting, to review a child's eligibility for special education services. To assist in determining the child's eligibility, a psychologist may administer more formal testing prior to this meeting. Initial, transition, and triennial IEPs include a psychologist who oversees the assessment process, reviews educational files, and leads the team in determining initial or continuing eligibility for special education services.

Additional meetings of the IEP team can be called by any team member (including by a parent) at any time if questions or concerns arise or changes to the IEP are necessary. When an IEP meeting is scheduled, it is considered a formal meeting and specified team members must attend, including an administrator, both a general and a special education teacher, any other team member who is contributing to that meeting, and, of course, the parents. Any changes agreed upon by the team will be documented in an IEP addendum. For minor concerns, for example, omissions or clerical errors, a nonmeeting amendment can be called for an IEP.

PREPARING FOR THE INDIVIDUALIZED EDUCATION PROGRAM MEETING

Arranging the date and time of an IEP meeting can be challenging if a large team is involved. One major difficulty is coordinating district members' schedules, workloads, and priorities with those of parents, especially parents who work full time. Trying to set a mutually agreeable time for all involved is often easier when done far ahead (e.g., at least four to eight weeks) of the actual due date of an IEP meeting. It is often the case that administrators and parents have the least amount of flexibility in their schedules, so they may be the first team members to approach. Once the date is set, sending out appropriate paperwork is both a legal requirement and a courtesy to team members. Written invitations and relevant IEP documents— including parents' rights documents—and assessment permission forms need to be sent to parents, and, of course, translated copies must be sent to non–English speaking parents.

Asking team members to prepare and submit assessment and progress reports ahead of time can be annoying to some; however, parents have a legal right to request copies of reports prior to the meeting. Establishing this expectation as best practice ensures that all are ready *prior to the meeting*.

During the preschool years, meeting or having a phone conference with parents prior to an IEP meeting is critical to establishing rapport with the family and determining the agenda for the IEP meeting. Moreover, it empowers families to continue taking an active role in the IEP process throughout their K–12 years. It is the early childhood special education (ECSE) teacher's professional responsibility to assist parents who are new to the process in understanding and participating in their child's IEP meeting. Arranging an informal home visit or phone conference to review the process of an IEP meeting and briefly sharing report results and draft educational goals helps families better understand what may be a threatening process to them. This also helps families become invested in the process and advocate for their child's needs. So often, families experience anxiety about the meeting because they do not know what will be said or reported by the other team members. This is counterproductive. Families experience enough worries about their children without IEP teams inadvertently adding to the worry by not making the effort to communicate prior to a meeting (see vignette below).

A Parent's First Individualized Education Program

I knew something was not quite right with my son when he was almost 3 years old. The pediatrician didn't say anything, but some of my family asked why he didn't play with his cousins or talk to them at family parties. His preschool teacher told me I could ask the school district if they would take a look at him, so I called. I didn't even know that kids under 5 went to public school! Anyway, I was given an appointment and took Sam in for some tests. The people were nice, but I felt like he didn't do very well for them. He knows his name and how to count to 20 and a lot of alphabet letters, but he wouldn't answer any of their questions or play with them at all. He just kept walking around the room. They told me we'd have a meeting in two weeks and talk about the results of the tests. I asked them what they thought of Sam right then, but no one really said anything, just told me that it would be better if I waited until the meeting. I was really nervous for the next week. I kept thinking about how Sam didn't do much during the tests.

About three days before the meeting I got a phone call from the school psychologist. She said she had some results, and if I wanted to, I could talk to her before the meeting so I'd know what was going to happen. I said I didn't have time to meet with her but could we talk over the phone. She said yes and spent about 15 minutes summarizing the results of the tests. She talked about what they observed in Sam and how my answers to their questions plus the test results pointed to the possible diagnosis of autism. I had been wondering about that because of what people had said to me, but it was really hard to actually hear someone tell me that was what my son might have. She told me a few more things about services, but I don't really remember what she said. After that, she asked if I was still planning to come to the meeting in a couple of days, and I said yes. She said it would be great if I could bring someone with me just to be there and listen for me—I didn't know I could.

The meeting was hard, but at least I already knew what they were going to tell me. I brought my sister with me, too, and it was nice to have her sitting next to me. This time I heard more of what the team was telling me about services and programs. I think the psychologist had said something about that on the phone. So, now we are starting a whole new stage in Sam's life. It's overwhelming, but I feel like the team took time to talk to me and listen to me. I feel like they care about what happens to Sam. I'm not sure if he does have autism, but at least people are helping him.

Of course, all families and teams are different, and some parents may have no problem being presented with all of the information for the first time at the meeting. The case managers of these teams can determine the most compassionate and professional approach for individual families as they establish relationships with them. Essentially, families need to know about their role in the planning process and their legal rights. Beginning this discussion in the months leading up to the transition to school services is essential so that the conversation happens multiple times, not just once. This is new and unfamiliar territory for most families of young children with disabilities. The more often they hear information, engage in discussion and planning, and have opportunities to ask questions, the more comfortable they will be once the IEP process begins. Actively encouraging parent participation in trainings or workshops on the subject gives family members opportunities to hear the information delivered in varying formats by different people, strengthening their understanding of the subject.

It should be noted that sometimes administrators discourage team members from preparing families for the IEP meeting based on the belief that such preparation leads to excessive demands on the part of parents and increases the likelihood of litigation. However, in our experiences, the reality is just the opposite. It is when parents feel that information or services are being withheld from them that they push back by bringing in a professional advocate.

Premeeting Legwork

In some cases, and whenever legally possible, premeetings with team members and parents may be helpful to ease anxiety about services and placement. When people attend meetings where some of the participants have information and others do not, the balance and equality among team members are lopsided. Trying to equalize information for all members often helps maintain better focus during the creation of the IEP.

Typically, IEP meetings are led by a case coordinator or manager. Initial meetings, transitions, triennials, or any meeting requiring major changes to an IEP, such as a change of placement, are usually led by an administrator and include the school psychologist. Annual meetings are coordinated by the special education teacher or primary service provider such as a speech therapist who knows the child and family well. In the annual meetings it may be easier to create a welcoming and organized atmosphere, especially when the family knows the teacher and enjoys a positive relationship with her. Usually, the annual meeting is a review of progress and, hopefully, with frequent teacher conferences occurring throughout the past year, the parents and service providers meet to formalize plans for next year with no surprises. Sometimes during initials or triennials, however, the delivery of testing results raises anxiety if the results have not been shared with parents ahead of time. Typically, this is not part of the annual meeting.

However, when there are several service providers attending, when parents need a translator, or when the meeting includes others because it is a transition or triennial, an IEP meeting can quickly become disorganized and possibly headed for disaster without careful preplanning. The following time line and list of considerations are helpful premeeting planning strategies. (See Table 4.3 for a time line for planning the meeting.)

COMING TO THE TABLE: THE MEETING

Using an agenda to keep a team meeting on track is helpful. The agenda delineates when items will be addressed throughout the meeting. Parents and other team members must resist the tendency to discuss placement first. Parents must understand, preferably prior to the meeting, what the agenda will be. In fact, all team members can be given a copy of a meeting agenda so all understand the protocol for

Table 4.3.   Preparing for an IEP meeting

4 weeks prior to meeting	• Arrange date and time with parents and other team members.
3 weeks prior to meeting	• Send invitation and permission-to-assess forms to parents for signatures (with copies for them to keep). • Arrange for translator as needed.
1–2 weeks prior to meeting	• Work on assessments and draft goals. • Arrange to meet or talk with parents about results and discuss possible goals.
1 week prior to meeting	• Check on specific location of meeting with administrator. • Remind all team members of date and time. • Verify who will translate and remind that person (if needed) of the meeting. • Request reports, goals, and so on be submitted by two days prior to meeting; give parents copies of reports.
Day before or day of meeting	• Check that the meeting room is unlocked and there are enough chairs for all participants to be seated comfortably around the table. • If parents are bringing children, arrange for age-appropriate toys to be available.

Key: IEP, individualized education program.

completing the IEP. Parents can be prepared to ask questions, present their views of their child's strengths and needs, and offer their own case for a preferred placement at the appropriate points in the meeting. See Figure 4.1 for a sample agenda beginning with introductions and ending with distribution of copies of the IEP and reports to parents. This sample agenda includes all possible areas that might need to be discussed at a meeting. We have summarized the key parts of most IEP meetings in the following eight steps to illustrate the main order of events.

1. Begin with Introductions and the Reason for the Meeting

This sets the stage for a welcoming meeting. Encourage team members to be punctual, because people arriving at different times after the start of the meeting requires repetition of introductions and review of material. Sometimes a team member may bring refreshments to share with the others. Parents often bring a photo of their child. Photographs often help to humanize the discussion: It is not just a legal process but a discussion about the needs of a particular child. Parents' rights, written in the primary language, must be offered to parents at this time, or prior to the meeting, with an offer to explain or summarize them, if requested.

2. Review and Provide Opportunity for Discussion of Assessments Results

This is an area where tensions can arise. Depending on how assessment results are delivered, family members can feel a variety of emotions from defensiveness to sadness or anger when they hear how their child performed on various tests. Imagine sitting at a table, surrounded by relative strangers, and hearing how poorly your child has performed, how many deficits he or she has, and how "low" he or she scores on tests as compared to "typical children" her age. Although it is important to deliver assessment results accurately, we have experienced profound

---

West San Gabriel Valley SELPA

SAMPLE IEP AGENDA

1. Introduction of IEP team members
2. Share purpose/outcomes of the meeting
3. Review of parent rights
4. Share assessment reports and discuss/determine present levels of performance
   a. General education teacher
   b. Special education teacher
   c. Psychologist
   d. Other specialists:
      i. Speech/language
      ii. Adaptive PE
      iii. Occupational therapist
      iv. Physical therapist
      v. Counselor
      vi. Etc.
5. Parent input
6. Review and determine eligibility criteria (initials and triennials only)
7. Develop goals and objectives
8. Develop individual transition plan (ITP)
9. Develop behavior support plan (BSP) - as appropriate
10. Discuss placement continuum - (services/program options needed)
11. Determine appropriate placement, services and accommodations/modifications
12. Review summary of notes taken during meeting
13. Clarify scheduled review date (remind participants that they may call an IEP team meeting at any time)
14. Sign required forms
15. Provide parent with a copy of IEP and reports discussed during meeting

---

Figure 4.1. West San Gabriel Valley SELPA: Sample IEP agenda. *Key:* IEP, individualized education program; SELPA, special education local plan area.

differences in how professionals choose to deliver the information, with lasting impact on families. Additionally, offering to review and summarize results with parents prior to the formal meeting may be time consuming but, ultimately, far more compassionate than waiting until all are gathered at the IEP meeting. If parents disagree with the assessment procedures or results, they have the right to request that an *independent educational evaluation* be administered.

3. Determine or Confirm the Child's Eligibility

If this is an annual IEP meeting, then eligibility has already been established. However, the purpose of initial and triennial IEPs is to determine initial or continued eligibility for special education services. Again, if the discussion of eligibility is new, parents need to be informed in a compassionate and sensitive way. Parents may know that their child has a suspected disability—after all, they have participated in the assessment process—but hearing a team confirm their suspicions can be devastating. Team members must allow families time to absorb this news. Suggesting a short break in the meeting, having a box of tissues, offering to bring parents coffee or water, or simply allowing some quiet time as the parent absorbs the news are ways for a team to show that they understand that this process is very difficult.

4. Discuss Areas of Child's Needs *and* Strengths

Needs and strengths may be considered during the reporting of assessment results. The team leader can either summarize the areas of need or ask individual service providers to summarize in order to move the discussion into development of appropriate goals. For some children with significant behavioral challenges and if a child's behavior is impeding learning, this may also be the point during an IEP meeting when a team considers the need for a behavior plan. Typically, with preschoolers, behavioral goals may be written as a first step before the team decides to create a formal behavior intervention plan, which becomes part of the IEP. (See Chapter 8 for discussion regarding dealing with difficult behaviors and documenting progress using positive behavior support plans.)

5. Discuss and Agree upon Proposed Goals to Meet the Child's Identified Needs

It is important to get a sense of parents' priorities regarding developmental goals as well as their priorities regarding level of access to school readiness and academic goals. For some parents, their primary concern may be behavior and social skills and acclimation to classroom routines rather than pursuit of grade-level curriculum goals. Parents should be reassured that social and behavioral goals are just as important as academic goals.

Well-written goals provide a clear picture of a child's present level of performance and a measurable plan for continuing to show achievement over the course of the next year. Goals should be individualized for each child and specific language should be used to describe what the child will learn during the next several months. Depending on the results of current assessments, goals may cover academic, social, and functional needs or may focus on just one area of development. Again, results of comprehensive assessments should indicate where a child's performance is affected by her disability; goals must be written to cover any affected area. Wright, Wright, and O'Connor (2009) referred to goals that are specific and measurable, that use action words, and that are realistic and time limited (SMART goals). Additionally, goals must be individualized for a specific child, not a broad statement applicable to any child, such as "Maria will show progress in reading comprehension." Table 4.4 provides samples of measurable goals written for a specific child.

6. Discuss Appropriate Educational Placement for the Child, Including How Supports and Services Might Be Provided in the General Education Classroom

Sometimes IEP meetings end up being more focused on placement rather than the goals and appropriate supports and services. Districts offering limited placement, such as only a special day class option, may enter the IEP meeting assuming that this will be the most appropriate setting for a preschooler. Parents who have had little contact with any team members to discuss the meeting may come

Table 4.4.   Sample Individualized Education Program goals

Prereading	By May 2015, given preschool books that are part of the Head Start curriculum, Maria will sit with a teacher and peers, maintain attention by helping to turn the pages, point to at least 20 object or action pictures when asked *wh* questions by her teacher, and stay with the small group for at least 15 minutes or until the story is finished with no more than one verbal prompt.
Social	By May 2015, during all opportunities for free-choice play at school (outside, classroom choice time, etc.), and two times per day, Maria will choose an activity from two picture cards showing her preferred activities, take the card to the area, and imitate peers playing in that area for at least 10 minutes, with teacher providing verbal prompts or gestures as needed to maintain contact with peers.
Self-help	By May 2015, during all clean-up periods at school and following one teacher prompt to the whole class, Maria will independently pick up at least four objects from the area she played in and place them on the appropriate shelves by matching the objects to their pictures, signing or saying "all done" when she is finished.
Communication	By May 2015, throughout all periods of the school day and with one teacher verbal or signed prompt each period, Maria will use at least 20 signs or words, in one- or two-word phrases, to communicate her wants and needs to peers or teachers, including *more, all done, stop, give me, drink, eat, ball, baby,* and so on.

Key: IEP, individualized education program.

to the initial IEP meeting with a high level of anxiety ("Where will my child go to school?"). They may be very concerned about the services their child will receive and where those services will be provided and may want to jump to these decisions before reports and goals are discussed. It is critical that all team members understand that placement is based on a thorough understanding of the child's strengths and needs, his or her goals, and the services and supports necessary for the child to reach those goals in a timely manner during the coming school year. By law, the placement must be in the "least restrictive environment." If some members of the team do not agree that the LRE for this particular child is with his same-age peers in a general education class room (or community-based preschool program such as Head Start), they must put forth specific data and arguments to make the case that adequate supports cannot be provided in the inclusive setting. Placement in special classes may occur "only when the nature or severity of the disability is such that education in regular classes with the use of supplemental aides and services cannot be achieved satisfactorily" (Musgrove, 2012).

In other words, the discussion should not focus on all the reasons why a child cannot be placed in an inclusive setting but rather what supports and services would be necessary for the child to succeed in the inclusive setting and whether or not those supports are feasible. If the team determines they are not feasible, then the next least restrictive option can be considered (for example, daily mainstreaming during music and centers in the Head Start program housed on the same campus). Before placement is agreed to by the family, they can request—or better yet, be invited—to visit and observe recommended programs, if they have not been shown possible sites prior to the meeting.

Another factor to consider when discussing placement and thinking about appropriate supports are the concerns and priorties that families have for their children. Some children are just beginning preschool and need functional, self-help, and social goals. A child whose goals focus on preliteracy and math skills may

Table 4.5.   Family priorities for their child and settings in which to meet them

Safety	Parents simply want a community program that will ensure their child's safety while they are at work. At this level, the child's educational goals are met in a separate classroom or school. The staff of the center may not have access to the child's goals or outcomes and special education supports may not be considered or funded.
Social	Social access is a family's priority in some early childhood settings. The child receives academic support in another program such as a special education preschool class in the morning and then joins typical peers in a child development center for the afternoon. This is sometimes referred to as a dual placement, and some special education supports may be available for the child to assist him or her in meeting social goals with typical peers. (Hopefully, an itinerant inclusion specialist would provide support in this setting.)
Academic	Some ECSE environments are co-located in early childhood programs, and children with disabilities are supported for all goals, academic and social. Children are served by teachers in a blended model or by itinerant inclusion specialists.

Key: ECSE, early childhood special education.

need very different supports than a child whose goals focus on behavior and social skills. In some instances, a child may be dually enrolled in two different programs, one of which emphasizes preacademic skills for part of the day while the other provides group child care for the rest of the day. These priorities will influence the type of support children might need in a particular setting. Table 4.5 illustrates the types of settings and related goals that may meet a family's priorities.

7. Discuss Supports and Services Needed to Enable the Child to Meet Goals

Once the goals are determined and placement has been discussed, the next question is "What kinds of supports or services will help the child achieve these goals in this setting?" There is always a range of options regarding types and intensities of possible support. Districts cannot offer only predetermined services for specific disability characteristics or child needs (e.g., "all preschool children qualifying for speech therapy will receive 30 minutes 1 time per week"). Just as there must be a continuum of LRE placement options, there should also be room for creativity and a range of options for teaching and learning solutions to help children meet goals in efficient and timely ways. For example, a short-term, 6–12-week articulation lab with reassessment before adding additional services may be more appropriate for a child's speech needs than a year of group therapy at 30 minutes each week. There are two types of services that must be considered to enable children to meet their goals: 1) related and supplementary aids and services and 2) accommodations and modifications.

Related and Supplementary Aids and Services   *Related services* are those required for a child to receive FAPE. Examples include direct therapies, such as S/L, OT, and behavioral interventions. Also included are more indirect services, for example, school health services, parent and teacher training, transportation, and counseling services.

Supplementary aids and services are those that are necessary to allow a child *access to participation in academic and extracurricular activities with typical peers.* These supplementary services should be made available to support a child in an inclusive setting with typically developing students after assessment and the team's individualized consideration of the child's specific needs. These supports may encompass the following (Wright, Wright, & O'Connor, 2009):

- Environmental needs (e.g., preferential seating)

- Levels of staff support (e.g., instructional support assistants, consultation for teachers)

- Planning time (i.e., for staff to collaborate)

- Specialized equipment needs (e.g., specialized furniture, eating utensils, writing objects)

- Pacing of instruction (e.g., break times)

- Presentation of subject matter (e.g., primary or sign language)

- Materials (e.g., assistive technology, Braille, large print textbooks)

- Assignment modifications

- Self-management assistance

- Testing adaptations

- Social interaction supports (e.g., Circle of Friends, social skills groups)

- Training for personnel (e.g., teachers, paraprofessionals)

Accommodations and Modifications   Accommodations and modifications are actions taken to ensure children's access to the general education curriculum and offer a means to demonstrate what they have learned given the accommodation or modification and in spite of their disabilities. Accommodations and/or modifications must be listed on the IEP and agreed on by the IEP team. At times, these words are used interchangeably. The following paragraphs will attempt to clarify these terms for the reader.

Accommodations do not change tests or academic assignments significantly. In elementary school, for example, a child may be given extra time to complete a worksheet or a quiet place to take a test, but he or she is still expected to complete all of the work. For preschool children, accommodations might also include some of the actions listed previously under supplementary aids, such as preferential seating (e.g., close proximity to teacher during circle time), allowing for breaks during instruction (e.g., taking a walk with an assistant when the classroom becomes too noisy), or the use of special equipment (e.g., a slant board to position a child to print or draw more easily).

Using appropriate accommodations allow the child to demonstrate his or her abilities and can help teachers understand how the child's disability may be interfering with performance. Common examples of accommodations for preschool children include using visual schedules, sitting close to adults, spending less time in preacademic work activities or large group periods, and using air cushions for seating or lap weights during group activities.

Modifications require more thought before prescribing, as they will change a test or school work significantly. Modifications may include reducing the amount of work a child is expected to complete or the number of concepts he is expected to learn. For a child with more significant intellectual disabilities, many of the grade-level academic standards may require significant modifications. For example, a preschool child with significant disabilities might be expected to print his name by tracing pre-drawn letters with yellow highlighter rather than independently drawing them like his peers do.

Modifications are used more often for children older than preschool age and affect classroom work requirements and testing. For example, a third grader may be expected to complete 50% of each math worksheet while peers will complete 100% of all problems. Chapters 6 and 9 offer specific accommodations and modifications for young children that can be used throughout the school day.

8. Conclude the Meeting with a Review of the Notes Taken During the Meeting and Obtain Required Signatures of All Team Members Present

Parents may choose to delay signing the agreement to eligibility, goals, services, and placement until they have an opportunity to thoroughly review the document and reports and discuss them with family members. This is entirely acceptable, as the information offered during the meeting may be overwhelming for many families, especially in an initial IEP meeting. It can be useful to arrange a follow-up date to meet with parents and answer any questions that they may have. If the team has determined that a follow-up team meeting is required to review either goals or a behavior plan, this is a good time to schedule that meeting, as all team members will be present.

While team members often feel pressed by busy schedules, they should resist the temptation to rush through the IEP process. A collegial and collaborative atmosphere can set the tone for true cooperation and problem solving. Not allowing time to encourage parents' questions and concerns can backfire. The IEP experience can be a confusing and emotional experience for most families. Figure 4.2 suggests some ways to help parents manage the process.

WHEN AGREEMENT CANNOT BE REACHED: NEXT STEPS

When agreement on any part of the IEP (e.g., eligibility, goals, services, placement recommendations) cannot be reached, the team needs to adjourn and either agree to meet again to come to resolution or move to the next level of decision making. At that level, the director or coordinator of special education or a person with similar authority will oversee disputed areas on the IEP, such as number of hours or types of services that require supervisory review. Teams can agree on parts of the IEP so that some services can continue while the disputed sections are being resolved. For example, a related service, such as speech therapy, may be implemented while discussions continue about the appropriate educational placement.

If a review of the IEP by a special education director, or someone in a related role of authority, does not resolve the concerns, then either parents or school personnel can access the due process options guaranteed in IDEA's procedural safeguards, such as *mediation*. Mediation is a process in which disputes can be resolved without litigation but with the help of a trained, impartial mediator. Once the request is made, the school district must follow through by contacting the appropriate local or state authority and arranging for the mediation.

Prior to the meeting

Attend an IEP or advocacy workshop if this is going to be your first IEP.

If you are interested in seeing any assessment reports before the meeting, ask for them.

Let your case manager know about any changes you may be asking for before the meeting so there are no "surprises."

Invite a friend or another parent to come with you for support.

Ask to discuss draft goals for your child with the appropriate service provider before the meeting.

At the meeting

Try not to come in either "on the defensive" or "ready to attack"!

Try the first meeting without an advocate; not every IEP needs one (but do bring a friend, a family member, or another parent).

Ask for a break during the meeting if you need to reorganize your thoughts.

If you feel strongly that you want an inclusive setting for your child, be clear in expressing this.

If you feel strongly that a more restrictive setting (like a special education classroom) would be a better fit for your child's needs, be clear in expressing this; you can let the team know that you may want (or not) to explore a more inclusive setting in 6–12 months.

Clarify the type of supports your child will have in whatever setting he or she will receive services.

Remember that "more" (services, supports, etc) may not always be "better."

If you meet resistance to placement or services at a meeting, trying asking team members what their concerns are about your request.

Ask for specific names and contact information of people at the meeting.

Ask that all requests and agreements or disagreements be logged in the meeting notes; be sure to read the notes prior to signing the IEP.

Know that it is okay to leave an IEP meeting with an unsigned IEP if you want to re-read it first.

After the meeting

Do contact key team members if you need to discuss actions following the meeting (e.g., school visits, agreed-upon assessments, etc.).

Do review and return the IEP with signatures (if you agree) in a timely manner so the team can begin implementing it.

Remember that you can call another meeting at any time if you feel that the team needs to reconvene to discuss any part of your child's plan. Any team member can do this!

Figure 4.2. Managing the IEP: suggestions for parents. *Key:* IEP, individualized education program.

Parents can also file an official complaint with their state's department of education at any time during this period. If these steps do not help to resolve problems, a *due process hearing* can be requested. This is formal and litigious and is used only as a last resort. Parents must formally request a due process hearing by writing a letter to the school district. A hearing officer will be assigned to the case, and both parties can bring evidence of their disagreement using witnesses and written information. At this point, attorneys are usually involved on both sides.

Ideally, team members are well versed in conflict resolution and effective communication skills, which are the topics of Chapter 5. The team's commitment to an ongoing problem-solving approach to meeting the needs of all children and families can significantly reduce the need to enter into formal dispute resolution and litigation.

The following story illustrates one family's journey through the special education system. "Tara's Journey" in the vignette below follows a child with Down syndrome from her infant services through elementary school. Tara's mother's memories highlight both the positive and problematic parts of the processes we've described in this chapter. This story puts a human face on a legal requirement.

Tara's Journey: One Parent's Memories of Individualized Education Program Meetings

Vivianna admits to feeling anxious each time an IEP meeting is scheduled for her daughter. Tara is almost 16 years old. Thirteen years of IEP meetings with the same school district, and Vivianna still feels nervous. She has attended meetings with four different special education directors, several speech pathologists and psychologists, two occupational therapists, and a different teacher every year, plus numerous other specialists called in at different times in Tara's young life. Probably the most consistent member of Tara's team has been the paraprofessional who has worked with Tara for more than six years.

The first IEP contact was the initial meeting with the school district when Tara turned 3 and left Part C services to go to preschool under Part B of IDEA. Vivianna remembers having no clue about what the transition meant. Both she and her husband thought Tara's future would be "a special education bus and a special education class." Tara's occupational therapist, a Part C early interventionist, began talking to Vivianna about the transition and what preschool services might look like for Tara. She spoke about assessments, placement options, and therapies. Vivianna remembers feeling quite overwhelmed at all of the changes that were going to happen when Tara turned 3.

The school district scheduled a transition meeting with the family about four months before Tara's third birthday. The meeting was held at Vivianna's home, which was under renovation. Vivianna felt as though she was being judged by the dilapidated state of the house and the quality of cars in the driveway. She remembers that no one asked her about the family's hopes and dreams for Tara. She does remember that she was told that the district had a "good preschool class" in a neighboring city and that Tara would get transportation there and back. When Vivianna asked why Tara needed to go to another city for her schooling she was told

(continued)

that this is where the class was. The meeting ended with Vivianna being told that she would be contacted at the beginning of the school year for another meeting. During the next two months, Vivianna began asking Tara's occupational therapist more questions about preschool. The thought of having to send Tara to another city made no sense to her, and she was having trouble accepting this as the only possibility. Through a series of phone calls initiated by the therapist, Vivianna spoke to a parent advocate and was advised to call the director of special education and ask for a list of preschools available to her daughter. Vivianna called and was told by the director that there was no "shopping list" of schools for parents to look at. Vivianna remembers feeling so nervous just initiating the phone call but then feeling even worse with the response, as though she'd overstepped her authority as a parent. She asked the parent advocate to attend the IEP.

That first meeting was very tense, and Vivianna felt that there was a guardedness to the atmosphere—probably because an advocate was now involved. She remembers praying before the meeting that she and her husband would appear united and not argue in front of the school team. Vivianna and her husband had decided to request that Tara attend a neighborhood preschool closer to their home, although Tara's dad was nervous about the request because he thought that his daughter would be too vulnerable in a busy preschool setting. Eventually, after several IEP meetings, the team agreed to provide support for Tara to attend a local Head Start program. Speech and occupational therapies were provided following much discussion, and Tara began preschool when she turned 3.

Vivianna's memories of subsequent IEP meetings involve a mix of emotions. She remembers thinking that sometimes discussions focused on "silly" things and that "we needed to pick our battles." She never felt that she could "let up or relax" while Tara was being fully included. Vivianna and her husband requested reports before meetings and read every word; they took IEP documents home to scrutinize before signing agreements because they felt that often things were left out or written in ways meant to deny supports or services for Tara. There was definite distrust on both sides of the table. Vivianna didn't want to cry, although she felt very emotional, because she "didn't want to look weak or vulnerable," and she often left meetings feeling like her opinions weren't respected. During one IEP meeting, Vivianna needed to take a break because she began crying and didn't want team members to make judgments about her based on her emotional reactions. Her reason for the tears? She suddenly felt overwhelmed because Tara's school time was going to change from a morning class to an afternoon class and Vivianna was going to have to change the times of the different therapies.

Vivianna remembers that she would see "a look in their eyes" that went from actively listening to her to shifting away whenever she brought up hopes or dreams for Tara that were "out of their control." She has good memories of one school psychologist who was assigned to Tara's case for several years during elementary school. He listened to Tara's parents. Vivianna remembers that she felt that his body language contributed to her feeling that he was truly hearing what they were talking about and he "took what I was saying … my fears, frustrations, fragmented sentences … then would summarize these into coherent thoughts, and come up with

(continued)

(continued)

solutions. He always returned phone calls and always told me what he was going to do." Vivianna summarizes her memories by saying he was someone who followed through, communicated that he cared, and was accountable to them.

The preschool years went well for Tara; her parents learned more about special education law and began to understand the convoluted system that they were thrust into because of their daughter's disability. They became more convinced that Tara and her peers were benefiting from her enrollment in a typical preschool setting. When Tara transitioned from preschool to kindergarten the family met with more resistance from the school campus. The principal told the classroom assistant that Tara's mother was in denial and Tara had no business being at the school. At the first parent conference, the kindergarten teacher asked Vivianna, "Who told you that Tara was ready for kindergarten?" Vivianna felt that she always needed to reassure teachers that she didn't expect her daughter to be learning the same things as her peers—she knew her daughter had significant disabilities.

At the last meeting of the kindergarten year, Vivianna remembers that the teacher told the team that, after teaching for 35 years, she had never had a class of young children that were so compassionate and kind and she felt the reason was because of Tara's presence in her classroom and her effect on her peers. Vivianna feels that her one wish during all the years that Tara has been included was that her teachers would have been provided with some training or expectations about what it meant to have a child with significant disabilities included in their classrooms—that the teachers didn't need to feel they had to teach Tara the same things as her peers and feel inadequate when they couldn't. She wished they had understood that they didn't need to have the same academic standards for Tara. Vivianna also felt that administrators at the IEP meetings set the tone of the meetings from the start. She feels that "the demons are starting to fade but they stay with me," and this is why she reads every word and every page of each report and IEP because she "needs to do whatever I need to do to help my daughter succeed." She and her husband continue to ask themselves, "Are we doing the right thing?" and they follow the advice of one of Tara's team members to ask themselves and other team members every six months how they are doing and how Tara is doing.

CONCLUSION

Trying to understand where a family is coming from is extremely difficult. Taking the perspectives of others involved in team meetings can be useful in beginning to understand their motivations and responses. While perspective taking is helpful, it is not a perfect approach to understanding others. When meetings are convened to discuss high-stakes outcomes for an individual, emotions can erupt. Dogaru, Rosenkoetter, and Rous (2009) reported descriptions of IEP experiences from families and service providers. The behavior and attitudes of service providers during the transition process created very emotionally charged memories of the experience as being either helpful or problematic. Their stories reflect our experiences: The emotional impact of the team process for transitional events in a young child's life is often determined by parents' positive or negative interactions with one or two key professionals. It is also important to understand the professional's perspective, as illustrated in the vignette below.

A Teacher's Thoughts

When parents stop attending their children's IEP meetings and check the box on the invitation that states "hold the meeting without me," I often wonder when they stopped attending meetings. Was it when their child was in preschool? In early elementary school?

I hear other team members say that the parents "just don't care" and that they "never show up for anything." I wonder when they stopped showing up? Or why we professionals think that the family doesn't care?

When the parents first attended meetings for their child, were the teams positive and helpful? Even when there were problems, were parents invited to help brainstorm solutions? Or were they given the message that *they* must be the problem? Did the first IEP teams create an uncomfortable, negative feeling about their child?

Did the team consider the possibility that the parents found the whole process of placing their child in a special education class to be terrifying, or that the realization that this was to be their child's future unbearably sad?

Were those first meetings welcoming and did the teams communicate that they cared about the education of the child? Or were they poorly run and disorganized, leaving parents with a sense that the meetings weren't that important?

Did the first teams work to communicate with parents about the importance of their role in their child's education? Did the team coordinator try to arrange meeting times that were convenient to parents? When parents began saying they couldn't attend, did a team member call them to ask why and try to address the barriers to attendance?

—Special Education Teacher

Attempting to understand and respect a family's perspectives is very important, though not easy. In hindsight, one family member's memories about their child's IEP meeting can be different from another member's. One parent may describe an IEP meeting as a positive experience, while his or her partner may remember it as being highly stressful and acrimonious. At best, professionals will try to put themselves in a family's place and personalize each meeting. But it is not possible to fully understand parents' experience of having a very young child whose future seems to rest with the people sitting around the table. The IEP meeting is an opportunity for a team of dedicated individuals to welcome and learn from the family, on behalf of their child.

REFERENCES

Cheatham, G.A., Hart, J.E., Malian, I., & McDonald, J. (2012). Six things to never say or hear during an IEP meeting: Educators as advocates for families. *Teaching Exceptional Children, 44*(3), 50–57.

Dogaru, C., Rosenkoetter, S., & Rous, B. (2009). *A critical incident study of the transition experience for young children with disabilities: Recounts by parents and professionals* (Technical Report no. 6). Lexington: University of Kentucky, Human Development Institute, National Early Childhood Transition Center. Retrieved from http://www.hdi.uky.edu

Individuals with Disabilities Education Act (IDEA) of 1990, PL 101-476, 20 U.S.C. §§ 1400 *et seq.*

Musgrove, M. (2012). "OSEP Dear Colleague Letter on Preschool (LRE), Feb. 29, 2012." Washington, DC: Office of Special Education Programs. Retrieved from http://www2.ed.gov/policy/speced/guid/idea/memosdcltrs/index.html

Roe, K. (2008). Perceived efficacy of individual education plans: A literature review. Research paper submitted in partial fulfillment of the requirements for the master of science degree in guidance and counseling, University of Wisconsin-Stout. Retrieved from www2.uwstout.edu/content/lib/thesis/2008/2008roek.pdf

Rosenkoetter, S.E., Whaley, K.T., Hains, A.H., & Pierce, L. (2001). The evolution of transition policy for young children with special needs and their families: Past, present and future. *Topics in Early Childhood Special Education, 21*(1), 3–15.

Turnbull, H.R., Stowe, M.J., & Huerta, N.E. (2007). *Free appropriate public education: The law and children with disabilities* (7th ed.). Denver, CO: Love Publishing Company.

Wright, P.W.D., Wright, P.D., & O'Connor, S.W. (2009). *Wrightslaw: All about IEPs.* Hartfield, VA: Harbor House Law Press.

5 Problem Solving and Conflict Resolution

Meeting the educational needs of young children with disabilities in inclusive settings involves teams of professionals and family members with very different areas of expertise and perspectives. In the United States, these educational teams consist of individuals representing a wide range of ages, social classes, cultures, ethnicities, linguistic backgrounds, lifestyles, and genders. While as a society we embrace this diversity, the day-to-day reality of working together as a team can be challenging. Positive attitudes and a willingness to collaborate are helpful attributes, but they are far from sufficient. Administrators and colleagues must create clear decision-making policies and procedures for dealing with conflict when it arises. Leaders can establish communication patterns and organizational structures that ensure a problem-solving approach to everyday planning and decisions. Such an approach can establish policies and communication patterns that anticipate—even encourage—differences of opinion and perspectives. Modern-day businesses, policy think tanks, and the entire technology sector of the U.S. economy have discovered that two heads—or two hundred!—are better than one.

Honest exchange of different perspectives can not only reduce conflict but also encourage thinking outside the box and necessary risk taking (Friend & Cook, 2007). This process, in turn, can generate creative ideas for providing more effective—and more efficient—services that support successful inclusion with same-age peers and ensure optimal learning opportunities for all children.

The word *conflict* generally has a negative connotation. Most of us avoid conflict. The degree to which individuals avoid interpersonal conflict is partly related to background and culture (Lynch & Hanson, 2011). Despite our avoidance of conflict, it is interesting to note that common dictionary definitions of "conflict" typically include the word *disagreement*, a word that is much less threatening than the connotations typically associated with conflict.

While differences of opinion, perspective, and knowledge are inevitable, they should be celebrated rather than avoided. These differences are the potential sources of ever more creative and effective solutions for successfully including children with disabilities in educational settings and for seeing that they have quality access to learning and relationships (Heron & Harris, 2001).

101

THE ROLE OF CONFLICT IN HINDERING INCLUSION

Today's array of technological supports, behavioral services and strategies, and proven teaching techniques provide tremendous resources for ensuring that young children with disabilities reach their highest potential. During the past 20 years, the field of early childhood special education has successfully demonstrated that these techniques can be implemented within inclusive settings. There has been a steady increase in acceptance of children with disabilities on the part of the general population, early childhood educators, and families of typically developing children. There is also increasing discussion about the principles of universal design (CAST, 2012), which support every individual's access to programs and settings, regardless of the particular challenges, including in early childhood education (ECE) (Schaff, 2005). These gains are significant, but one of the most common challenges to successful inclusion of young children with disabilities is deeply rooted: *poorly managed conflict* (Connor & Ferri, 2007).

As Cook, Klein, and Chen (2011) point out, the development of effective educational programming for young children with disabilities requires a collaborative problem-solving approach in order to meet children's unique and sometimes complex needs. Very often, the failure of inclusive programs, or lack of success for any given child, is not due to a lack of funding, the complexity of the disability, or a lack of commitment to the philosophy of inclusion. Rather, the lack of skills in resolving common conflicts is often the culprit. It may seem that the business of including 3- and 4-year-old children in typical preschool settings would not be a particularly contentious endeavor. However, everyday conflicts can easily arise because of some unique challenges experienced in preschool inclusion, which are not typical in K–12 programs.

For example, an ECE teacher, who earns a low salary and has little training related to working with children with disabilities, may be resentful of the early childhood special education (ECSE) consultant who places extra demands on his or her time and responsibilities. Or a collaborating preschool special education program and a Head Start program—each administered by different agencies—must deal with challenges regarding decision-making authority and the appropriate chain of command for employees. Another common source of conflict is different views of curriculum and academic expectations. While the ECE program may adhere strictly to a specific curriculum such as High Scope or the Creative Curriculum, a district ECSE program may focus primarily on children's individualized education program (IEP) goals and allow teachers flexibility in developing and adapting curriculum.

Several unique characteristics of early childhood inclusion were introduced in Chapter 1. These set the stage for conflict in a number of ways.

Lack of parity: In the United States, special education teachers, as well as therapists, are typically more highly trained and better paid than teachers in early childhood education settings. Statistics provided by Career and Job Search Resources (2013) suggest that the average annual salary for preschool teachers is $22,700, compared to $46,400 for special education teachers and over $60,000 for speech-language pathologists (SLPs), occupational therapists, and physical therapists. Despite this difference in pay, the early childhood classroom teacher typically has daily responsibility for the entire class, while therapists and special education consultants are usually responsible for only one or a few children who have a disability. Also, in many early education programs, the ECE teacher is closely supervised and may not have the authority or flexibility to make changes in curriculum or daily classroom routines without supervisor approval. The special educator, however, may have much more autonomy and flexibility. Finally, early childhood teachers may feel invaded by the number of itinerant service providers and specialists who come in and out of their classrooms to observe the children with special needs. Since the specialist's focus is on the child, he or she may not be respectful of the role of the ECE teacher. The teacher may feel like she herself is being observed and critiqued. In these situations, it is easy to see how lack of parity can evolve into the early childhood teacher's perception of unfairness and lack of respect, as well as possible concerns about his or her own competence. These feelings can be deadly ingredients in the soup of conflict.

Multiple agencies: The service delivery settings and administrative responsibilities in ECSE inclusion are highly variable. While federal law mandates that children with disabilities must be placed in the least restrictive environment (LRE), it does not suggest what those settings should be or what kinds of administrative structures should exist. K–12 education (including both general and special education) is regulated in each state and municipality by a single entity, for example, a state department of education. However, at the preschool level, ECE and ECSE service delivery systems are rarely managed under the same agency or authority. A study by Odom et al. (1999) described several different program settings in which inclusive early childhood programs were housed. For example, Head Start grantees manage their own Head Start classrooms at the local level under the auspices of the federal government. However, the children with disabilities placed in a Head Start program are likely to be served under the jurisdiction of the local school district and the state department of education. In addition, certain services (e.g., behavior therapy, occupational therapy, speech-language pathology [SLP], physical therapy) may be provided via subcontracts with nonpublic agencies.

Lack of single administrative authority: With multiple agencies come multiple administrators and lines of administrative responsibility. For example, classroom teachers in ECE settings often are overseen by mid-level supervisors, who in turn are under the management of a program director. However, the individuals providing specialized services (e.g., ECSE consultant, speech-language therapist, behavior specialist) for the child with a disability may each be under the supervision of different managers or administrators. Successful preschool inclusion can be undermined by lack of collaboration, of respect, and of clear lines of communication among these responsible administrators and supervisors.

Number of key players: It is often the case that providing effective special education programming for young children with disabilities is labor intensive and multidimensional. The Individuals with Disabilities Education Act (IDEA) of 1990 (PL 101-476), Part C, which relates to early intervention for infants and toddlers, requires that appropriate therapeutic, developmental, and educational services be provided within a multidisciplinary team, which includes the family. As a result, when young children with disabilities transition into preschool services at age 3, they often continue to be eligible for and receive many of these services. Furthermore, providing support in an *inclusive* setting adds even more key players (the ECE teacher, ECE paraprofessionals, and ECE supervisory personnel). Thus, the sheer number of individuals, each with his or her own obligations and perspectives

Table 5.1. Key players and supervisors for one child in a district–Head Start partnership classroom

Key player	Supervisor(s)
Head Start ECE teacher Head Start paraprofessional	Head Start site supervisor and Head Start program administrator
ECSE consultant or co-teacher (district)	Special education director (district)
Speech-language pathologist (SLP) (district)	SLP supervisor (district)
Behavior specialist (agency)	Applied behavior analysis (ABA) supervisor and ABA agency manager
Family members	NA

Key: ECE, early childhood education.

(and different supervisors to whom they are accountable), can create a ripe environment for potential conflict. Table 5.1 provides an example of a list of key players and supervisors for one child with special needs in an inclusive Head Start program. There are 11 individuals, *not counting family members*.

By definition—that is, *by law*—the business of providing educational program plans and services to young children with disabilities involves multiple individuals, many of whom are also decision makers. Just consider the number of individuals often present at a contentious IEP meeting. Then consider the number of additional key players who are not at the IEP meeting (e.g., paraprofessionals, bus drivers, in-home service providers, child care providers, non–public agency personnel, and contractual service providers). The numbers of different individuals with different objectives and perspectives often feels like a cast of thousands. It goes without saying that the more key players, the greater the potential for conflicts, although it should be noted that conflict can occur with any number greater than one.

SUBSTANTIVE VERSUS AFFECTIVE CONFLICT

Ellis and Fisher (1994) identified two basic types of conflict: substantive and affective. *Substantive conflict* arises from intellectual differences and is content based. It comes about because individuals naturally differ about priorities, intervention strategies, curriculum philosophies, best practices, service delivery procedures, and so on. The presence of numerous key players automatically increases the potential for many different views on such issues. This type of conflict, when managed properly, can make a healthy contribution to the team process and problem solving.

In the example below, while there are legitimate differences of opinion based on *substantive* issues, the group problem-solving approach leads to solutions that may very well be better than the initial preference of any single individual.

The family of a child with significant communication and behavioral issues requests clinic-based speech-language services and behavior therapy once per week. The classroom special educator co-teacher feels strongly that the off-campus services will not generalize to the classroom. The administrator is concerned about escalating costs.

The proactive administrator calls a meeting of the IEP team. As a result of the shared problem-solving process, the team agrees to a three-month trial of weekly, in-class consultation from the district SLP and occupational therapist. The SLP and occupational therapist will jointly present a brief after-school in-service to the classroom staff so everyone understands the S/L and OT approaches. The co-teacher agrees to assume primary responsibility for serving as the link between the therapists and the staff in terms of follow-through with strategies. The team agrees to reconvene after the three-month trial to evaluate the effectiveness of the plan.

Affective conflict arises from emotional and personality factors. In rare cases, a coworker may suffer from a serious personality disorder and may demonstrate paranoia, anger management difficulties, and so forth. More often, however, affective conflict results simply from poor communication skills and misunderstandings or from genuine emotions and personal challenges associated with working as a member of a team. For example, organizational or policy changes might cause one to fear losing status or even fear losing one's job. An expectation that each team member must share and discuss justifications for his or her recommendations may lead to embarrassment or loss of self-esteem in an individual who has limited experience or limited self-confidence. These common realities of group process and decision making can lead to *resistance to change*. Figure 5.1 provides examples of common sources of resistance within educational teams. Being able to understand others' perspectives and the reasons for team member resistance is critical to avoiding conflict.

Unfortunately, when not properly managed, these affective issues can lead to very serious conflict. Consider the following scenario.

Shelly is a newly hired lead teacher in a community-based preschool program. The program has a commitment to inclusion, and currently there are three children with special needs in Shelly's classroom. Support for the children is provided by an ECSE itinerant consultant from the local school district. Shelly is an experienced early childhood teacher who loves working with young children, and she takes pride in her knowledge and expertise. However, she has had very little experience working with children with special needs. The preschool has developed a reputation for welcoming young children who have autism. One of the children in the classroom, Frederick, though high functioning academically, has very severe autism.

After a short period of time, Shelly becomes increasingly anxious about Frederick's behavior and discovers that her usually effective discipline strategies don't seem to work. She notices that classroom staff are beginning to ignore her suggestions. They often comment that Shelly should follow the suggestions of Amanda, the district ECSE consultant, "who always knows how to fix these

---

Fear of loss of status: Many individuals are fearful of change. For example, individuals may be concerned that if job responsibilities change, they will not be competent to take on new roles. They fear losing the respect of their peers. Individuals who are very competitive may fear being viewed as weak by their competitors.

Fear of loss of control: Some personalities seek a sense that they are in control of themselves and their work environment. Perceived or real threats to that ability to maintain control is a common source of resistance to change if the persons themselves are not the change agent.

Preference for the current status—general view that change is always disruptive: "If it ain't broke, don't fix it"; "Don't rock the boat."

Perceived threat to the existing social order: Many individuals find great comfort and social support in their workplace. Anything that threatens this social comfort zone may be resisted.

Figure 5.1.   Sources of resistance. (Adapted from Project Vision, 1993.)

kids." Shelly has met Amanda twice and has been put off by the way she rushes into the classroom, jokes and chats with the staff, then distracts Shelly from whatever she's doing at the moment to try to talk about Frederick.

This scenario can easily result in serious affective conflict. Shelly's early feelings of inadequacy about her skills with children who have disabilities are leading to feelings of defensiveness as staff seem to compare her negatively with the special education consultant. She is aware that Amanda has more training, makes more money than she does, and seems to have much more independence and authority in her position, which seems very unfair. She also perceives Amanda as being disrespectful toward her and sees her as the reason the staff seem to question Shelly's authority. Shelly fears that she is losing her status as the competent leader of the classroom team. She no longer takes pride in her role as lead teacher and starts to wonder if this is the right field for her. At the same time, Amanda senses that Shelly doesn't like her and is somewhat resistant to her consultation and strategies for supporting Frederick. Amanda is concerned that his behaviors may escalate and feels she should mention this to Frederick's parents.

The classroom assistants now feel that they are walking on eggshells. Shelly seems to reject their suggestions and isn't very friendly. One of the assistants thinks maybe they should tell Amanda about their frustrations with this new teacher. And so it goes.

If the ECSE consultant, Amanda, has been well trained in conflict resolution and problem solving, she will realize what is happening and will take steps to mitigate Shelly's understandable emotional reactions and her increasing resistance. She will acknowledge the possibility of her own (inadvertent) role in Shelly's reactions. She will be more mindful of how she communicates with Shelly and will proactively engage in more collegial problem solving with Shelly around Frederick's challenges. She will resist the pull toward siding with the classroom assistants.

DYNAMICS OF CONFLICT AND CONFLICT RESOLUTION

Two major factors related to both the sources and the effective resolution of conflict are understanding 1) others' *perspectives* and 2) the effects of certain kinds of *communication styles.*

Perspective taking: It is important for the professionals involved in planning and implementing effective inclusion support to be able to understand and manage the resistance that may be caused by team members' fears of loss of status, control, or respect. The ECSE teacher who is trained in consultation can play a critical role here. The teacher's ability to understand the different perspectives of each key player often enables him or her to assume an informal leadership role in dealing with immediate conflict. In the vignette about Shelly, successful resolution will depend, in part, on Amanda's awareness of Shelly's perspective about her own competence and status in the classroom.

Communication style: Another major source of conflict is communication style. Cultural differences in communication style can cause misunderstandings that lead to emotional conflict. For example Euro-American communication style is much more direct, competitive, and confrontational than the styles of most other cultures. The highly competitive nature that is typical of U.S. culture and the belief in a *zero-sum game* (that your gain is my loss, and vice versa) is another example of a cultural characteristic that often feeds conflict. One might assume that cultural predispositions for more collectivist, communal organization of families and communities would naturally produce better team members than individualistic cultural backgrounds. However, this is not necessarily true. The tendency to *not* express one's disagreement in order to avoid confrontation, or loss of face, may inhibit the free flow of ideas essential to effective problem solving.

The term *cultural* used here refers to something much broader than *ethnicity*. Note Edward T. Hall's classic 1966 definition of culture: "those deep, common, unstated experiences which members of a given culture share, which they communicate without knowing, and which form the backdrop against which all other events are judged" (Rogers & Steinfatt, 1999, p. 79*)*.

Relevant to the important role of culture in interpersonal communication is an entire field of study referred to as *intercultural communication*, which is defined as follows: "the exchange of information between individuals who are unalike culturally…. Individuals may be unalike in their national culture, ethnicity, age, gender, or in other ways that affect their interaction" (Rogers & Steinfatt, 1999, p. 79).

Personality styles can also influence the ways in which team members communicate. For example, one individual may be by nature very quiet and introverted; another might be very outgoing and confident; while another has a sarcastic, sometimes caustic sense of humor. For example, a school psychologist begins a team meeting by saying, loudly and sarcastically, "Well I guess we're here to talk about our favorite student again." While he or she may have meant it as an ironic, slightly humorous comment, others in the group may view it as mean and disrespectful of the child. As a result, a teacher who is often quiet and tends to defer to the administrator and specialists may be even less likely to voice his or her positive views of the child being discussed.

Effective team members will become aware of their own communication habits and their possible effects on others. They will also develop sensitivity to different styles in others and will inhibit their own inclination to react negatively to certain individuals.

DEVELOPING AN ONGOING PROBLEM-SOLVING APPROACH: PRACTICAL, DAY-TO-DAY INGREDIENTS OF COLLABORATION

Inclusive programs are difficult to sustain without a collaborative, problem-solving approach. Without understanding the nature of conflict and with little training in collaborative communication and problem-solving approaches, it is likely that, over time, conflict will undermine the good intentions of educational personnel and families. Below we present a discussion of the causes and dynamics of conflict and practical ways to manage and resolve them.

In settings in which the stakes are high (e.g., success or failure for young children with challenging disabilities) and there are multiple key players (e.g., child, family members, administrators, ECE teacher, ECSE teacher, therapists, psychologists), conflict is inevitable. For most people, conflict is uncomfortable. As a result, individuals working in a group environment may inadvertently undermine group collaborative processes. They may unconsciously and automatically seek to avoid conflict rather than engage in it and solve problems. For example, managers may become more authoritarian to reduce the time and conflict associated with differing views of team members. Alternatively, staff in nonleadership roles may avoid expressing views that differ from the authority figure's or from the dominant views and philosophy of the group.

Despite these challenges, in modern society generally, and particularly in the context of multidisciplinary special education service delivery, it is important to develop an attitude of acceptance of conflict. Rather than using emotional energy to avoid conflict, a better goal is to establish healthy ways of using the focused attention that conflict often generates to create even better outcomes for children. Isaura Barrera (Barrera, Kramer, & Macpherson, 2012) has described an effective approach to the kinds of differences in culture and mindsets that often provoke conflict related to meeting the needs of young children with disabilities and their families. It is called *skilled dialogue*. An important aspect of skilled dialogue is referred to as *third space*, which suggests that the ability to process two contradictory ideas at the same time can lead to completely new understanding and creativity. The tendency toward polarization and the inability to view something from a very different perspective than your own fuels conflict, whereas Barrera's third space can lead to creative problem solving. Being able and willing to understand each other's point of view allows for the evolution of a new idea or solution that neither party would have thought of on its own.

Developing a Collaborative Communication Style

Many aspects of how co-workers talk to each other can make or break the effectiveness of a collaborative team. Communication style is at the core of real collaboration, as described by Friend and Cook (2007). Collaboration is not simply working with other people. Rather, it is adopting a collaborative communication style and a problem-solving approach in the ongoing processes of providing teaching and support for students who have disabilities. Certain ways of communicating will facilitate problem solving, while other communicative behaviors will interfere with establishing collaborative relationships and thus interfere with problem solving. One's communication style includes both verbal and nonverbal communicative behaviors. Regardless of the role of the individual (e.g., ECSE consultant, ECE co-teacher, SLP itinerant, administrator, supervisor, or parent), awareness of the kinds of communication styles that can interfere with collaboration, and development of one's own skills in both verbal and nonverbal communication, will go a long way toward setting the tone for effective problem solving. When this occurs, conflict is mitigated, and when conflict does arise team members are prepared to address it productively.

The following section provides examples of both nonverbal and verbal communicative behaviors that may present barriers to effective communication, as well as those that support the development of problem solving and positive working relationships among team members.

Nonverbal Communication   While most of us are very aware of what individuals *say* in a meeting or conversation (their verbal behavior), we are much less consciously aware of their nonverbal communication and how dramatically it may affect us. Most individuals are actually very sensitive to the nonverbal behaviors of others, although usually at an unconscious level. Unfortunately, however, individuals are almost never aware of their own nonverbal communications. Non-verbal communicative behaviors can have a greater effect—positive or negative—than the words actually spoken. The literature describing the role of nonverbal behavior (see, for example, Burgoon, 1994; Rogers & Steinfatt, 1999) reveals that in many situations nonverbal communicative behavior conveys as much or more meaning than the actual words used by the speaker (Friend & Cook, 2007).

The successful team player must learn to keenly observe and accurately inter-pret other people's cues. Equally important is accurate self-awareness of the impact of his or her own nonverbal behavior on others. In order to identify their own non-verbal communication habits, ECSE consultants may want to consider videotaping themselves in a communicative interaction. It is important to determine if there are ways in which one's own behavior may exacerbate conflict rather than miti-gate it. Equally important (though admittedly difficult when working with teams of diverse personalities and cultures), it is important for the ECSE team member to try to avoid misinterpreting the nonverbal behaviors of others. Following are some examples of nonverbal communication that team members should be aware of.

Eye contact: There are wide variations in how eye contact, or the lack thereof, affects the communication process. In mainstream U.S. culture, making eye contact when speaking to someone is expected. On the other hand, in other cultures, direct eye contact may be viewed as seductive behavior (e.g., on the part of a female toward a male) or disrespectful (e.g., a child toward an adult.) In main-stream U.S. culture, individuals who do not make direct eye contact may be viewed as disinterested, untrustworthy, or extremely shy. These impressions could all be incorrect.

Facial expression: It is important to be aware of one's facial expression. Some individuals may be unaware of their inappropriate smiling or look of irrita-tion. Facial expressions that are incongruent with the mood of a group discussion or with an individual's emotions can set the stage for conflict on an emotional level, even when there are no substantive issues. For example, a group may be engaged in a particularly emotional staff meeting where strong feelings and dis-agreements are being expressed. The administrator joins the group late and is insensitive to the mood. If he or she is smiling and upbeat, the administrator may have difficulty facilitating the group process. In another situation, the group may be engaged in sharing funny stories about their classrooms. If a colleague joins the group with a look of anger or disgust, this can have a surprisingly last-ing effect on group cohesion. Again, there are significant cultural differences related to facial expression; in some Southeast Asian cultures, for example, smiling may express embarrassment or distress (Chen & Chan, 2011). See Klein and Chen (2001) for more detailed considerations of communication styles and child-rearing practices when working with children and families from culturally diverse backgrounds.

Back channeling: In U.S. culture, *back channeling* is an important behavior on the part of the listener, because it indicates attention and interest in what the speaker is saying. Back channeling includes both verbal expressions (e.g., "No kid-ding?", "Oh my!") and nonverbal behaviors (e.g., head nodding or intonated vocal-izations such as "hmm" that express interest or agreement with what the speaker is saying). These often have the effect of validating the speaker. In cultures in which back channeling is a common pragmatic feature, the absence of back channeling is often viewed as disinterest or disagreement. Thus, lack of responsiveness from team members can inadvertently undermine the effectiveness of the team process.

Use of silence: Individuals have different levels of tolerance for silence in conversation or in group discussion. One of the goals of collaborative teaming and problem solving is ensuring that all members of the group actually participate. There are huge differences among members of any group in their comfort level with speaking and their willingness to express differences of opinion. Unfortunately, because some members are very comfortable talking in a group (and some would love to hear themselves talk), group decision making and problem solving can often become dominated by one or two individuals. Also, many of us are not comfortable with silence and rush to fill more than a few seconds of pause. However, the purposeful use of silence can encourage greater participation of all members.

Body language: What you do with your body in a communication situation can send powerful messages. It is important for collaborators to be aware of their own body language as well as to accurately read other people's body language. Examples of body language and its effect on interactions in mainstream U.S. culture include *mirroring movement* and the use of *personal space.*

Mirroring the movements or body postures of your communication partner generally conveys synchrony and agreement. If two people are having a dialogue and one person leans forward, if the other also leans forward he or she will be perceived as being supportive and in agreement. On the other hand, if the first person leans forward and the conversation partner leans back (an opposite response), that movement may be perceived as disagreement or retreat.

An individual's perceptions of body language can also be influenced by the use of personal space, sometimes referred to as *proxemics.* Cultures differ significantly on what is considered the appropriate distance between people in public and private situations (e.g., the appropriate distance between two strangers at a bus stop compared to good friends having a conversation). Thus we may unconsciously make negative judgments about people when we feel they have violated our own norms for personal space. For example, the term *standoffish* has probably evolved from differences in these social norms.

Listening: Perhaps one of the very best nonverbal communication strategies is simply listening. Very often, group members are not really listening carefully, or at all. They may be much more focused on making a point, constructing their next response or comment, or winning the argument. One of the great skills of collaborative teaming and problem solving is learning how to listen. In addition to really listening, both our nonverbal and our verbal behaviors can communicate to others that we are truly listening and that we care about what others have to say.

Verbal Communication   Just as nonverbal communication behaviors can significantly influence collaboration effectiveness, both positively and negatively, so can verbal communication behaviors. Below are specific verbal strategies that demonstrate that what team members say and how they say it can make or break the problem-solving process (adapted from Cook, Klein, & Chen, 2012).

Build rapport: This may seem trivial, but in potential conflict situations, using neutral comments ("Can you believe the traffic!"), humor and self-deprecation ("I'm getting more forgetful in my old age"), genuine compliments ("That's a great tie!"), and offers of amenities ("Can I get anyone coffee?") can have very positive effects by diffusing tension and creating an air of camaraderie.

Avoid talking too much: The best negotiators and most effective team members listen more than they talk. If you are talking, other people are not talking. Problem solving and conflict resolution require that everyone fully participate in the communicative process. The more you dominate the conversation, the less other group members will honestly share their different ideas. As other members of the team participate less, true collaboration erodes. They may simply give in and stop sharing their views on other possible solutions.

Openly acknowledge and encourage different ideas and perspectives: Tension and defensiveness can sometimes be reduced by simply acknowledging that there are disagreements and different views. It is often helpful to give examples of those different views and invite people to correct or clarify assumptions and express additional views. Over time, in any organization, it is possible to create a culture that allows sharing different views and purposely trying to think outside the box. In this way, people's defenses about voicing unworthy ideas or being shot down are greatly reduced. Disagreements (i.e., conflicting ideas) become an expected part of the process for decision making.

Ask others for their views: Rather than asking whether individuals agree or disagree, ask the question more broadly: ask "John, how do you see the situation?" or "Angelina, since you see him from a different perspective at home, what are some of your thoughts about Miguel's recent behaviors?"

Use reflective listening: Team members want to be heard and understood. Use language that reflects that you are hearing what people say and that you are interested in really understanding their message (e.g., "It seems like you're saying that the situation is getting worse, not better").

Use these skills to solve problems: These communication styles can become part of the "rules of engagement" for problem-solving discourse. A problem-solving, collaborative approach would require that each team member (i.e., teachers, therapists, parents, paraprofessionals, and administrators) honestly express their concerns, their areas of agreement, their questions, and their creative ideas. There should be an explicit goal for all members to learn to use communication styles that express disagreements as well as strong emotional reactions in such a way as to enrich the discussion rather than inflame or destroy collegial relationships.

ESTABLISHING A PROBLEM-SOLVING WORK ENVIRONMENT AND A CULTURE OF COLLABORATIVE COMMUNICATION

One key to conflict management and resolution in the inclusive preschool environment is finding ways to create and maintain opportunities for everyday interactions among adults that support open honest communication. Program managers and administrators (or persons who find themselves in de facto leadership roles) can create routines and policies that expect—even require—that all key players express their ideas and concerns. This will help staff be fully engaged in finding solutions to problems as they arise. It will help them push the envelope in creative ways and thus achieve the best possible outcomes for children. Some examples of these routines and policies follow.

Date: January 15, 2001

Target child: Brandon S.

Age: 3 years, 5 months

Case manager: S.K., inclusion specialist

Team members: B.L. (mother), R.T. (speech-language pathologist),
  A.L. (preschool teacher), L.M. (district paraprofessional)

Agenda

1. Child progress reports (formal or informal) from each team member

Social/behavior:

Communication:

Curriculum participation:

2. Review of goals and concerns from previous meeting

Successes:

Effective strategies:

Issues and concerns:

3. New action plan

Who:

What:

By when:

4. Date of next meeting: _____

_____

Figure 5.2. Sample team meeting agenda.

Regular debriefing, planning, and problem-solving meetings should be on the calendar. These meetings should be routinely scheduled events, not just called when there is a problem. The point is to ensure regular proactive communication. An efficient agenda should be used in each meeting. (See Figure 5.2 for an example of a meeting agenda related to one of the case studies presented in the chapter appendix.) One common challenge is that staff who work in early childhood programs may be paid only for the hours the children are present. Unlike district programs, there are no lesson planning periods or staff development time. The most effective programs are able to find creative ways of dealing with this, such as the following:

- Coming to work 20 minutes early on Fridays, taking turns bringing donuts

- Getting permission to dismiss children half an hour early one day per month

- Combining problem solving and planning with happy hour or an after-school potluck

- Using e-mail listservs to collect members' ideas and suggestions

- Meeting during recess one day per week or per month (for example, at a picnic table at the edge of the playground), rotating staff so that one certified staff person is always supervising, while volunteers, student teachers, older peer tutors, and so forth monitor playground activities and safety

It is important that every effort be made to include itinerant specialists in these collaborative meetings. The input of therapists and part-time one-to-one assistants—and sometimes family members and administrators—should be included and welcomed to the regularly scheduled meetings. Opportunities to build relationships are crucial to ongoing problem solving and team building.

The key is not how often the team meets but that it meets regularly and predictably on a weekly or monthly calendar. If the last Friday of every month for 20 minutes is the only available meeting time, then so be it. The key is to honor that commitment and engage in honest discussion of the children's and the program's needs, challenges, and successes. The content of the meetings should address whatever is most important to the team.

With regular use of the preceding strategies, disagreement loses it potential for confrontation and hostility and can come to be valued as an opportunity for broadening perspectives and thinking creatively. These can lead not just to solutions for problems but also to exciting new ways of making the program more fun and effective for children and adults. *Create a classroom culture of collaborative communication and problem solving, characterized by both the opportunity of and responsibility for each person to speak honestly and respectfully about his or her perspectives of progress and challenges.*

ASSESSING COLLABORATIVE COMMUNICATION AND PROBLEM SOLVING IN INCLUSION SUPPORT PROGRAMS

A successful inclusion support program requires some kind of formative assessment. Since collaboration is the cornerstone of a successful program, assessing the effectiveness of adult collaboration can be as important as assessing student outcomes. Such collaboration is a complex process, as it involves developing interpersonal and communication skills as well as technical expertise in order to ensure the following, as described by Gately and Gately (2001); Rice, Drame, Owens, and Frattura (2007); and Wiggins and Damore (2006).

- An understanding of nonverbal as well as verbal messages of team members

- Communication among team members that is honest and open

- Frequent, productive, flexible, and sensitive communication

- Philosophies, goals, and activities that are jointly developed and planned

- Identification and resolution of barriers to effective collaboration

- A prevalence of positive feelings and views toward collaboration

- Clarity, understanding, and acceptance of collaborative roles

- Accountability for collaborative roles and responsibilities

- A collaborative process that is user friendly and respects participants' values and decisions

- Effective instructional strategies that are analyzed and adapted

It is important to recognize that adults themselves need support to provide inclusion support services for children in collaborative ways. As adults develop collaborative teams, they must understand what each person can contribute, develop common goals, plan together, and reflect on the effectiveness of their work together. Each inclusion support team can develop its own list of important collaborative goals and activities and create a rubric to assess its collaborative efforts. Collaborative teams will encounter obstacles, and they will need support in problem solving to overcome these obstacles. The time spent developing relationships will result in better services for children; better services for children is the goal of inclusion support.

To identify the resources that are important for effective inclusion support, it is helpful to consider the following recommendations for early childhood inclusion support providers developed by Lieber et al. (2002).

Teachers should

- Have a positive attitude toward change

- Take the initiative

- Be flexible

- Develop communication strategies

Administrators should

- Support a shared philosophy

- Support adequate meeting times

- Support working toward a common goal

- Support team members' sharing of their expertise

- Support team members' use of collaborative skills

- Support team members' sharing of the work

USING A SYSTEMATIC PROBLEM-SOLVING PROCESS WHEN NECESSARY

In any fully engaged organization there may be disagreements that cannot be resolved easily. The complexity of some children's disabilities, the number of key players and specialists, as well as the passions and emotional investment of family members can often overwhelm even the most collaborative team. Fortunately, there are well-established procedures that can be used to manage such an impasse. As mentioned earlier, during the past decade there has been an explosion

---

1. Preparation (prior to first meeting)
2. Entry (as face-to-face meeting commences)
3. Define the problem
4. Generating possible solutions: Brainstorming
5. Action plan and implementation
6. Follow-up
7. Recycle problem-solving steps (as needed)

Figure 5.3. Seven-step problem-solving approach. (*Source*: Kurpius, 1978.)

of interest and development in the phenomenon of conflict resolution, including techniques and processes of negotiation, mediation, and dispute resolution. Some of these have been inspired by the years of work of the Harvard Negotiation Project (e.g., Fisher, Ury, & Patton, 2011; Ury, 2007). A detailed, multistep conflict-resolution procedure has also been described by Heron and Harris (2001). Kurpius (1978) described a somewhat simpler version, outlined in Figure 5.3.

The process of providing effective inclusion support for young children with disabilities will inevitably involve solving difficult problems and meeting specific challenges. The inability to meet these challenges can lead to failed inclusive placements. The following process is an example of a simple but systematic way of approaching situations that are interfering with the child's access to supportive, successful early education experiences. Equally important, over time the implementation of such a procedure, when needed, can support the collaborative team's development of skills necessary for an ongoing problem-solving approach. It will also support members' comfort level in dealing with conflict whether it arises from very real challenges presented by the complexities of children's needs (i.e., substantive issues and disagreements) or the everyday clashes or misunderstandings that may arise from different communicative and cultural styles, personalities, and perspectives (i.e., affective issues).

While such a process is admittedly time consuming, recognizing when it is necessary will save time over the long run, increase successful solutions for children, and decrease the likelihood of costly litigation. It could be useful, for example, in a conflict regarding parents' request for use of specific teaching techniques, which teachers feel are inappropriate and harmful, or when disagreements arise between two staff members who have long-standing, intense personality differences regarding classroom responsibilities.

Seven-Step Problem-Solving Technique

1. Preparation (Prior to First Meeting)   Once it is determined that a problem cannot be resolved within the regular planning meeting, or that the tension around a particular issue is clearly increasing, it is important to prevent further escalation. (There will be a point where team members become so entrenched in their views *and* in their antipathy toward one another that a systematic approach must be used.) A team leader (e.g., lead teacher, administrator) will arrange a meeting. Prior to the meeting, the ECSE co-teacher or consultant can play a crucial leadership role even when he or she is not the "official" person to preside over the meeting. It is very important to determine who the key players are (to ensure they are actually present at the meeting) and to try to clarify expectations and perspectives of key members of the group regarding the nature of the issues to be discussed. Information can be obtained via phone call, e-mail, or preferably face-to-face informal conversation. Gathering information related to different opinions about the nature of the problem—or even about what the problem *is*—can allow the ECSE member to play a facilitative role or even a de facto leadership role in the actual the meeting.

2. Entry (as Face-to-Face Meeting Commences)   The term *entry* refers to the brief period in which team members are arriving and getting settled. Many factors during this stage can either help set the stage for a positive collaborative process or start things off on the wrong foot. Even the physical environment can have a positive or negative effect. For example, a long rectangular table subliminally encourages individuals to pick sides and invites the group leader to sit at the head of the table. Both of these features tend to decrease the collegiality of the group and increase polarity and adversarial relationships (such as supervisor versus employees, general educator versus special educator, families versus district personnel). Note that a well-trained collaborative problem solver can have a positive effect on the process simply by sitting next to the person with whom he is most likely to disagree. On the other hand, a round table—especially one with snacks in the center—can facilitate a feeling of equality and collegiality within a team.

Simple amenities can also help establish group rapport, for example, offering coffee and casual, neutral conversation like "I can't believe this weather." A sense of humor can also create a positive mood (although sometimes it can inadvertently be misunderstood or offensive). On the other hand, displays of negative affect (e.g., scowling facial expression, sarcasm) can create a toxic atmosphere before the meeting even begins. Stress, frustration, and feeling rushed are realities for all members of any team. Nevertheless, team members who are committed to ongoing collaborative problem solving can learn to be fully present and engaged in listening to and understanding others' perspectives.

Another important goal during this entry stage is to establish the rules of engagement for the process the group will use to define the problem and to plan any action it will take. In true problem solving, the process is as important as the outcome. Engaging in a conflict-resolution process similar to the one described here not only increases the likelihood that a real solution will eventually be achieved but also establishes a team culture that values the development of skills and practices that over time not only decrease toxic conflicts but also strengthen the team's cohesion. This in turn can lead to creative ideas through which the team ultimately discovers new and better ways of meeting the needs of both children and adults.

3. Define the Problem   Perhaps the most common mistake in conflict resolution is not understanding individuals' perspectives and beliefs about what the problem actually is. For example, team members may be using the phrase "Michael's difficult behavior" without ever checking in with each other to describe exactly what that behavior is. One person may be referring to noncompliance, for example, when Michael has difficulty transitioning from one activity to another and screams when the teacher tries to prompt him to leave one activity for another or to put away toys. Another may consider the problem to be the loud tantrum behavior, which is disruptive to the class, and less concerned about the noncompliance and the need for assistance in transitioning from one activity to another. Another member's view of the "problem" may be a strong belief that the staff does not have the time or the skills to deal with a child with special needs.

In any inclusive early childhood classroom, there are many problems to be solved; indeed, that is the very nature of any educational endeavor. *However, teams cannot solve a problem until the problem has been carefully described and the group agrees that, for now, this is the problem to be addressed.* Defining and selecting a problem is often a surprisingly difficult process. But it is an invaluable step because it helps clarify different team members' perceptions and views, and it also begins the process of understanding the parameters and specific characteristics of the problem. (This conversation highlights the importance of including a team member who has expertise in the area of positive behavior support. See Chapter 8.)

Another advantage of this step is that it often leads the group to better insights and encourages focused thinking about appropriate solutions. However, it is critical that the group not proceed to the next step of suggesting solutions until consensus is reached about the problem to be solved.

One practice that works very well is for the team to adopt a "rule" that requires each member to present his or her view of what specific problem should be addressed. Members should be assured that other problems can be addressed later, but a consensus must be reached regarding which problem the group will immediately focus on. Once selected, it should be written down on chart paper or a whiteboard or projected on a screen, where everyone can view and edit the problem description. Only at this point should the group proceed to the next step.

4. Generating Possible Solutions: Brainstorming

In this step, all members engage in brainstorming possible solutions to the agreed-upon problem. The biggest challenges to the effectiveness of this step are egos and competitiveness. It is natural for individuals to want to suggest the "winning" idea. Each team member has his or her own area of expertise (and thus his or her own lens through which to view the problem) and his or her own beliefs about what strategies will work best. It can be helpful for the team leader to remind the group—with a bit of humor—that brainstorming is not a contest to see who can generate the best solution. Rather, the goal is to generate as many ideas as possible. Brainstorming is widely recognized as an effective process for increasing creativity and generating new ideas and ways of thinking. Fisher, Ury, and Patton (2011) refer to the importance of encouraging wild ideas: anything goes, no matter how seemingly implausible.

It is important to adhere to the rules of brainstorming:

- Participants should be seated side by side (e.g., in a semicircle, along one side of a table), facing a whiteboard or chart paper with the description of the problem selected.

- Someone must write down each idea.

- Everyone must contribute.

- All ideas are acceptable during the brainstorming process itself. (Avoid discussion of different ideas; this is simply brainstorming at this point.)

- Negative criticism is not allowed.

- Each idea—without the name of the person who suggested it—is written down and visible to the group.

- After brainstorming is completed, the group can begin to identify the most promising ideas from those suggested.

- Begin by placing a mark next to those ideas the group thinks are most promising.

- For each promising idea, identify what is effective about the idea and suggest improvements and ways to make it more realistic and so forth. (This is where the discussion begins.)

- Select the solution to try first.

It is often suggested that the person who would be responsible for implementing a solution have the opportunity to select which plan to try first. For example, once the most promising solutions are identified, the classroom teacher who will be implementing the procedure in his or her classroom should be able to select the plan to try first.

An important goal in shared decision making is to make sure all parties feel that they participated in the process. Good brainstorming sessions can support this. If this is not the case, then ultimately the implementation of a teaching strategy or an inclusion support plan may fail, because those responsible for actually carrying out the plan were not active participants in the decision-making process. It is important to keep in mind that the goal of conflict resolution is not always to gain consensus. Rather, it is to agree on a strategy or a policy to implement, with the understanding that the team will have an opportunity to reconvene and debrief regarding the effectiveness and/or shortcomings of the solution decided on. This approach can diminish the tendency of some members of the team to be invested in getting credit either for the belief that the strategy would not work or for coming up with the "winning" strategy. The shared decision-making process should be about which of the most promising solutions to try first, not which solution is the best.

For example, the speech-language pathologist is convinced the PECS (Picture Exchange Communication System) is the best solution for decreasing a child's behavioral outbursts. The behavioral consultant is strongly committed to attempting to decrease the disruptive behaviors using an extinction procedure. The teacher is interested in learning and implementing the PECS procedure. The group decides to try the PECS procedure for six weeks, then assess progress.

5. Action Plan and Implementation   Once a particular solution is selected, a written action plan is drawn up. The action plan must include the following:

- A detailed description of what the intervention is

- Who is responsible

- What each person's role is

- Where it takes place

- How often and for how long

- Date of follow-up meeting to describe results

Figure 5.4. Extreme team and dream team.

6. Follow-Up It is critical that the action plan include a date for follow-up. This does not have to be a formal meeting, but key players must connect somehow, for example, by phone or e-mail, to describe results. It is not helpful to view the purpose of the follow-up as assessing the success or failure of the plan. Those members who were invested (either way) in a particular solution may see themselves as winners or losers depending on the outcome. It is particularly important that the ECSE consultant or co-teacher avoid being invested in seeing his or her own ideas validated. The belief that because you are the "expert" on the area of disabilities you have to have all the answers will not contribute to genuine collaborative team processes. Rather, the purpose of the follow-up is to consider the experiences and results of implementing the plan as data to be examined.

- If the solution seems to be working, the team can simply schedule the next follow-up date.

- If it shows promise but needs to be tweaked, the relevant key players could make those changes to the original plan and continue the plan for some specified period of time before another follow-up check.

7. Recycle Problem-Solving Steps   If the solution selected does not appear to be effective, some members of the group may choose to meet again and select another promising solution from the previous brainstorming results. In some cases, when the problem really has not been solved, there is a tendency for team members to retreat to their corners and their original positions in the conflict (saying, "I told you so" or "I knew that wouldn't work"). However, it should become a matter of course that some problems are more difficult than others to solve. The group should return to the drawing table, so to speak, to debrief and recycle the problem-solving procedure again. The cartoon in Figure 5.4 humorously compares teams that use genuine collaborative problem solving to those who don't.

CONCLUSION

How teams manage conflict can "make or break" the effectiveness of the educational support plans for children in inclusive settings. Using collaborative communication styles, embracing conflict, understanding and validating a wide range of perspectives, and allocating adequate time and space for creative problem solving can harness conflict on behalf of the children we serve.

Appendix 5A

Two Case Studies—Jonny and Brandon

This chapter has presented a great amount of detail describing conflict resolution, perspective taking, and collaborative problem solving. We believe this focus is warranted in light of the importance of conflict resolution and collaborative problem solving in successful preschool inclusion. The following are two real-life examples of challenges and solutions often experienced by early childhood special education (ECSE) and early childhood education (ECE) practitioners in their efforts to provide supportive, inclusive early childhood experiences for young children with special needs. The first case study, of "Jonny," presents the perspectives and frustrations of an itinerant inclusion consultant's with the kinds of conflicts that can arise related to preschool behavioral challenges. The second case study, of "Brandon," presents a description of a case in which emerging conflicts were managed and averted through staff and administrative collaborative communication and willingness to think outside the box to find solutions.

Case Study 1: Jonny Goes to Kindergarten

Jonny is a 5 year old with a diagnosis of Down syndrome. He was successfully included in a co-teaching blended program with great Head Start and district special education support. This year, Jonny began full-day general education kindergarten with an itinerant inclusion specialist managing his case. Jonny's individualized education program (IEP) team included the following members:

- Inclusion specialist
- Parents
- School psychologist
- Kindergarten teacher
- Resource specialist (special education teacher at the school)
- Speech therapist
- Occupational therapist

(continued)

- School principal
- Paraprofessional
- School nurse

The variety of members on Jonny's IEP team reflects his developmental and behavioral needs. Jonny is cognitively 2–3 years younger than his peers. He uses one-word utterances to express his wants and needs. Jonny likes looking at books and labeling pictures. His fine motor skills are limited. He recognizes his printed name, labels two colors, and rote counts to five. The team agreed on academic goals in the areas of reading comprehension; letter recognition; mathematics (colors, shapes, and numbers); printing; and increasing attention and participation to a variety of school tasks (not just those he chooses) based on present levels of performance.

Social behaviors are of greater concern. Jonny has a difficult time attending for more than 2–3 minutes during work periods. He often uses cursing, spitting, and hitting to protest or try to escape class work. Jonny also uses these same behaviors to gain attention from both peers and adults, even during play periods when he is engaged in high-interest activities of his choice. His IEP team prioritized three major social goals: communicate with peers and adults using appropriate phrases, play with peers by following play rules, and reduce escape and protest behaviors through the implementation of a personalized behavior plan.

Supplementary aids and services were discussed to ensure adequate supports for Jonny in the kindergarten classroom. A paraprofessional has been assigned as an extra classroom assistant to supervise Jonny throughout the school day and assist with implementing the behavior plan. The team agreed that Jonny would continue to receive weekly speech and occupational therapies.

Kindergarten began in September. The first two weeks were very difficult. Jonny kept asking, "Home?" He looked tired. He refused to do any work and insisted on wandering around the room or sliding under desks throughout the day. He hit several peers during recess and used swear words to call the paraprofessional names. The teacher talked to the inclusion specialist and suggested that the team think about dismissing Jonny earlier in the afternoon, allowing him to go home early.

The teacher thought, *I can't teach with the disruptions caused by Jonny. I want to have him in my class, but I have to make sure the other 19 children are learning. Seems like going home early isn't a bad thing!*

The inclusion specialist suggested that the team set up a data collection plan to note when these behaviors occurred to determine whether or not his behavior deteriorated at certain days or during certain activities or times of day. The inclusion specialist also created a simple picture schedule for the teachers to use. She explained that the schedule might help Jonny learn the new classroom routine and would provide clear information about when he could go home. She used laminated black and white drawings symbolizing each period of the kindergarten day including a "home" card.

The inclusion specialist thought, *I can't believe it! We haven't finished two weeks of school and you already want him to go home early. No strategies, no discussion, just "send him home when he asks." I do not think this is a very good way to help a*

(continued)

child understand that school is not just an option. Guess I'd better try some strategies fast to show that Jonny can *handle the full day.*

During the next two weeks, Jonny used the picture routine each day and used fewer requests to go home, but other negative behaviors occurred multiple times each day with no noticeable pattern. Jonny enjoyed being rewarded for on-task behaviors, but his interest in what was observed as high-preference, rewarding activities or objects was inconsistent. He liked stickers or stamps, one or two edible rewards, and books read to him, but his interest shifted from day to day. The inclusion specialist began to suspect that the plan wasn't being fully implemented.

The inclusion specialist thought, *Whew this is one tough kid! I thought the behavior plan would show a spike in bad behaviors but then we'd start seeing some positive responses by now. Maybe they are trying to undermine his success.*

Meanwhile, the paraprofessional worried about her relationship with Jonny: *I don't think Jonny likes me. He calls me names and won't listen. No one is really helping me understand how to respond to him.*

The resource specialist began to question the placement: *I think this is the wrong place for this child. He should be in a special education class.*

Eight weeks into the school year, the team—including Jonny's parents—met to discuss the teacher's concerns and review the existing behavior plan. Some members were more vocal than others, and each person perceived different problems. One item all members agreed on was that Jonny looked and acted tired often. His parents described sleeping habits that could indicate possible sleep apnea (a common health issue for children with Down syndrome, characterized by restless sleep, snoring, waking, and sitting up to take deep breaths before lying down again). The team asked the school nurse to follow up with the pediatrician for a referral for sleep apnea testing.

The principal later reflected on what she had learned in the meeting. *I didn't realize there were so many concerns. As much as I'd like to be more involved with this case, I have to run a school! I've certainly spent enough time listening to complaints from Jonny's teacher and from parents of children in his class. I need to listen to my teachers.*

The inclusion specialist began to have doubts. *This is going to be a fight all year long, I can tell. The kindergarten teacher has all these high expectations for Jonny. She keeps saying "he knows what he's doing." I agree, in part, but I think he's overwhelmed. I keep trying to explain to the teacher that Jonny is a little boy with severe cognitive delays; he's more like a 2- to 3-year-old, not a 5-year-old. Both Jonny's mom and dad say they don't know where he gets the bad language from.... He has an older teenage brother so maybe he's overhearing him or television shows. Another frustration … and no control. I'm concerned about the reports of sleep problems. Let's hope the parents and pediatrician follow up.*

The occupational therapist was having similar doubts. *Jonny responds well to sensory input, but he's been displaying a lot of the negative behaviors with me, too. I'm not seeing much progress in the regular classroom.*

The parents thought, *The team doesn't want Jonny at school. They don't think he can learn. He was doing so well in preschool! We need to talk to the doctor, but they keep telling us it'll take about two months to get the test. Where will Jonny be then?*

(continued)

During the next few months the team members were frustrated by a lack of follow through from Jonny's pediatrician. The referral for a sleep apnea test was rejected. The doctor failed to follow through with parent requests for additional testing for allergies. Finally, after persistent calls and e-mails from the school nurse, the doctor agreed to provide appropriate referrals. Unfortunately, no tests were scheduled until the summer following kindergarten. Meanwhile the school team continued to review weekly data, and Jonny missed several days of school throughout the second trimester due to a variety of colds and flu-like symptoms. His sleeping habits continued to be poor, according to his parents. The data showed no improvement in off-task behaviors. In fact, several weeks showed spikes in one behavior or another.

In spite of the ongoing concerns, Jonny was showing progress in several of his academic goals: his fine motor skills were improving, he recognized names of more classmates, he labeled more colors, and he was counting to 13 with one-to-one correspondence increasing to 5 objects.

This inconsistency perplexed the inclusion specialist. *I cannot figure out why the negative behaviors are continuing at such a high rate, other than my feeling that the sleep issue is a contributing factor. There are many days when Jonny just seems exhausted.*

A final IEP meeting was scheduled for near the end of the school year to review the progress and determine first-grade placement. As the meeting date approached, the inclusion specialist met with key players. All members had different ideas on how to solve the problem based on their experiences with Jonny and their perspectives.

The parents wanted Jonny to stay at his neighborhood school and move to first grade with peers. They were worried about the need to change schools if the team recommended a more restrictive placement (which was not available at his current school). The school principal was ambivalent. She clearly enjoyed her interaction with Jonny whenever she saw him in class or on the school campus. However, she had fielded complaints throughout the year (usually based on Jonny's negative interactions with peers: spitting, cursing, or hitting). The school psychologist had observed Jonny a few times in the classroom but deferred to the inclusion specialist's recommendations. Both the speech and the occupational therapist observed that Jonny did fine in the one-to-one therapy setting.

At the end of the year, the kindergarten teacher did not feel she could recommend that Jonny move to a regular first-grade class. It had been a difficult year for her. *I really feel like I failed. I wasn't able to help him improve his social skills and work habits. And I know his parents are really disappointed.*

The resource specialist insisted that a special education classroom was necessary for the following year. The paraprofessional assigned to Jonny was tired of the constant negative behaviors (many directed toward her throughout the school day).

The inclusion specialist was convinced that Jonny's behavior would improve over time and as he matured but acknowledged that the team had been unsuccessful in its attempts to support the development of social skills and reduce Jonny's episodes of inappropriate behaviors. She also continued to have serious concerns about the medical issues. *I feel like I've failed! I really want to recommend continued inclusion for*

(continued)

Jonny, but as I observed him and the adults he interacted with, I did not feel he was truly included in the classroom most of the day. We weren't able to make any kind of significant changes in his behaviors and, even though he's shown much academic progress, his social behaviors are not appropriate.

Jonny's father did not agree with the decision that he could not attend a regular first grade. *Seems like Jonny would've been okay going to regular first grade, but even the inclusion specialist didn't think so. I'm disappointed, but everyone says that placement in the special education class will still provide opportunities to be mainstreamed with his typical peers for certain activities. I really hope we can work on getting him back into regular education.*

Jonny's mom was exhausted. *This year has been really hard. I'm so frustrated with the doctors! I'm really worried. We have to get Jonny in for tests this summer. I'm almost relieved we don't have to keep meeting like this. I've taken a lot of time off from work. I'm just tired of fighting. Maybe in the next year Jonny will settle down and stop the swearing and spitting.*

At the IEP meeting the team agreed to a first-grade placement in a special education classroom. Team members left the meeting with a variety of feelings, described previously. The inclusion specialist felt relief that a decision had been made but with a sense of failure in her inability to change Jonny's behaviors. She felt that working with children's disruptive behaviors was one of her strengths and had really thought that she would be effective in working with Jonny and his team to change those behaviors. She also felt a sense of frustration with the resource specialist, because she felt that there had been little commitment to positive change in the inclusive setting. At the same time, she acknowledged that this was an exceedingly difficult case behaviorally, so she tried to acknowledge the resource specialist's feelings from that perspective. She felt a strong alliance with Jonny's parents and knew they were unhappy with

Table 5A.1.   Jonny: Team perspectives and issues

Team member	Perspective
Parents	*We want our child to go to school with his neighborhood friends. He's such a happy child and we know he likes school. Why won't he behave for the teachers?*
Kindergarten teacher	*I want to include this child, but I don't know why he won't learn like other children. I've always felt so effective with young kids. I feel like I've failed this year.*
Special education teacher	*He is in the wrong setting and it's not good for him or the other students in his class. A special education class would be so much better for Jonny. Maybe later, when his behavior gets better, he can come back to regular ed.*
School psychologist	*My job is to support the team with the decisions they make. Not everyone is in agreement with this placement. I'd like to be more helpful, but I have so many other cases that need my time this year. It's just easier if Jonny goes to a special ed class.*
Inclusion specialist	*I want this child to be successful. I want to show the naysayers that this is a good decision. I think everyone thought I'd do a better job. Parents are disappointed, teacher's frustrated, and I feel completely ineffective.*

(continued)

(continued)

Table 5A.1. (continued)	
Team member	Perspective
Paraprofessional	*I'm overwhelmed and tired; this little boy is a handful and, no matter what anyone says, I feel responsible for his learning and safety and the safety of his peers. I wish I had more training on how to handle these behaviors. I've never had a child this challenging!*
Speech therapist	*I can handle him in therapy. Even though he tries his behaviors on me I can ignore them because we're in a small group setting. I can see why the teachers are frustrated; I can't imagine trying to teach Jonny in a class of 20 other children.*
Occupational therapist	*I want to help the team with the behaviors, but he's challenging for me, too! I know we're supposed to offer strategies in the classroom, but this is one case in which I feel like I'm out of ideas. Seeing him in the clinic by himself would be so much easier, not that that would help his schooling.*
Principal	*I like this little boy and his family, but I'm spending a lot of time listening to teacher concerns and the concerns of parents of the other children in his kindergarten class. I have a lot of other things to think about, not just Jonny. I thought the special education staff would be more helpful and effective, but it feels like they are trying to get me to make the decisions that they are more trained to make.*
School nurse	*It's frustrating trying to get responses from doctors. I agree that Jonny would really benefit from a full medical workup, but we have to wait so long when families don't have comprehensive medical plans. I'll just have to ask everyone to be patient, which I'm sure they don't want to hear.*

the decision, although they did realize that the lack of improvement in Jonny's social behavior was of great concern to the entire team.

Conclusion

This case demonstrates the complexity and frustrations that can be associated with difficult behavioral issues. Unresolved conflict is often the result of many different, competing perspectives. There is no bad faith effort in this story, just many different—though valid—perspectives (see Table 5A.1). It should be noted that despite many perspectives, the team continued to meet and communicate. While the goals for a successful inclusive kindergarten experience for Jonny were not realized, escalation of conflict was kept in check.

Case Study 2: Making It Work with Brandon

Brandon was found eligible for early intervention services on the basis of communication delay, particularly social communication and atypical behavior patterns suggestive of autism spectrum disorder. At age 2 years, 6 months, in preparation for the transition IEP from early intervention to preschool services, Brandon was assessed formally

(continued)

and found to have difficulty with adaptive skills of communication, daily living, and socialization, performing at around the 12-month level, and was found to meet the diagnostic criteria for autism.

Brandon's IEP goal areas included the following:

- Social /pragmatic communication skills, including appropriate language responses

- Independent transition and appropriate participation in daily routines

- Increased social engagement and participation in peer play

At age 3, as per the district IEP team recommendations, Brandon was placed in a preschool special education class. This was a high-quality special education classroom serving children with a wide range of complex disabilities. This special day class program had a reputation for meeting the individual needs of each child and was led by a highly trained teacher who had special expertise in the area of assistive technology. However, Brandon's parents became concerned that the special day class (SDC) placement was not appropriate for their son. They reported regression in his communication skills and an increase in inappropriate behaviors. They became concerned regarding the lack of appropriate peer social and communication models in the SDC and requested placement in an inclusive preschool setting.

In response to this request, the district agreed to explore possible inclusive placement options. The district had already established a cooperative partnership with a church-affiliated ECE program that was receptive to including children with special needs. Because of *previous positive collaborations* with district personnel, the ECE program director was open to accepting Brandon and even offered to increase the number of hours her one floating assistant could spend in Brandon's classroom. (This increased the number of hours an extra adult was available in Brandon's classroom without additional cost to the district.) The team agreed that when the assistant was in the classroom she would not function primarily as a one-to-one support provider for Brandon. It was believed that assigning a one-to-one assistant would interfere with Brandon's priority goal: development of peer social skills. Rather, the program assistant would be an extra hand in the classroom, providing assistance as needed under the direction of the classroom teacher. This would allow the ECE teacher to focus more attention on Brandon.

It is important to note some interesting things about the beginning of this case:

- Because the key district actors (administrator and professional staff) in this program had a history of working collaboratively with families, the parents' significant unhappiness with the initial placement was not viewed as a major threat or problem. In many districts, there is an automatic push-back and resistance to parent complaints.

- These same actors had also worked hard over the years to establish respectful collaborative relationships with community partners, partly due to a history of valuing inclusive opportunities for students.

- As a result, they were able to use their political capital to obtain a positive response from the teacher at the private preschool and a willingness to take on the challenge of including Brandon. Also, because of positive history, the teacher readily

(continued)

agreed to allow her one classroom floating assistant to spend some extra hours supporting Brandon.

It might be said that "collaborative relationships beget more collaborative relationships." Unfortunately, it is also the case that previous conflicts often lead to more conflicts and resistance.

Brandon's Behavior and Participation Challenges

Behavioral and participation challenges that presented the greatest difficulty for the ECE classroom staff (one full-time teacher and one part-time classroom assistant) were the following:

- Isolation—preferred standing in corner playing with trucks

- Difficulty making transitions from one activity to the next without total prompting

- Difficulty engaging with materials in different centers due to very limited, perseverative interests (cars and trucks)

- Tantrums expressing resistance to certain activities, particularly art activities, apparently related to tactile sensitivity.

Brandon's Inclusion Support Plan

To ensure Brandon's success in the inclusive preschool placement, the district realized the importance of providing high-quality yet flexible support to both Brandon and the staff. Therefore, a *collaborative consultation* model of support, providing 60 to 120 minutes of inclusion support per month, as needed, was written into Brandon's IEP. This service would be provided by a highly experienced ECSE consulting teacher and a well-trained special education paraprofessional assistant who worked under her direct supervision. The amount of time spent per week was limited but flexible and depended on the needs of the child and/or classroom staff. Visits occurred at different times of the day to ensure observation of Brandon in a range of activities The ECE teacher and the ECSE inclusion consultant collaborated to plan the roles and strategies of the two part-time paraprofessionals working with Brandon (one an employee of the preschool and the other a district special education staff member). The amount of support per month was gradually decreased over time in order to prevent the common problem of a child's overdependence on one-to-one adult support

This model of support combined expert and collaborative consultation provided by the ECSE teacher and direct support provided by the paraprofessionals during those activities in which Brandon most needed support. The ECSE consultant observed Brandon for approximately 30–45 minutes during each visit. Her consultation activities included the following:

- Direct observation and data collection regarding Brandon's performance in different activities and his progress on IEP goals

- Modeling specific strategies for staff (e.g., how to scaffold Brandon's transitions or participation in activities using his existing skills and preferences, such as playing with cars)

(continued)

- Debriefing with the ECE teacher at the end of each observation or briefly after school

The consultant demonstrated or provided suggestions and/or brainstormed ideas regarding the following:

- Brandon's tactile sensitivity and associated behaviors of crying and refusal to participate

- Specific strategies to help Brandon make transitions throughout the daily schedule: verbal reminders (e.g., "First we have circle, than we go outside"), decreasing physical prompts (e.g., physically leading or directing Brandon's attention toward the appropriate area of the classroom), and use of visual supports such as a picture schedule

- Occasional discussion of Brandon's challenges with curriculum content and materials and possible modifications

Collaboration with Speech-Language Pathologist

In addition to the inclusion support already described, Brandon also received small group pull-out speech-and-language therapy support once per week. However, even though the group therapy service was provided at the school site, the speech-language pathologist (SLP) used a pull-out model. The SLP did not spend time observing Brandon in the classroom and provided minimal consultation to the teacher regarding Brandon's goals and progress. In order to provide this important exchange of information between the SLP and the teacher, the ECSE consultant took on the additional role of conferring with the SLP and sharing her recommendations for classroom generalization of newly acquired communication skills with the classroom teacher. While this arrangement was not ideal, it avoided confrontation with the SLP and provided the information needed to the teacher.

Role of the Special Education Paraprofessional

Back at the district office, the ECSE consultant and the district paraprofessional would discuss the specific supports the paraprofessional should use in her weekly visit to the classroom.

The direct support provided by the paraprofessional (one visit per week, or every other week, under the supervision of the ECSE consultant) included the following:

- Providing decreasing prompts and cues to assist with Brandon's transition from one activity to the next

- Offering specific enticements to support difficult transitions (e.g., at lunch time use of a 5-minute warning, placing his favorite truck on the lunch table, using a preferred chair)

- Using successive approximation to encourage Brandon's participation in those activities that were the most aversive to him (e.g., placing a small dab of paint on the back of his hand, providing a variety of utensils during finger paint activity)

(continued)

- Writing notes regarding Brandon's performance in each goal area, which were then shared with the ECSE consultant

Home visits were provided by the ECSE consultant once every four to six weeks to go over Brandon's progress and challenges and provide information to his parents so they could support classroom goals and activities at home. For example, duplicates of books and materials used frequently in the classroom were provided in the home so parents could familiarize Brandon with them and reinforce concepts taught in the classroom.

Specific Challenges and Solutions in Year 1 of Inclusive Placement

Curriculum and materials: Initially curricular challenges centered mainly on content and structure of circle time. Circle time was long and required attention to materials that the ECSE consultant strongly believed to be developmentally inappropriate for many of the students, not just Brandon. However, the consultant did not frame her concerns in this way. Rather, she communicated to the ECE teacher that Brandon was having difficulty focusing on the materials and content because they were not engaging for him. Also, because the teacher was new and relatively inexperienced, the consultant focused on the most simple-to-implement strategy. She suggested that Brandon sit close to the teacher and thus close to the materials. She also made attractive name cards for the teacher to use when taking attendance so that Brandon could use his print recognition strengths to learn his classmates' names.

These changes required no extra prep time on the part of the ECE teacher, and she was able to easily incorporate them into her usual routine. Over time the teacher began to note that several children in the class (not just Brandon) were at developmental levels somewhat lower than the materials being used and that some of Brandon's adaptations were helpful for several of the children.

Snack time: Another challenge was snack time. Brandon was an extremely picky eater and also uncomfortable with close proximity to other students at lunch, where many children were all seated around a single table. The accommodation that worked easily was to initially allow Brandon to eat at a separate table and gradually transition him to a "special" assigned seat preferred by him.

At the end of year 1, progress had been achieved in the following areas:

- Though participation in activities and interactions with peers was still minimal, he tolerated proximity of other children and engaged in parallel play.

- Brandon was able to make transitions appropriately and generally followed the daily routines and tolerated activities without major emotional episodes.

- As a result of these gains, it was possible to decrease the level of support.

- The team was able to collaborate with the preschool's program administrator to select which second-year teacher would be most appropriate for Brandon.

Year 2 Goals and Support Strategies

There was a significant decrease in level of support needed in year 2. There was no longer a need for direct support in the classroom. The support model used was

(continued)

observation and consultation provided to the classroom teacher by the ECSE inclusion consultant. Year 2 goals focused on the following:

- *Moving beyond Brandon's achievements in parallel play to cooperative play and communicative interactions with peers:* The primary focus became more specifically aimed at the development of social and pragmatic communication skills. The inclusion consultant continued to provide a liaison between the SLP and the teacher to ensure that Brandon's social communication skills were prioritized. For example, Brandon's preferred play partners were encouraged to use certain comments (e.g., "Let's play race cars!") and questions (e.g., "Which car do you want, Brandon?"). The paraprofessional was trained to prompt and scaffold Brandon to respond with pragmatically appropriate language (e.g., "Okay!" or "I want the blue one.").

- *Decreasing sensory issues—for example, tactile sensitivity—and increasing voluntary participation in sensory activities:* Behavior-management issues related to Brandon's tantrums and anxiety around sensory activities decreased, but his general reluctance to engage in activities and his lack of cooperative play skills continued to be a concern.

- *Preparation for the kindergarten classroom environment, including observation and consultation with receiving kindergarten teacher:* Based on team input and considerations of the demands of the kindergarten environment, concerns related to development of Brandon's *listening* skills were addressed (e.g., independent use of headphones to listen to a story).

By the end of year 2, Brandon participated voluntarily and appropriately in most activities, made transitions without support, tolerated proximity of peers, and engaged in parallel play and some associative play. Brandon continued to be a picky eater and had some toileting issues. Primary concerns were social communication and listening skills. While Brandon had made major progress during year 2, school readiness expectations of the kindergarten environment were of great concern to the parents. The inclusion support provider agreed that one more year in the inclusive preschool setting would significantly increase the odds for successful grade-level achievement in kindergarten. A request for an additional preschool year was granted by administrators of both the private preschool and the district special education program.

Kindergarten Transition

As part of Brandon's transition to kindergarten, his inclusion support team, including the school psychologist, produced a very thorough assessment and description of his strengths, needs, and learning style. Planning for the transition was carried out by key players, including Brandon's parents, the ECSE inclusion support consultant, the school psychologist, SLP, and, particularly important, the receiving kindergarten teacher. Brandon successfully transitioned to a 5-day inclusive kindergarten in which a strong focus was placed on speech, language, and social pragmatic goals. He had a very successful year. At the time of writing this book in 2013, Brandon is currently included in first grade, *without support*, and doing well!

(continued)

(continued)

Keys to Success

Several of the characteristics of successful inclusion that are described in this book were evident in this case. These include the following:

- Individualized, customized, flexible support plan

- Administrative support (both ECE and ECSE) and willingness to think outside the box

- Efficient support staffing, decreasing over time

- Consultant's ability to establish a supportive, collaborative relationship and get buy-in from ECE teacher by focusing on specific needs of the child, rather than on ECE teacher skills or program characteristics

- Effective, meaningful support for ECE teacher, particularly adaptations of materials, types of accommodations, and ease of implementation (The teacher felt supported and respected, not critiqued, by the inclusion consultant.)

- Continuing support and communication with the family, enabling them to understand and reinforce goals and strategies in the classroom and to freely express concerns and priorities

- Individualized planning conducted for the transition to a general education kindergarten, including collaboration with the receiving teacher

By any measure this was a success story. Although it could have easily been an all-too-familiar tale of conflict and costly fair hearings, a collaborative problem-solving approach significantly changed the trajectory of one little boy's educational achievement.

REFERENCES

Barrera, I., Kramer, L., & Macpherson, T. D. (2012). *Skilled dialogue: Strategies for responding to cultural diversity in early childhood* (2nd ed). Baltimore, MD: Paul H. Brookes Publishing Co.

Burgoon, J.K. (1994). Nonverbal signals. In M.L. Knapp & G.R. Miller (Eds.), *Handbook of interpersonal communication* (pp. 229–285). Newbury Park, CA: Sage Publications.

Career and Job Search Resources. (2013). Retrieved from http://www.careeroverview.com

CAST. (2012). Universal Design for Learning *Guidelines version 2.0*. Wakefield, MA: Author. Retrieved from www.udlcenter.org/aboutudl/udlguidelines

Chen, D., & Chan, S. (2011). Families with Asian roots. In E. Lynch & M. Hanson (Eds.), *Developing cross-cultural competence* (pp. 234–311). Baltimore, MD: Paul H. Brookes Publishing Co.

Connor, D., & Ferri, B. (2007). The conflict within: Resistance to inclusion and other paradoxes in special education. *Disability and Society, 22*(1), 63–77.

Cook, R., Klein, M.D., & Chen, D. (2012). *Adapting early childhood curricula for children with special needs* (8th ed.). Upper Saddle River, NJ: Pearson.

Ellis, D.G., & Fisher, B.A. (1994). *Small group decision making: Communication and the group process* (4th ed.). New York, NY: McGraw Hill.

Fisher, R., Ury, W., & Patton, B. (2011). *Getting to yes* (3rd ed.). New York, NY: Penguin Group.

Friend, M., & Cook, L. (2007). *Interactions: Collaboration skills for school professionals* (5th ed.). Boston: Pearson.

Gately, S.E., & Gately, F.J. (2001). Understanding co-teaching components. *Teaching Exceptional Children, 33*(4), 4–7.

Heron, T., & Harris, K, (2001). *The educational consultant: Helping professionals, parents, and students in inclusive classrooms* (4th edition). Austin, TX: PRO-ED.

Individuals with Disabilities Education Act (IDEA) of 1990, PL 101-476, 20 U.S.C. §§ 1400 *et seq.*

Klein, M.D., & Chen, D. (2001). *Working with children from culturally diverse backgrounds.* Albany, NY: Delmar.

Kurpius, D. (1978). Consultation theory and process: An integrated model. *Personnel and Guidance Journal, 56*, 335–358.

Lieber, J., Wolery, R.A., Horn, E., Tschantz, J., Beckman, P.J., & Hanson, M.J. (2002). Collaborative relationships among adults in inclusive preschool programs. In S.L. Odom (Ed.), *Widening the circle: Including children with disabilities in preschool programs* (pp. 81–97). New York, NY: Teachers College Press.

Lynch, E., & Hanson, M. (2011). *Developing cross-cultural competence: A guide to working with children and their families* (4th ed). Baltimore, MD: Paul H. Brookes Publishing Co.

Odom, S.L., Horn, E.M., Marquart, J.M., Hanson, M.J., Wolfberg, R., Beckman, P., ... Sandall. (1999). On the forms of inclusion: Organizational context and individualized service models. *Journal of Early Intervention, 22*(3), 185–199.

Rice, N., Drame, E., Owens, L., & Frattura, E.M. (2007). Co-instructing at the secondary level: Strategies for success. *Teaching Exceptional Children, 39*(6), 12–18.

Rogers, E.M., & Steinfatt, T.M. (1999). *Intercultural communication.* Longrove, IL: Waveland Press

Schaff, J.I. (2005). Universal design for learning and its implications in the early childhood educational classroom. *Exceptional Individuals, 29*(6), 16–19.

Ury, W. (2007). *Getting past no.* New York, NY: Penguin Group.

Wiggins, K.C., & Damore, S.J. (2006). "Survivors" or "friends"? A framework for assessing effective collaboration. *Teaching Exceptional Children, 38*(5), 49–56.

6 Strategies that Support the Needs of All Learners

Once the inclusive *placement setting* for a child and the particular features of the *support plan* have been determined, work can begin on ensuring that the classroom team, the physical environment and materials, and the teaching and curricular strategies are designed to meet a child's individual learning and developmental goals. When the team works well together and assumes the daily, creative problem-solving approach described in this book, teaching becomes the fun part. This chapter addresses the nuts and bolts needed to implement an early childhood program that meets *all* children's learning needs, but in particular those of children with disabilities. From the overarching principles of the universal design for learning (UDL) to the most specific strategies used within classrooms by adults and peers, this chapter describes ways to help young children with special needs become true participants in their preschool settings. A classroom community can be created in which there is a shared value among children and adults alike that learning is fun and the process (not just the product) is important in its own right. The realization that learning is accessible to every learner is inspirational. This kind of classroom spirit is palpable. Classroom cohesion and student achievement are predictable by-products of such an environment.

Fortunately, within the field of early childhood special education there are many well-established strategies with which to design specific interventions to enable all children to achieve their potential. These strategies are often as appropriate for typically developing children as for those with special needs. Many textbooks are available that describe these strategies in detail (see, for example, Cook, Klein, & Chen, 2011; Downing, 2008; Sandall & Schwartz, 2008). Odom and Wolery (2003) have described basic tenets and evidence-based practices, which comprise what the authors refer to as a "unified theory of practice" in early intervention and early childhood special education (ESCE) (p. 165). These are summarized in Figure 6.1. The strategies described throughout this book consistently reflect these practices.

Many of the practices and principles described by Odom and Wolery (2003) have also been described by Cook, Klein, and Chen (2011), who refer to them as "general instructional strategies" (p. 130). These are widely used, well-established, basic strategies that support all children's learning and are discussed in greater

- Children's families and their homes must be viewed as primary contexts within which to nurture children's learning and development.

- Strengthening relationships between caregivers and children, supporting peer interactions, and establishing collaborative teams and partnerships are essential to positive child outcomes.

- Child learning occurs best through opportunities for active participation in contingently responsive environments.

- Adults play a key role in teaching and learning by skillfully mediating children's experiences.

- Children's participation in more developmentally advanced settings, with appropriate assistance, is essential for their increasing independence.

- The effective practice of early childhood special education is individually and dynamically goal oriented.

- Successful transitions across programs require careful planning and support, including training for the next environment, and interagency agreements.

- Families and programs are influenced by the broader context, that is, by their culture and communities.

Figure 6.1. A unified theory of practice in early intervention/early childhood special education. (*Source*: Odom & Wolery, 2003.)

detail throughout this chapter. While we offer many specific and evidence-based strategies and examples, our suggestions are by no means exhaustive. Both regular early childhood programs and special education programs use variations and combinations of these.

Increasingly, the principles of UDL are being applied to designing early childhood education environments and programs (Sadao & Robinson, 2010). UDL is committed to the universal acceptance of human differences and to designing educational environments that can meet the needs of all learners, regardless of their characteristics and abilities. The foundations of universal design include multiple means of expression, engagement, and representation. Their applications to ECSE are immediately apparent:

Multiple means of expression: There are many ways of communicating to others, such as facial expressions, spoken and written words, sign language, pictures, drawing, and high-tech communication devices.

Multiple means of engagement: Learning cannot occur without the child's attention and engagement. Teachers must discover and provide ways for children to be engaged in learning experiences based on their interests and abilities. The possibilities are unlimited. While some children easily engage in social interaction with peers and adults, others may prefer movement activities, tactile sensation, or music and sound. Some children may be captivated by manipulation of objects or cause-and-effect exploration.

Multiple means of representation: Teachers must find multiple ways of representing the world and conveying information to young children. Teachers rely on spoken words, storybooks, and photos as the primary means of representation. However, some children with disabilities may derive meaning more easily from songs, adults' use of consistent gestures or manual signs, picture schedules, or touch cues.

This chapter considers the many interwoven dimensions of the preschool classroom and provides suggestions for practices and strategies that create learning environments that can meet the needs of all children.

DEPLOYING ADULTS IN THE CLASSROOM

In order to provide a preschool environment where children can engage and learn, all adults in that setting must be aware of their roles and responsibilities. How many adults, where they are, and what they actually do in the classroom can be major factors in the success or failure of an inclusive preschool program. Administrators and classroom teams should take into consideration how the activities and behaviors, and even the *locations*, of the adults in the classroom will support or impede children's learning and sense of belonging. Equally important, systematic deployment or assignment to areas and tasks in the classroom will increase safety. This is particularly an issue with large groups in large outside play areas.

An example of one approach to deployment of adults in the early childhood setting is the "zone defense system" described by Casey and McWilliam (2005). During each period of the day, adults are assigned to a specific area or activity in the classroom. For example, one adult may be assigned to work directly with children in a carefully planned learning activity, and the second adult takes care of all other classroom tasks, including toileting, phone calls, and setting up the next activity or area. This may help to increase child engagement while simultaneously maintaining ongoing setup and addressing child care needs. When the number of adults available is ample, this design can work well. The environment is carefully planned so that children have multiple opportunities to engage with objects and materials in clearly defined interest areas around the classroom. Equally important, the adults assigned to key areas have a good understanding of the high-probability interests and learning for a particular class zone and facilitate engagement by being focused and available at that center, without distractions. Meanwhile, other adults can deal with behavioral or toileting needs or set up next activities. Thus, transition time is lessened because activities are set up and ready to use without wait time. As transitions become more orderly and predictable, behavior problems decrease. The adult positions can change as needed.

Teacher-Student Ratios and Class Size

Keep in mind that more is not always better. Adults sitting behind students at circle time, chatting with colleagues on the playground, or simply assisting at the craft table where there is already one adult and only three or four children may not be adding to children's learning and could interfere with peer socialization. If some children do need extra, intensive supports, then the role of the adult—often a para-educator—should be carefully delineated and monitored. There will be some children whose major needs are behavior regulation and social interaction skills. For them, the classroom's greatest resources will be their other classmates. The best adult coaches will decrease their own involvement over time.

The model of inclusive support (e.g., consultation, co-teaching) is a primary factor in making decisions about deployment of classroom staff. For example, a child placed in a co-teaching setting has the daily support of the ECSE co-teacher and assistant working under that teacher's supervision. However, if the inclusion support model being used is itinerant consultation, the child may receive less direct specialized support. In this case, the training and skills of the regular classroom staff will be critical. The use of well-trained and supervised paraeducators may be necessary to allow the child opportunities to adequately and meaningfully access the inclusive setting.

Use of Paraprofessionals and One-to-One Assistants

In some inclusive settings, additional paraprofessionals may be assigned to the classroom as extra classroom assistants or as "one-to-ones" to help meet a specific child's needs, including health or safety concerns. While some teachers and parents see the extra adult in the classroom as a bonus for that child with special needs, we have often observed these extra adults used in ways that do not necessarily benefit or enhance a child's learning or engagement. In fact, an untrained paraprofessional may cause more segregation of the child if he or she provides constant supervision or shadowing to the exclusion of peers. Using a zone defense–type system as described or providing very specific assignments defines a clear purpose for each adult in the classroom. Sharing student goals and providing ongoing training and supervision can help classroom assistants become more active participants in the early childhood setting.

DESIGNING THE CLASSROOM ENVIRONMENT

Assessing the preschool environment is an effective practice to ensure that classroom demands and supports are congruent with children's strengths and needs. Abilities and needs are assessed within the context of the surrounding environment: peers, adults, routines, and materials. Specific instructional strategies are addressed using an individualized inclusion plan and monitoring progress. Embedding functional goals into everyday activities and routines with opportunities to practice across different settings and people is one of the most highly researched, evidence-based, and recommended approaches (Hollingsworth, Boone, & Crais, 2009).

The Physical Environment

Accommodating children with disabilities will require special adjustments to the physical environment. For example, a preschool classroom may require more room for movement between areas if a child uses a walker or wheelchair. Putting a sticky mat (cut from no-slip carpet backing) on tables during meals or when working with blocks or other manipulatives prevents objects from sliding away from a child. Using different types of seating may be necessary to support the physically challenged child. Heavy stools or phone books wrapped in carpet backing (so they cannot be kicked aside) can support a child's feet when chairs are too tall to allow a child to comfortably engage in fine motor activities. Cushions or taped-together phone books can be inserted behind a child's back to decrease the depth of a chair and increase a child's ability to sit comfortably and attend to peers and adults rather than constantly shifting around trying to get stable and comfortable.

For some children, sitting in large group for circle or rug time may be too difficult if shelves offer easily accessible and enticing toys. When designing an environment that supports attention and learning through play, it is essential to consider where group activities are held, how to arrange shelves containing play objects, and how to change the look of areas in the classroom depending on their use (e.g., when using the block area for both block play and rug time).

Visual Supports

Visual cues can be another simple but very effective environmental support. Most children with disabilities—particularly children on the autism spectrum or with speech and language disorders or auditory-based learning disabilities—are much better at processing visual information than auditory information. In fact, this is probably true for many of us. One obvious advantage of visual information is that it lasts longer than speech signals, which are very complex and fleeting. In addition, printed information is concrete and tactile, because it can be presented on manipulatives like picture cards or in a book.

The fleeting nature of auditory information can be particularly evident when what is being presented is *language*. Teachers sometimes forget that the adult's speech is incredibly complex and rapid. Unlike a written record or a picture, words that are spoken cannot be retrieved by the listener unless they are repeated. Some children with significant auditory processing and communication difficulties may even find the sound of people talking to be unpleasant or absolutely meaningless. Individuals with autism often report this phenomenon (Valentine & Hamilton, 2006). Pictures, written symbols, or actual objects, on the other hand, are static and, within limits, can last as long as needed. Even for children who do not have visual or severe cognitive impairments, pictures are easier to perceive, process, and make sense of. Also, unlike speech input, which is constantly changing and slightly varied with every repetition, visual stimuli, like print, pictures, or objects, are more consistent and predictable. The visual schedules described in the TEACCH program (Mesibov, Shea, & Schopler, 2004); the use of visual cues in "structured work systems," which help task analyze the steps of an activity (Carnahan, Harte, Dyke, Hume, & Borders, 2011); and the pictures or drawings used in "Social Stories" (Gray, 2006) are all examples of approaches used successfully with students who have autism. It should be noted that children who have Down syndrome—and probably most children with disabilities—can benefit from visual supports (Janse van Vuren, 2009; Oelwein, 1995).

Visual Schedules as Support for Daily Routines

A picture schedule is quite helpful if the child understands the relationship of pictures with the daily routine. Objects can be used in lieu of pictures for children not developmentally ready for two-dimensional representations. Systematically presenting the schedule prior to the start of a transition, labeling the expected actions, and providing verbal encouragement or physical help is often enough of an intervention to help a child cope.

In some cases, children may resist transitions to activities that are unpleasant for them. If a child does not like small group time during kindergarten because he or she has learned that small group means fine motor work—which the child dislikes—then he or she will probably resist leaving the playground if the next activity is small group work. Additional strategies may need to be tried with visual and verbal reminders:

- Consistently use the visual schedule but pair the transition with foreshadowing ("We need to clean up and come inside in 5 minutes").

- Use the visual schedule but add a special "job" to engage the child in the actual transition (e.g., ringing the bell, counting all classmates as they line up, carrying in a basket of outside items).

- Pair the undesired activity—small group work—with a high preference activity for the child, such as distributing work materials to peers or using special markers to color at the beginning of the small group activity.

- Use a behavior chart that targets positive and cooperative transitions ("When you walk into the class and sit down, you can put a sticker on your chart").

Structured Work Systems

Using approaches such as structured work systems for children with autism to help organize their play or work periods is one strategy found to be effective in promoting engagement (Carnahan et al., 2011), especially in busy environments that rely heavily on verbal directions. The structured work system differs from the typical visual schedule, which is used to remind them of the activities in their daily schedule and where to go next. The structured work system visually conveys to the child the specific sequence of steps to complete a task or a series of tasks. The system helps to answer the following questions for the child:

1. What is the activity? (Picture of puzzle)

2. How much work is required or how long will the activity last? What will signal that the activity is finished or that progress has been made? (Picture of child putting puzzle pieces in correct slots, followed by a picture of completed puzzle)

3. What happens next? (Picture of next activity)

A structured work system is often useful for children who are familiar with the activities but engage in off-task behavior or are disorganized or rigid in their play. Teachers can also create work stations where students can learn to independently complete a series of school readiness tasks with very little supervision.

Space does not allow for an exhaustive discussion of the many uses and applications of visual supports. For more comprehensive coverage of this topic, see Cohen and Sloan (2007).

TEACHING STRATEGIES TO ENGAGE AND SUPPORT CHILDREN

Motivation, Attention, and Engagement

Whether implemented informally as a common sense approach to all learning or as the key principle of the many iterations of *applied behavior analysis* (ABA, discussed in Chapter 8), it is not disputed that *motivation* is a key to learning. All learners pay attention to and seek out objects and experiences that are positive and pleasurable. (Conversely, learners will ignore stimuli that are not motivating and attempt to escape from or stop stimuli that are noxious or unpleasant.) A closely related critical learning prerequisite is *attention*. Children cannot learn if they are not paying attention. Paying attention to something or someone the child finds positively motivating leads to *engagement*—this engagement further enhances attention, creating a wonderful self-sustaining context for learning. This process is further enhanced when there is a skilled adult available to provide the "just right" scaffolding and language input. Young children learn best when they are physically active and engaged with materials they can touch and feel. They even master symbolic language skills (and emergent learning of symbolic representations of literacy and mathematics) best when those symbols represent familiar people, places, and things; stories; and meaningful experiences.

The simple fact that children must be motivated and engaged in order to learn is routinely violated in some preschool environments. We have observed classrooms where well-meaning, qualified teachers focus on the need to cover planned lessons, cope with large groups of preschool-age children, or simply try to present lessons without noting whether or not all children are involved. The popular concept of the 1980s referred to as *developmentally appropriate practice* was based, in part, on the reality that children learn best from materials and activities that are not too far beyond the developmental level of the child. This is somewhat related to the concept of the *zone of proximal development* as described by Vygotsky (1980). The zone of proximal development is described as the difference between what the child can currently do independently and how the child performs with assistance from an adult or more capable peer. Learning happens most when support is provided within that zone. Thus, teaching efforts that are below the level at which the child is already capable cannot promote new learning. Targeting a skill that requires performance beyond what the child can do with assistance may be wasted effort and can cause frustration for both the teacher and the learner. More than once in past decades this issue has arisen with regard to the introduction of abstract academic learning goals at earlier and earlier ages.

The casual observer of many preschool classrooms (that may or may not include children with disabilities) can often identify children for whom the goals, teacher instructions, and learning activities or materials are simply not appropriate. Some children are not engaged because they are not motivated and do not pay attention. Without motivation, attention, and engagement, learning cannot occur. This is true for typically developing children and may be even more so for children with significant learning challenges.

It is also the case that skilled teachers can help create motivation, attention, and engagement regardless of whether the child is with same-age typical peers or in a segregated special education classroom. In some ways it is easier in an inclusive setting than in a segregated setting, because typical peers act as role models for children with disabilities. The following sections focus on specific adult-child interactions and instructional strategies that emphasize these concepts of attention, motivation, and engagement.

Social Mediation of Experience

Perhaps one of the most intensively studied phenomena related to early childhood learning is the role of responsive interactions with adults. One of the first descriptions of this was posited by Vygotsky (1980), who described the central role adults and more competent peers play in young children's learning. This is often referred to as *social mediation of experience*. Any child's learning can be enhanced by the degree to which important adults in his or her life pay careful attention to the child's interests and efforts and help the child reach new levels of competence and understanding by providing the "just right" language input or physical support. This kind of support is referred to as *scaffolding* and has been described particularly as it relates to child language learning by Bruner (1983). A teacher must be able to estimate a learner's current level of skill or knowledge and provide scaffolding that supports more complex behavior, just beyond what the child could do independently (i.e., within the zone of proximal development). Skillful, experienced teachers do this automatically. In fact, recent research examining what is particularly defining in human DNA suggests that the ability to "teach" in this way appears to be a uniquely human characteristic (Rubin, 2007).

Adult-Child Communication

As early as the 1970s and 1980s, research clearly revealed the important relationship between caregiver communicative input and responsiveness and the development of child language and literacy (Cross, 1984; Owens, 2008). Reading the child's cues, establishing joint attention, being responsive to the child's attempts to communicate, using and repeating key words, recasting one's own utterances, and expanding the child's communications by adding syntactic structure and semantic information and new vocabulary are evidenced-based communication strategies (see, for example, Mahoney & Perales, 2003; Mahoney, Boyce, Fewell, Spiker, & Wheedon, 1998). Figure 6.2. provides examples of these simple language-input strategies. While these responsive language interactions seem simple, they are surprisingly difficult to teach adults. It may be that, because of the belief that teaching requires predominantly *teacher-initiated* prompts and directives, following a child's lead during play without providing adult-initiated prompting and direction is difficult for teachers to implement (Kohler, Anthony, Steighner, & Hoyson, 2001). However, good teaching, especially for children with disabilities, requires the educator to have the ability to listen to and watch the child carefully and use the responsive communications described in Figure 6.2.

Naturalistic Teaching

Naturalistic teaching refers to following the child's lead and expanding on his or her play choices within natural environments. Naturalistic teaching strategies are described by Kohler, Anthony, Steighner, and Hoyson (2001) and Downing (2008). The following list offers examples of types of strategies used:

- Using novel materials

- Joining in the activity with the child

- Inviting the child to make choices

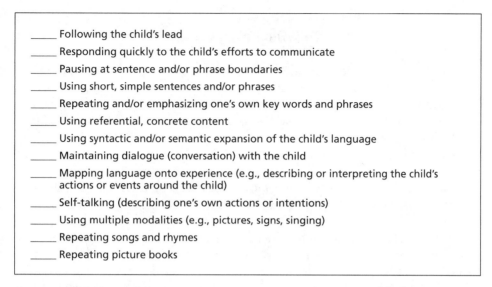

_____ Following the child's lead

_____ Responding quickly to the child's efforts to communicate

_____ Pausing at sentence and/or phrase boundaries

_____ Using short, simple sentences and/or phrases

_____ Repeating and/or emphasizing one's own key words and phrases

_____ Using referential, concrete content

_____ Using syntactic and/or semantic expansion of the child's language

_____ Maintaining dialogue (conversation) with the child

_____ Mapping language onto experience (e.g., describing or interpreting the child's actions or events around the child)

_____ Self-talking (describing one's own actions or intentions)

_____ Using multiple modalities (e.g., pictures, signs, singing)

_____ Repeating songs and rhymes

_____ Repeating picture books

Figure 6.2.   Adult support of early language development: Communication input checklist.

- Using a time delay (e.g., waiting for a response from the child, providing a prompt, then waiting again for a response)

- Using incidental strategies (e.g., place items out of reach, pretend to forget an object, block a child's access to a desired item "by accident"), also referred to as _violation of routines_

- Using questions, making comments

- Encouraging the child to expand on his or her requests

- Inviting interaction with peers

Naturalistic teaching strategies are much easier to implement than complex planned prompts and procedures that take more adult time and can be difficult to implement on a consistent basis in the inclusive setting.

Following the Child's Lead   Another way to look at naturalistic teaching and perhaps one of the simplest and most powerful teacher behaviors in ECSE is _following the child's lead._ Simply put, the adult is attentive to the interests and behaviors of the child. This concept is also related to adults' use of responsive language input strategies as described earlier. Following the child's lead is particularly critical when working with children with severe disabilities, who may have low initiation rates, seemingly limited interests, or minimal communication abilities. By following their actions, however minimal or even repetitive, the teacher begins to establish a relationship with the child. Rather than the adult initiating a plan and trying to pull the child into it, the adult follows whatever the child is doing and slowly, over a period of time (from minutes to days depending on the child, the adult, and the environment) becomes knowledgeable of what interests that child has and can begin using strategies to create communicative turn taking. The following vignette illustrates this idea.

Following Wing's Lead

Wing is a 3 year old with a diagnosis of autism. He plays alone and has a limited repertoire of interests. He rarely uses words functionally: For example, he does not ask for something he wants. He does not seek out adults or peers to play with at school. During outside play, he sits in the sandbox and flips sand around with a small shovel. His teacher has tried leading him to the bike area or the water table with no success. He always wanders back to the sandbox and shovel. One day his teacher sits down next to Wing in the sand. As he shovels sand around, she picks up a shovel and begins to copy his actions. When Wing shovels sand, she shovels. When Wing stops, she stops. As she continues to follow his lead, he begins to show some agitation and turns away. His teacher doesn't move but waits for his next action. Wing looks back and—as if he senses that she's not going to pull him away from the sand area—begins to dig in the sand again but this time watching his teacher for her reaction.

　　This activity is repeated over the next two days. Wing doesn't show agitation anymore. In fact, he begins to make fleeting eye contact with his teacher when she sits down and follows his lead. She begins to label his actions with single words: dig, shovel, sand, stop, and go. During one session, his teacher imitates Wing but expands on his actions by getting a pail and putting the sand in the pail. She moves a second pail close to Wing. Wing watches, shovels some sand, watches his teacher shovel sand into her pail, and then he imitates her action by using the pail close to him. As the days continue, Wing's teacher sometimes "hides" the shovel or the pail or covers the sand area. Wing begins to use single words and gestures to ask for items that are part of this activity that he has become used to sharing. Little by little, similar play scenarios are used in other settings as all teachers become more used to following Wing's lead. He begins to tolerate peers joining in the activities and by the end of the school year has shown much improvement in social skills and communication.

CREATING EFFECTIVE AND PRACTICAL DAILY SCHEDULES

Arranging the daily schedule to meet the developmental needs of all children in a classroom is challenging. While some preschools offer individualized schedules for children (e.g., eating snacks when they are hungry, moving to small group activities when they choose to), it is our observation that many preschools, especially state- or federally funded schools like Head Start programs, set daily schedules in place for teachers to follow. Often, a daily schedule must be strictly adhered to when multiple classes share the same playground and space is limited to a specific number of children at any one time. Schedules are important to follow when special education classrooms join community preschool classrooms for mainstreaming activities or send children back and forth for reverse mainstreaming. Another reason for maintaining a daily schedule where children move in groups from one activity to another may be due to staffing. In many preschool classrooms, the ratio of children to adults is 10:1. This does not allow for much flexibility in the schedule.

So, daily schedules must be carefully designed to provide a balance of low- and high-energy activities, sitting and moving, teacher-directed and child-initiated activities, and so on. Large group activities such as circle time must include a mix of movement and sitting activities. More and more time seems to be devoted to teaching literacy to preschoolers in a developmentally inappropriate approach, requiring far too many minutes of sitting and listening and teacher-led activities. For young 3 year olds (and many 4 year olds), children with intellectual or other disabilities, or children learning English, these large group periods often become behavior struggles as teachers try to teach children who are not attentive, motivated, or engaged.

As demonstrated in the daily schedule in Figure 6.3, opportunities to meet most goals or outcomes are possible throughout the course of a well-organized day. While the possibilities are endless, planning how to approach each part of the day and what to focus on specifically becomes the challenge when considering the child with disabilities. While most typical children learn routines and develop skills easily in a well-run program, the child with special needs may simply not pick up how to follow a sequence or join in play without additional cues and scaffolds.

EMBEDDING INSTRUCTION IN DAILY ROUTINES

When a child with disabilities attends a regular preschool program, teachers worry that, without periods set aside to work on goals throughout the day, the child will never learn the skills necessary to reach those goals. Early childhood staff members may feel ill equipped to provide appropriate opportunities for a child to practice skill acquisition. There is a pervasive belief among early childhood educators that children with disabilities require intensive, specialized, individual or small group instruction and therefore learn better in a special education classroom. For some children with very complex and intensive needs, this may be the case. However, as discussed previously, there is no clear evidence to support the belief that children with disabilities generally do better in segregated classrooms. There *is* evidence that many children with disabilities do better in inclusive settings. Research conducted by Horn, Leiber, Li, Sandall, and Schwartz (2000) has suggested that well-written, developmentally appropriate, and functional goals can be fully met in a high-quality early childhood program. According to McBride and Schwartz (2003) these approaches have three simple but powerful characteristics:

1. Functional skills are targeted.

2. Instruction is embedded into a child's everyday routines and activities.

3. A child's interests, initiations, and resulting natural consequences are given precedence over teacher-initiated activities.

McBride and Schwartz caution that, because supporting children's learning of specific skills during planned activities may be initially difficult for teachers, it is very important to provide adults with enough support to understand, plan, and implement the specific interventions needed to help children learn the targeted skills.

Time and activity	Child actions and embedded opportunities for learning
8:00 a.m. **Arrival**	Greeting teachers and peers—language and social skills: *"Hi, Mr. Dan."* Finding cubbies; prereading; locating name, and picture: *"I see Sam. There's me."* Putting belongings in cubby; self-help skills–dressing, sequencing; large and small motor skills: *Taking off sweater, pulling boots off, putting shoes on*
8:00–8:45 **Settling in** *Transition cue at end: play song to gather children on rug*	If table toys are provided—fine motor, language, and social skills: *"You can choose blocks or art." "Do you want the red blocks or the yellow blocks? How many?"* If free choice—planning, language, and social skills: *"Do you want to go to house area or science area?" "Let's play with friends."*
8:45–9:00 **Large group** *Transition cue to snack: describe/show snack; dismiss peers by color of clothes, "Who's wearing blue?"*	Singing—language, fine motor, and social skills: *"Let's sing, Good Morning," "Tell your friend 'hello, Sara,'" "Put your hands together for 'Wheels on the Bus.'"* Calendar and daily planning—preacademic skills in math and reading: *"Today's a school day. It's Monday," "We have three things to do today," "Let's write our plan."* Story—preacademic skills, reading, and listening comprehension: *"We'll read about the silly mouse. Let's see what happens. Ready?"*
9:00–9:30 **Mealtime/snack time** *Transition cue for cleaning up: 5-minute warning, then big trash can brought in*	Washing hands—self-help, sequencing, and motor skills: *Encourage independence after teaching steps* Finding place at table—planning, literacy if looking for name, and gross motor skills: *"Find your placemat. Look for your picture/name."* Serving food: motor, language, and social skills: *"Can you open your milk?" "Ask Jaylene for the crackers," "What do you need? Give me___?"* Eating food—self-help and social skills: *Holding spoon or fork, scooping food, passing bowls to peers* Cleaning up—self-help, organizing, and motor skills: *Throwing trash away, stacking plates*
9:30–9:45 **Toilet** *Transition cue for small group: show objects representing activity*	Dressing—self-help and language: *Requesting help, buttoning, zippering* Diapering or using toilet—self-help, language, and sequencing: *Using descriptive words (cold, wet) and concepts (up/down)* Washing/drying hand—self-help and sequencing: *"What's next?" "First we wash, and then we dry."*
9:45–10:00 **Small group activity** *Transition cue for choice time: show cards with pictures representing available play areas; limit choices for some children*	Art, journals, books: preacademic—sequencing activities (e.g., cutting, gluing, painting, printing, drawing, building; language skills: *"Let's draw a face, first a circle, then our eyes. What's next?" "Do you want the red paper or the blue paper?")*

Figure 6.3. Sample daily schedule with learning opportunities across developmental domains.

Time and activity	Child actions and embedded opportunities for learning
10:00–10:45 **Free choice or work time** *Transition cue for clean-up: give 5-minute warning to individual children who need foreshadowing; blink lights or ring bell and start singing a clean-up song*	House area—pretend play; language, and social: *Use play scripts like "Taking sick baby to the doctor."* Math area—fine motor, preacademics in math and language: *"How many?"* Quiet area—literacy, with books; language; social skills; block area for motor skills; planning; social and language: *"Where can the cars go? Do we need a garage? Let's ask Amir if we can help to build."* Science area—preacademic science, language, and social Art area—fine motor, sequencing, language, and social: *"I can make a snake with my play dough. What can you make?"* Computers—fine motor, language, and preacademic: *Learning to use the mouse; understanding cause and effect—click the mouse and something happens on the screen*
10:45–11:00 **Clean up** *Transition cue for outside play: verbal reminder plus use of object or picture to symbolize outside*	Clean up—language, social, self-help, matching, and sorting: *"Where do the cars go? Find the picture." "How many blocks go there? 1, 2, 3, 4."*
11:00–11:35 **Outside** *Transition cue for large group: give 5-minute warning to individual children who need foreshadowing; sing a song*	Bikes: gross motor and social: *"We need to wait for a turn. Count with me."* Sand/water—social, language, sensory, and measurement: *"Wow, that's a lot of water in the big bucket! My cup is little. I have a little bit."* Climbing structure—gross motor, social, and language: *"You are up high!" "We need to wait to go down the slide."* Running/hiding—gross motor and social: *"I'll count to 10. Where are you? I can't catch you!"*
11:35–11:50 **Large group** *Transition cue to go to cubbies: sing goodbye song; dismiss peers by showing name tags with pictures, "Who's this?"*	Singing—language, fine motor, and social: *"Hold hands with friends and let's sing." "Which song should we sing: the fish song or the alphabet song?"* Daily review—language: *"What did we do today? First? Then?"* Story reading—comprehension, literacy
11:50–12:00 **Goodbye**	Finding cubby—literacy and self-help: *"What do you need? Yes! Your backpack." "Let's put the book in; let's zip up."* Dressing—fine and gross motor Leaving—language and social: *"Goodbye, friends. See you tomorrow."*

Looking at the efficiency of instructional procedures is an important consideration for children in inclusive settings. The number of children that early childhood teachers are responsible for can certainly have an effect on the number of possible interactions and opportunities for targeted teaching opportunities with a child with special needs. The use of naturalistic, responsive teaching interactions and communication during normal daily routines can often increase teaching effectiveness while decreasing the need for specific planning of targeted instruction. A teacher's spontaneous presentation of materials and ideas, as well as his or her responsiveness, can very effectively help many children acquire knowledge. For example, a teacher can consistently use playtime opportunities to remark on the colors of toys children are playing with but without creating structured teaching steps and trials to teach colors: "Oh look! You have the blue truck, and Jenny has the yellow truck" (Daugherty, Grisham-Brown, & Hemmeter, 2001). Of course, some children with more intensive needs may need more targeted instruction.

The Role of Responsive Adult-Child Language Input

As mentioned earlier in this chapter, one of the most well-established bodies of evidence related to the development of infant and early childhood communication skills is the role of responsive adult language input and adult-child interactions. These communication strategies can be easily embedded into everyday routines in the classroom, and they do not require additional teacher time or planning. They are equally effective for both typically developing children and children with special needs, as well as with English language learners. Chen, Klein, and Osipova (2012) have described the use of language and communicative interaction strategies with dual language learners who have disabilities. There is perhaps no other teacher behavior that generates more impact than their *talking* to children. See Weitzman and Greenberg (2002) for an excellent resource for teachers on this topic.

The following vignette illustrates how teachers can embed teaching into the preschool routine. The ECSE consultant supports language and preacademic learning using naturalistic strategies and building on the child's interests. She also helps Sam learn self-regulation strategies and decrease his disruptive behavior at the end of his school day.

Sam

Sam's ECE classroom teacher expresses concern to the ECSE inclusion consultant that Sam is having difficulty following the last 45 minutes of his preschool routine. He is hungry, tired, and ready to go home. As peers begin their snack time, he often eats his snack quickly then grabs whatever food is still available from a nearby peer. He begins to cry as snack time is cleaned up and often lunges for the door before it is opened, yelling "Mommy, mommy, mommy!" The teacher thinks that maybe Sam should go home early to avoid all of this noncompliant behavior.

The ECSE inclusion consultant observes him during this time period. After conferring with the teacher, she offers to bring in a visual schedule to help Sam predict what will come next and see that his mom will be coming to pick him up after the good-bye song. The inclusion consultant realizes, however, that even if Sam understands the schedule, it won't prevent him from taking peers' snacks. She and the teachers decide to seat Sam at the head of a table next to a teacher and a more assertive peer,

(continued)

(continued)

seated out of arm's reach. Teachers are also coached to remind Sam verbally when he is almost finished with his snack: "Sam you have one more cookie and then you're all done"; "You've finished half your banana, almost done." This does not stop the whining or attempts to grab peers' food, however.

The inclusion consultant adds another strategy. She brings markers and paper to the snack table. As Sam finishes his food she reminds him that he is almost finished but shows him the paper and markers and suggests that they write a note to his mom about wanting more snacks. Sam looks interested in this novel turn of events. The inclusion consultant asks him to choose a colored marker (he has a goal to identify and label several colors). Then she asks Sam what he wants to tell his mom. One of Sam's communication goals is to use 4–6 word sentences to express wants and needs. He begins to whine and say "Mommy!" The inclusion consultant says, "Dear Mommy, I want __ " and writes the words on the paper. She pauses and looks expectantly at Sam. Sam watches the paper and words and says, "Want more cookies." Quickly the inclusion consultant writes his words. (Sam has a literacy goal of recognizing several letters in the alphabet.) She draws a simple picture of large and small stick people, labels one "Mommy" and one "Sam." (Sam has another goal of recognizing and printing his name.) Sam continues to watch and says, "Want cookie!" The inclusion consultant draws a "cookie" held by the mommy figure. The children are still finishing their snack, so Sam is invited to write his name at the end of the note. He asks for a different color marker by saying the color name ("I want red") and draws a squiggly *S*.

The inclusion consultant asks Sam to help her fold the note and reminds him to hold it until his mom arrives. She asks him to check his visual schedule before going to sit in a cube chair on the rug next to peers. The low chair helps him stay in one place on the rug and allows the lead teacher to sit next to him using her body to block access out of the chair when Sam's mom arrives. This time he calls out "Mommy" when he sees her but appears happy to hold his note and sit in the cube chair until she finishes signing him out for the day. She comes over to him and he shows her the note, saying, "Mommy, more cookies!"

Sam's teachers will continue to use the strategies with Sam. The inclusion consultant first models and then discusses the suggestions with them: They use a novel, motivating activity to get his attention (note to mom), embed this activity into the routine, and address several goals during the course of this activity. Later, teachers encourage both Sam and his peers to begin writing their own letters to families and friends about a variety of subjects. Finally, this activity serves to help Sam maintain control of his behavior so there is no need to send him home early.

WORKING WITH TYPICAL PEERS

Another strategy for providing support to a child with a disability in the typical preschool setting is coaching his peers. Providing typical peers with specific directions and training to enhance their understanding of the peer with special needs helps with building friendships. For example, a child with autism may rebuff peers due to an inability to interact socially or communicate easily. Peers may find these behaviors difficult to relate to and begin avoiding the child. When an adult steps in to provide support and encouragement to peers, they learn to be more persistent, use play objects of high interest to the child, and wait longer for positive responses or acknowledgment from the child than they might normally do with other children.

Encouraging Peer Interactions

Peer interactions in the inclusive preschool classroom can range from being "best buddies" to adopting caregiver-type roles or from having occasional misunderstandings due to lack of appropriate communication to demonstrations of outright hostility depending on the characteristics of children's personalities in the classroom and the types of and severity of disabilities represented in those peers with special needs. We have seen typical children befriend, protect, speak for, and "boss" their peers with disabilities. Many of the interactions are based on adult modeling and guidance, while others seem to reflect the distinctive makeup of class personalities. Han, Ostrosky, and Diamond (2006) explored the development of children's attitudes toward their peers. Past research shows that children attending inclusive programs are more accepting of differences in others. However, although preschool children seem to understand disability when represented by equipment such as hearing aids or a wheelchair, "hidden" disabilities like autism and cognitive delay are more difficult for children to comprehend. (Diamond & Innes, 2001).

Young children base their perceptions of others on knowledge that they possess ("Babies can't talk; if you can't talk, then you must be a baby."). Children in the inclusive setting are less inclined to play with peers with disabilities when compared to the amount of time they play with other typical peers, but children with special needs *are* included in classroom activities and parallel play situations for a majority of the school day. Social participation may be at a lower level, but the interactions are quite high in routine classroom activities. Diamond and Stacey (2000, pp. 66–67) provide the following suggestions to help peers interact with and accept their peers with disabilities:

- Provide therapies (such as speech or occupational therapy) in the classroom setting so peers can observe and participate.

- Allow typical peers to experiment with and use adaptive equipment and encourage them to try different equipment or augmentative communication tools brought in for specific children.

- Check the environment for barriers to children being able to sit together for group activities and try to arrange for similar seating. For example, cube chairs are used in classrooms to provide extra support for children with physical or sensory needs but still have a low seat option so children are not noticeably higher than their peers when sitting on the rug. The chairs are also used by typical peers on a rotating basis.

- Find opportunities to focus on a particular child's special skills or talents so that peers do not view him or her as the child who always needs help.

Addressing Peer Attitudes and Social Behavior

Children develop attitudes about others based on their observations of differences from themselves. They learn from the attitudes of their family members and others around them. Han et al. (2006) summarized much of the research about attitudes of young children toward disabilities. They note that children can have either positive or negative attitudes toward a person based on negative or positive experiences with that individual. Providing positive experiences for typical children with their peers with disabilities during the preschool years can help children form more positive attitudes toward those with special needs. Adults need to actively engage children in positive interactions with peers, as shifts in attitude do not happen simply with proximity. Adults are needed to model appropriate peer responses to a child with a disability. They need to help typical peers practice waiting for a child to respond to them, as response times in a child with special needs may be slow. Timmy's story as presented in the following vignette, describes the work of integrating one child with disabilities into peer activities with adult help.

Timmy

Timmy is 4 years old. He does not play with peers. He has autism. Teachers encourage peers to play with Timmy when they are outside by offering verbal suggestions: "Go and ask Timmy if he wants to play." Timmy runs from the children each time they approach. At first, the ECE staff think that Timmy is playing a chase game with the other children, but as they observe, they notice that peers are getting frustrated with Timmy never reciprocating their attempts to play with him. In fact, the frustration overflows as a couple of boys from his class begin to hit at Timmy whenever they are close to him. When the inclusion specialist arrives for a regular weekly visit, the teachers explain the situation. Based on their observations, he realizes that the typical peers need to approach Timmy in a way that doesn't make him run off, get his attention appropriately (without hitting him), and wait for his response. Timmy needs help to stop and respond to peers, but the typical children need to do the same with Timmy. The inclusion specialist joins children on the playground and finds out that the typical peers are hitting Timmy because they are angry with him: "He never listens to us! He always runs away! He doesn't like us!"

The specialist begins to model how to approach Timmy by calling his name, gently tapping him on the shoulder, and waiting for him to turn toward the child initiating the interaction. Timmy needs adult help to respond. Once he looks toward the child, the specialist helps the child use simple language to ask Timmy to play: "Want to run with me?" Knowing that Timmy likes to run, the specialist helps him respond by modeling a head nod (they'll work on a verbal response later) and then holds Timmy's hand and runs with the peers. This interaction is repeated a few times each day by the teaching staff, and within a few weeks Timmy is responding to peers' requests without the need of an adult model. The next step will be to help Timmy learn to take turns chasing and being chased by peers—actually playing a game.

When considering actively supporting the development of positive peer attitudes, teachers and others may find the following suggestions helpful:

- Understand adult attitudes toward different types of disabilities.

- Encourage true friendships, not pity.

- Help children see similarities first and value and celebrate differences.

- Avoid judgments of others based on physical looks or characteristics.

- Give information to families (with permission from parents of children with disabilities).

- Answer children's questions with answers *appropriate to their developmental level* (both typical peers *and* children with special needs).

Children learn to interact with their peers with disabilities when teachers coach them in skills to encourage play. Embedding social skills interventions across domains and throughout the school day rather than using an isolated social skills training approach is effective in increasing children's ability to play together. Providing systematic opportunities for social interactions in a variety of settings and with different peers and adults helps children with special needs actively engage in play with their typical friends (Strain & Hoysen, 2000). Teachers can use the following three steps to create a classroom where all children have opportunities to participate and interact:

1. Create the environment: arrange small playgroups; use toys that encourage interaction (house area toys, blocks); use toys to support familiar routines or themes (post office, pizza restaurant); use high-interest or preferred toys and objects. Identify peers who are interested in the target child's favorite toy or activities.

2. Teach social interaction skills to children: use play scripts; teach turn-taking and sharing skills before an activity occurs (preteaching); provide modeling and opportunities for practice; prompt and reinforce appropriate social skills; reinforce positive social behavior during high-interest group activities.

3. Use peers in social interaction interventions: teach socially competent peers to use incidental teaching strategies; reinforce these peers as they use peer-mediated intervention; assign peer buddies.

In addition to these strategies, Hollingsworth (2005) adds the need to involve all children in activities, implement these interventions throughout the school day, and train paraprofessionals to implement interventions and observe results.

When children cooperate, the suggestions can work well. However, peers need ongoing support to help them deal with a child's negative behaviors, especially if the behaviors are loud and emotional, such as tantrums. Tantrums and challenging behavior in young children with disabilities, if not addressed immediately, can result in their removal from inclusive settings due to the disruption to peers and adults. Using functional behavior analysis (FBA), social skills interventions, and the involvement of peers in these interventions can reduce challenging behaviors and enhance positive peer interactions in some studies (Blair, Umbriet, Dunlop, & Jung, 2007). This topic is addressed further in Chapter 8.

Harnessing Peer-Mediated Interventions

Peer-mediated approaches have been researched over several years. Kohler, Greteman, Raschke, and Highnam (2007) reported consistently positive results in the use of these procedures to enhance the length of engagement and amount of reciprocity in children with autism.

Typical children were coached in a *stay, play, and talk* approach: stay with your friend, play with your friend, and talk to your friend (Goldstein, English, & Kaczmarek, 1997). For example, a child, Caitlyn, is playing alone, picking up stones. A peer notices and joins her activity (stays). The peer finds a box to put the stones in (plays). The peer says, "Here's a box. Let's put the stones in the box" (talks). Both children are praised by adults for their interactions. Children with autism responded positively to these peer interactions, and the interactions were maintained over time with less adult input and praise.

Peer-mediated interventions (PMI) have four characteristics that support reciprocal and beneficial relationships between children (Harris, Pretti-Frontczak, & Brown, 2009):

1. The interventions address a range of targeted skills across activities and routines. Typical peers are taught to support social routines, use communication strategies, and teach preacademic skills, such as counting, throughout the day.

2. The interventions provide multiple opportunities for learning and practice. Daily pairing with typical peers throughout activities increases the number of teaching and learning opportunities.

3. The interventions are practical for teachers. Peers are coached to provide ongoing support for children with disabilities when teachers are leading a large group or busy with other students.

4. The interventions increase children's involvement throughout daily preschool activities (with encouragement and interaction with typical peers).

Harris, Pretti-Frontczak, and Brown (2009) recommend that teachers make time to coach peers in PMI strategies. Both peers and activities need to be carefully chosen and not overused so that the interactions do not become burdensome. Teachers also need to monitor peer interactions to ensure that peers do not do everything for their counterparts with disabilities.

Although a specialist's job is to help the child with disabilities gain access to the typical environment, it is important that access includes building relationships with the other children in that classroom. One of the major challenges is finding time to train and support ECE staff in understanding the importance of encouraging typically developing students to engage their peers with disabilities and then coaching typical peers in using peer-mediated procedures to enhance the quality and length of interactions (Kishida & Kemp, 2009). Although several approaches in the research describe interventions requiring much adult training and support, we believe that there are practical solutions to enhancing peer engagement once adults agree on the importance of *all* children being engaged with each other during play periods in the preschool environment. However, the importance of adult training and support cannot be underestimated if teachers are serious about providing supportive environments for children with disabilities to learn appropriate social skills.

Using Visual Scripts and Joint Action Routines

Play scripts and *joint action routines* have long been described in the literature as useful play-based strategies to support language development in young children (McLean & Snyder-McLean 1978; Cook et al., 2011). A similar intervention is the use of "social stories" (Gray, 2006). Especially for children with autism, the use of visual scripts (words and pictures used to describe events or activities and used to encourage engagement in these events or activities with others) to aid in play and social interactions can be useful in learning and using appropriate play and social behaviors. Ganz and Flores (2010) suggested that visual scripts are most helpful for children who have some verbal skills. The scripts are used during activities to help cue the verbal responses and sequence of elements in a particular activity or play routine. (Visual scripts should not be confused with *visual schedules*, which help a child anticipate and transition to the next activity within the daily routine.) The following sequence is suggested for effective use of visual scripts:

1. Choose a familiar theme, for example, playing restaurant or taking a camping trip, and prepare related setting and materials, or choose more sensorimotor play themes, like making snakes and balls from play dough or via finger painting.

2. Choose goals and/or objectives related to individual child's communication or social skills and needs.

3. Write the script for the child (based on the child's developmental levels for language and attention span) and provide picture cues and/or instruction cards for each step.

4. Teach the script:
    *   "Red play dough, please."
    *   "Thank you."
    *   "I make snakes."
    *   "Next I make balls."
    *   "All done now."

5. Teach peers to use instruction cards with target child.

6. Implement play scripts several times per week in small playgroups (sometimes one other peer is enough).

SUMMARY

The early childhood special educator must not only know the various approaches and strategies for meeting children's needs in the preschool setting but must also be able to communicate and demonstrate that knowledge to others in order to provide practical, everyday solutions. We have suggested many ideas for enhancing child learning. We have attempted to describe the types of approaches and interventions that we feel are both efficient and effective in early childhood settings. Do all of these strategies and approaches work every time in every inclusive setting? Is implementation feasible in every typical ECE setting? It is up to each inclusion support team to be creative and to consider and decide what will work best for them and their program. Fortunately, there are many effective configurations of supports and strategies from which to choose. While challenging to do, the opportunity for ECE and ECSE teachers, specialized service providers, pareducators, families, and children to use these strategies as they work together on behalf of young children's learning can be very satisfying—and fun!

REFERENCES

Barton, E.E., Reichow, B., Wolery, M., & Chen, C. (2011). We can all participate! Adapting circle time for children with autism. *Young Exceptional Children*, *14*(2), 2–21.

Blair, K.C., Umbreit, J., Dunlap, G., & Jung, G. (2007). Promoting inclusion and peer participation through assessment-based intervention. *Topics in Early Childhood Special Education*, *27*(3), 134–147.

Bruner, J. (1983). *Child talk*. New York, NY: Norton.

Carnahan, C., Harte, H., Dyke, K.S., Hume, K., & Borders, C. (2011). Structured work systems: Supporting meaningful engagement in preschool settings for children with autism spectrum disorders. *Young Exceptional Children*, *14*(1), 2–16.

Casey, A.M., & McWilliam, R.A. (2005). Where is everybody? Organizing adults to promote child engagement. *Young Children*, *8*(2), 2–10.

Chen, D., Klein, M.D., & Osipova, A. (2012). Two is better than one: In defense of home language maintenance and bilingualism for young children with disabilities. In R.M. Santos, G.A. Cheatham, & L. Duran (Eds.), *Supporting young children who are dual language learners with or at-risk for disabilities. Young Exceptional Children Monograph Series, No. 14* (pp. 133–147). Missoula, MT: Division for Early Childhood, Council for Exceptional Children.

Cohen, M.J., & Sloan, D.L. (2007). *Visual supports for people with autism: A guide for parents and professionals*. Bethesda, MD: Woodbine House Inc.

Cook, R., Klein, M.D., & Chen, D. (2011). *Adapting early childhood curricula for children with special needs* (8th ed.). Upper Saddle River, NJ: Pearson.

Cross, T. (1984). Habilitating the language-impaired child: Ideas from studies of parent-child interaction. *Topics in Language Disorders*, *4*, 1–14.

Daugherty, S., Grisham-Brown, J., & Hemmeter, M.L. (2001). The effects of embedded skill instruction on the acquisition of target and nontarget skills in preschoolers with developmental delays. *Topics in Early Childhood Special Education*, *21*(4), 213–221.

Diamond, K.E., & Innes, F.K. (2001). Young children's attitudes toward peers with disabilities. In M. Guralnick (Ed.), *Early childhood inclusion: Focus on change* (pp. 159–178). Baltimore, MD: Paul H. Brookes Publishing Co.

Diamond, K.E., & Stacey, S. (2000). The other children at preschool. *Young Exceptional Children Monograph Series*, *2*, 59–68.

Downing, J. (2008). *Including students with severe and multiple disabilities in typical classrooms* (3rd ed.). Baltimore, MD: Paul H. Brookes Publishing Co.

Ganz, J.B., & Flores, M.M. (2010). Supporting the play of preschoolers with autism spectrum disorders: Implementation of visual scripts. *Young Exceptional Children*, *13*(2), 58–70.

Goldstein, H., English, K., & Kaczmarek, L. (1997). Interaction among preschoolers without disabilities. *Journal of Speech, Language and Hearing Research*, *40*, 33–48.

Gray, C. (2006). *The new social storybook: Illustrated edition*. Arlington, TX: Future Horizons.

Han, J., Ostrosky, M.M., & Diamond, K.E. (2006). Children's attitudes toward peers with disabilities: Supporting positive attitude development. *Young Exceptional Children*, *10*(1), 2–11.

Harris, K., Pretti-Frontczak, K., & Brown, T. (2009). Peer-mediated intervention: An effective, inclusive strategy for all young children. *Young Children*, *64*(2), 43–49.

Hollingsworth, H.L. (2005). Interventions to promote peer social interactions in preschool settings. *Young Exceptional Children. 9*(1), 2–11.

Hollingsworth, H.L., Boone, H.A., & Crais, E.R. (2009). Individualized inclusion plans at work in early childhood classrooms. *Young Exceptional Children, 13*(1), 19–35.

Horn, E., Leiber, J., Li, S., Sandall, S., & Schwartz, I. (2000). Supporting young children's IEP goals in inclusive settings through embedded learning opportunities. *Topics in Early Childhood Special Education, 20*(4), 208–223.

Janse van Vuren, M. (2009). Visual supports for children with Down syndrome. Dublin, Ireland: Down Syndrome Centre. Retrieved from http://www.downsyndromecentre.ie

Kishida, Y., & Kemp, C. (2009). The engagement and interaction of children with autism spectrum disorder in segregated and inclusive early childhood center-based settings. *Topics in Early Childhood Special Education, 29*(2), 105–117.

Kohler, F.W., Anthony, L.J., Steighner, S.A., & Hoyson, M. (2001). Teaching social integration skills in the integrated preschool: An examination of naturalistic tactics. *Topics in Early Childhood Special Education, 21*(2), 93–103.

Kohler, F.W., Greteman, C., Raschke, D., & Highnam, C. (2007). Using a buddy skills package to increase the social interactions between a preschooler with autism and her peers. *Topics in Early Childhood Special Education, 27*(3), 155–163.

Mahoney, G. Boyce, G., Fewell, R.R., Spiker, D.M, & Wheeden, C.A. (1998). The relationship of parent-child interaction to the effectiveness of early intervention services for at-risk children and children with disabilities. *Topics in Early Childhood Special Education, 18*(1), 5–17.

Mahoney, G., & Perales, F. (2003). Using relationship-focused interventions to enhance the social-emotional functioning of young children with autism spectrum disorders. *Topics in Early Childhood Special Education, 23*(2), 77–89.

McBride, B.J., & Schwartz, I.S. (2003). Effects of teaching early interventionists to use discrete trials during ongoing classroom activities. *Topics in Early Childhood Special Education, 23*(1), 5–17.

McLean, J., & Snyder-McLean, L. (1978). *Transactional approach to early language training.* Upper Saddle River, NJ: Merrill/Prentice Hall.

Mesibov, G.B., Shea, V., & Schopler, E. (2004). *The TEACCH approach to autism spectrum disorders.* New York, NY: Springer.

Mirenda, P., & Beukelman, D.R. (2006). *Augmentative and alternative communication: Supporting children and adults with complex communication needs* (3rd ed.). Baltimore, MD: Paul H. Brookes Publishing Co.

Odom, S.L., & Wolery, M. (2003). A unified theory of practice in early intervention/early childhood special education: Evidence-based practices. *Journal of Special Education 37*(3), 164–173.

Oelwein, P. (1995). *Teaching reading to children with Down syndrome: A guide for parents and teachers.* Bethesda, MD: Woodbine.

Owens, R.E. (2008). *Language development: An introduction* (8th ed.). Boston, MA: Allyn & Bacon.

Rubin, J. (2008). The ape that teaches. Retrieved from http://www.pbs.org/wgbh/nova/body/ape-teaches.html

Sadao, K.C., & Robinson, N.B. (2010). *Assistive technology for young children: Creating inclusive learning environments.* Baltimore, MD: Paul H. Brookes Publishing Co.

Sandall, S.R., & Schwartz, I.S. (2008). *Building blocks for teaching preschoolers with special needs* (2nd ed.). Baltimore, MD: Paul H. Brookes Publishing Co.

Strain, P.S., & Hoysen, M. (2000). The need for longitudinal, intensive social skill intervention: LEAP follow-up outcomes for children with autism. *Topics in Early Childhood Education, 20*(2), 116–122.

Valentine, V., & Hamilton, J. (2006). Q&A: Temple Grandin on autism and language. NPR interview on July 9, 2006. Retrieved from http://www.npr.org

Vygotsky, L.S. (1980). *Mind in society: The development of higher psychological processes.* Cambridge, MA: Harvard University Press.

Weitzman, E., & Greenberg, J. (2002). *Learning language and loving it.* Toronto: The Hanen Centre

7

Disability-Specific Challenges and Strategies in Inclusive Preschool Programs

With invited contributors Beth A. Moore, M.A., Sue Parker-Strafaci, M.A., Sherwood J. Best, Ph.D., Sara Chen Ling, M.A., Janice Myck-Wayne, Ed.D., Jennifer Symon, Ph.D., BCBA-D, and Michelle Dean, Ph.D.

This text has focused on the challenges of and solutions to providing support for preschool-age children in inclusive early childhood settings. These issues and strategies are, for the most part, applicable to any child with special needs. This chapter addresses some of the unique and interesting challenges that often characterize specific low-incidence disabilities. We have included the voices and expertise of several of our colleagues in the field with disability-specific knowledge and strong clinical expertise and experiences: Sue Parker-Strafaci and Beth A. Moore on visual impairment, Sherwood J. Best and Sarah Chen Ling on physical and health disabilities, Jennifer Symon and Michelle Dean on autism spectrum disorders, and Janice Myck-Wayne on hearing loss.

Information provided in this chapter extends the strategies discussed conceptually in Chapter 6. Early childhood special educators and other providers responsible for coordinating or providing inclusion support should be familiar with the unique challenges often presented by low-incidence disabilities and know how to access the specialists who can provide information and strategies when needed. Most children with low-incidence disabilities in inclusive settings receive at least some itinerant support from disability specialists. The early childhood special education (ECSE) professional who establishes relationships with these specialists will be able to engage in meaningful, knowledgeable problem solving on behalf of children whose disabilities require very specialized supports and solutions.

This chapter describes specific characteristics, intervention strategies, and examples of children's experiences in inclusive settings. It also offers information related to various learning, developmental, and behavioral characteristics that are commonly associated with children diagnosed with visual disability, autism spectrum disorder, hearing loss, and physical and health disabilities. However, it is not the intent of the authors to present stereotypes of children who wear particular labels. Each child has his or her own unique strengths and challenges and is a mosaic of different learning styles and personality characteristics.

The goal of this chapter is to provide information that will help early childhood special educators be mindful of the unique challenges children may face. All key players are encouraged to proactively seek out ongoing, collaborative, problem-solving relationships with disability specialists and find creative and exciting ways to ensure children's success in inclusive early childhood settings.

Inclusion Practices for Children with Visual Impairment

Beth A. Moore and Sue Parker-Strafaci

If you look around a typical preschool classroom, you will likely see how children with normal vision develop readiness concepts simply through visual exposure. A child recognizes a letter or connects the word chair to the physical one he sees and sits on. Much of education is built around visual cues, and this presents a challenge to providing an appropriate and stimulating curriculum for very young children with visual impairments. The following vignette about one child with visual impairment illustrates both the challenges such children face and the solutions that educators and other professionals can provide.

LULU

Lulu is a 6 year old with a complete vision loss due to a condition called Leber's congenital amaurosis. Her only functional vision is a small amount of light perception. She wears glasses for protection. She has typical cognition. In addition to visual impairment (VI) services, she has also received orientation and mobility training and occupational therapy.

A teacher of the visually impaired for her school district first started working with Lulu when she was 2 years, 7 months of age. She was already receiving early intervention services from a nonpublic agency child development consultant. As she approached preschool transition age, the VI teacher provided weekly in-home service for early intervention, as did the child development consultant.

Lulu honed many skills through her home intervention that prepared her and her family for her integration into a typical preschool. She practiced her tactile discrimination in a great variety of ways. She loved small wind-up toys and could tell them apart. She was an excellent auditory learner, having had an environment rich with narrated stories, music, and dialogue with her sister and parents. She had appropriate concept development due to exposure to many natural environment experiences.

As Lulu approached preschool age in the spring of the following year, her administrator, her child development consultant from a nonpublic blind service agency, the VI teacher, and her mother started discussing what the options were for preschool. A nonpublic center-based program for children with visual impairments, including reverse mainstreaming, was one option. Lulu's mother visited that program and was familiar with the site, as that was where Lulu received her occupational therapy (OT).

Lulu's school district had formed a relationship with a local private preschool that had experience including another student with a different disability. This provided a

(continued)

second possible school option. Lulu's mother visited the program and felt it would be the best fit for Lulu. The team agreed that Lulu would have a one-on-one assistant provided and trained by another blind service agency. The VI teacher would continue her instruction in braille and concept development. She would continue receiving OT at a separate private site and she would receive mobility training onsite at the pre-school. She would attend the preschool two half-days per week, as was typical of all of the students.

Prior to the start of school, the child development consultant, the mobility instructor, and the VI teacher met with the whole staff of the school. They provided an in-service on vision impairment in general and described Lulu's particular condition, what the staff could expect in the way of Lulu's needs, and what services would be provided. Topics and activities included the following:

- Description of blindness and visual impairment and Lulu's particular eye condition

- Introduction to what braille looks like

- Overview of the role of a sighted guide and beginning cane travel

- Awareness of the need to verbally describe what is being presented in class

- Opportunity to experience different kinds of visual disability using simulation goggles

- Explanation that the students in class will most likely reflect the attitude of the teacher in response to the student that is being included

- Examples and demonstration of adapted materials and technology

- Importance of the concept that the instructional assistant needs to be perceived as being there for the whole class and teacher, not just for a particular student

- Allaying of safety concerns, for example, playground activities and movement in classroom

- Description of classroom labels and tactile and braille materials

Preschool Year Two

For Lulu's second year in preschool, her school sessions were three half-days per week. She continued to have a one-on-one assistant, VI service increased to two times per week, and onsite mobility training occurred two times per week. She also continued her offsite occupational therapy. In summer she attended a pre-K session prior to her beginning kindergarten. VI services were increased to three times per week to help prepare her for the transition to kindergarten.

Overall the early intervention and preschool experiences were very successful. The focus during her time at the preschool was on social skills and school behavior in general. The day consisted of the following:

- Circle time

- Outdoor play time with both varying and consistent activity choices

- Snack time

(continued)

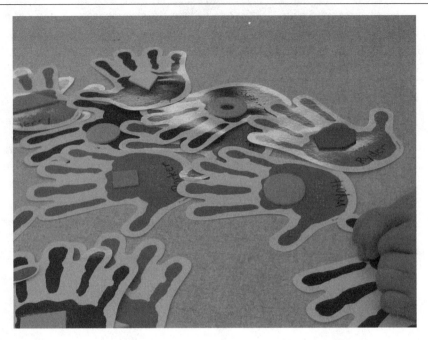

Figure 7.1. Children's name tags with raised, tactile identifiers.

- Table activity centered on themes
- Indoor free-choice playtime
- Craft time centered around themes
- Trips to the local library
- Music (weekly)
- Physical education (twice weekly)

Lulu's summer pre-K program geared the students up for a more academic day, in anticipation of the transition to kindergarten. For instance, in preschool Lulu had learned to recognize her classmates' name cards via a different raised tactile symbol on each card (see Figure 7.1). The braille symbols for each classmate's name were also on each card. As her instruction in braille increased, the large tactile symbols were removed, leaving only the brailled name on each card. Her instruction in braille continued, with the expectation that she would know her alphabet, numbers, and be able to read the pre-K level Braille Patterns Program books by fall.

Transition to Kindergarten

For Lulu's transition to her regular neighborhood kindergarten, several essential steps were taken. The principal at the school was made aware of her imminent attendance several months before school started. He was able to then make a determination of

(continued)

what teacher and class would work the best for Lulu. Lulu's team was able to have her instructional assistant from her preschool, previously an employee of the Braille Institute, become an assistant for the public school district. Her mobility instructor worked with Lulu several times throughout the summer to orient her to her new campus. The VI teacher had as many materials as possible brailled for Lulu prior to the start of the school year. An in-service was arranged for the whole staff prior to the start of the school year.

Lulu had a very successful kindergarten year! The VI teacher's services were increased to four days per week for 45 minutes each. The team had all of the small weekly reading books brailled prior to the start of school. Lulu's daily math sheets were difficult, as they were very visual and did not transfer well to use with an image enhancer. So the team used manipulatives and the braille writer to expose Lulu to the concepts being presented. Through ongoing assessments, Lulu demonstrated that she was performing at grade level or above. She was able to use her braille skills to perform in a functional academic manner.

Lulu also made many friends in her kindergarten class. (She knew some of them from her preschool, which was important to her integration.) However, she experienced some difficulties related to her frustration with the need to delay gratification, now that she was part of a larger group. Part of the problem stemmed from the necessity of having a one-on-one instructional assistant. There were also safety concerns, provoked by some head bumps she suffered. Striking a balance between safety and independence was a delicate process. Her support team wanted the regular school staff and parents to be assured of her safety. However, bumps and bruises do happen, even among sighted kindergarteners. On some occasions, the problem was clarifying who was responsible for supporting Lulu at any one time. Her peers often wanted to participate by being her sighted guides. It is often difficult even for adults to realize the vigilance necessary to ensure safe travel for a child who is blind.

Lulu's inclusion assistant summarized her experiences this way:

"Even though I received training on working with children who are visually impaired, nothing really prepared me until I started working with Lulu. I fell back on my child development education and reminded myself what was developmentally appropriate for a child her age and made tactile modifications."

"The biggest problem I encountered with Lulu is she wants everything for her to be 'just like everyone else.' That is not always possible, and in some cases the class was learning something visually that wasn't adequately adapted so she could participate. Understandably, this caused a lot of frustration for her. Lulu is an extremely smart little girl and was very capable of managing in a 'regular' classroom. She was given the freedom to learn both in braille as well as using adaptive materials with her peers. She had no difficulties making friends or keeping up with the class. In fact, I think sometimes she challenged them to keep up with her!"

It is important for teachers of the visually impaired who provide preschool consultation support in early childhood classrooms to keep the following recommendations in mind when providing services:

(continued)

(continued)

- Respect the overall structure of the program and try to fit your instruction in seamlessly.

- Support the classroom teacher through adapted materials and suggestions for best placement (for example, location of the student's "cubby," the best place for the child at meal or snack times, or where the student should sit for circle time).

- Help the regular educator find ownership of the student's education.

- Be aware of the fact that having a student with visual impairment in a class inevitably entails interruptions to the class, including other adults coming in and out and space being needed for materials. Be respectful of the teacher and ask for input and understanding.

- Include the whole class in learning tactilely.

- Lead the way in ensuring that the student with visual impairment experiences all activities in some manner. Encourage thinking outside the box in how something can be adapted. Don't allow the mindset that "She can't see it, so she can't …"

- Encourage the student to think of the classroom teacher as his or her teacher, too. Don't allow him or her to be instructed only by the assistant or specialists.

Conclusion

Full inclusion can be a very successful model for delivery of services in the preschool years. The key ingredient is preparation of the immediate team, in depth, and of the whole school staff, in general. Lulu's kindergarten teacher told the VI teacher that the in-service training was important, but she feels it needs to be repeated. She feels that the staff hadn't fully absorbed the fact that Lulu will be part of the school throughout her school career. Now that they have experience with her being on campus, they will be more aware of what questions to ask and what their particular concerns might be.

The regular education teacher expressed that she was never comfortable with being fully responsible for Lulu on those occasions when none of the support staff were present. The expectation that a regular educator should have the competency to deal with a student who is visually impaired without support staff is not a realistic goal.

The role of parents as part of the education team is also central to children's success in the early years. While the rest of the team's priorities may not always be exactly the same as those of the parents, it is the team's responsibility to help families understand how to navigate the system to better understand their options and rights.

COMMON CHALLENGES TO INCLUSION OF CHILDREN WITH VISUAL IMPAIRMENTS

A child with visual impairment can benefit from the same visual environment as his or her peers; however, the environment must also include opportunities that allow the child to learn by touch (e.g., encouraging tactile exploration of objects) or visual modification (e.g., increasing visual contrast, enlarging the display)—the same concepts a sighted child would develop through visual exposure. Young children with visual impairments need opportunities to learn through a variety of modalities: touch, hearing, smell, and even taste and movement.

The Child with Low Vision

Knowing the degree of vision loss the child may have will assist in determining what type of adaptation is necessary. Often children who are defined as having low vision may not appear to have any visual deficits during normal play. A closer look might indicate that the child may be making his or her own accommodations, such as bringing an item closer during an art project or tilting his or her head to one side to get a better view. This type of visual behavior is known as *eccentric viewing*. The child is accommodating to better view the item. It is commonly recognized that allowing the child to use his or her vision to his or her best ability is recommended over trying to correct the child.

In many cases overadapting the environment can limit the child. Becoming a good observer of how the child accommodates to the activity helps educators anticipate possible curriculum adaptations. Another consideration is the amount of *visual clutter* in the child's viewing area. This refers to unnecessary materials in the child's experience area that make it difficult for the child to locate an item visually. For instance, if a child is eating a snack and the snack is the same color as the table, the child may not be able to successfully be independent in the activity. However, if the background is a contrasting color, the child may be able to see the snack and maximize his or her success. This also could apply to activities in the classroom. The child with low vision may also have challenges making choices throughout the day. If the activities change frequently, it would be helpful to provide the child with a narrative of what is happening and what activities are being offered.

Knowing the angle of the child's best vision is also helpful during circle-time activities. Initially asking the child to sit to the right or left of the teacher may also allow the teacher to hand the child the book so he or she can look closely. Provide a contrasting color background when asking a child to use vision to complete a task. Allow the child to use his or her vision, which may mean they can see best when looking to the side. Talk with the child about any changes in the room setup or activities offered, but also allow the child to use his or her auditory, spatial, and vision skills to navigate the environment independently.

The Child Who Is Totally Blind

The child with total vision loss can certainly benefit from an inclusive environment, as described in Lulu's experience in the opening vignette. The preschool curriculum is a hands-on experience. This type of learning provides the foundation for all children and is ideal for the child who is totally blind. A team approach that offers best-practice supports is necessary to maintain the quality of the child's preschool experience.

Imagine the child's introduction to the activity. Does he or she have enough information to work on an art project? You will need to verbally describe what the activity is: for example, "We're pasting lots of things, like crepe paper, buttons, string, and leaves on our paper. This is called a *collage*." Help the child tactually locate the items necessary to engage in the activity: teacher moves child's hand to touch items and says, "You can feel the crepe paper and the leaves here, on your right side."

Some children with visual impairment may be tactually defensive and not want to touch what you are asking them to touch. Offer and encourage a child to try something, but do not force the child by moving his or her hand unless the child allows you to. As teachers we often encourage children to try new experiences that include sensory experiences. Getting messy is part of being a kid! While this is true for all children, special considerations are usually needed when planning activities that include a child with a visual impairment.

Setting up the environment to support the child's safe autonomous exploration may provide the best outcomes. Consider adopting a hand-under-hand approach (i.e., the child's hands are on top of yours) rather than the typical hand-over-hand approach if the child is showing that he or she needs or wants help. Observe how the child approaches the task, watch, and listen for apprehension or uncertainty. Offering the activity when you sense the child is interested, open, and prepared will provide a much more successful outcome for the child, peer, or teacher.

SUGGESTED ADAPTATIONS FOR THE ENVIRONMENT AND ORIENTATION FOR A SUCCESSFUL PRESCHOOL EXPERIENCE

In the very beginning of the process of choosing a program, communicate the goals of an inclusive experience with family members, teachers, and specialists. Find out the major concerns and obstacles in preservice meetings. Determine who the parent's point of contact will be among the general education preschool teacher or specialists.

There are several specific elements that will support the inclusion process. Specialized training for paraprofessional and teaching staff that reflects the adaptive needs of the child's visual diagnosis is very important. Areas such as the degree and type of vision loss, adaptations for specific learning activities, and ongoing assessment of the child's developmental progress should be discussed regularly.

Prior to the child's first day, orient him or her to the classroom. During this time the child will have a chance to meet his or her teacher and others who will be interacting with him or her daily. Allow time for the child to explore the inside and outside play equipment. Preferably offer time when there are no or few children in the space the child is exploring. Come back for another visit when the child's classroom peers are present so he or she can hear the differences between an empty classroom and a busy one.

Initially, invite the child to sit next to you at circle time. Allowing the child access to a book or object to help represent circle time prior to the beginning of circle will reduce the child's anxiety about what is happening. As you become more familiar with the child's ability to access information, such as the amount of usable vision and how he or she uses it in the classroom, place the child to the left or right to best support his or her use of vision.

Observe the child's interaction with the environment. Notice if he or she has "mapped" out the room; for example, does he or she freely move from the snack table to circle time? Familiarity with the environment may be incremental, and you may notice that a child chooses to stay in a particular area because the child feels competent there. Describe the environment in terms of activities that are available. Sharing that the block area is open but the house area is closed will help a child make choices and increase his or her level of independence.

Try not to perform tasks for the child. All children need help with various tasks, but do not assume that the child with visual impairments needs help. Describe the task ahead, pause, and watch how the child approaches the task, then offer to help if needed. In the classroom do the following:

- Adapt classroom books. A simple shape book can be made accessible by adding texture or outlining the shape with a glue gun.

- Reduce visual clutter by reducing the number of items on a table at one time.

- Use high-contrast materials (e.g., a black placemat on a light-colored table) to help the child visually locate materials. Also, eliminate busy backgrounds that compete with what the child is trying to see.

Table-top activities can become busy and cluttered, and a child who is visually impaired working within a group of children at the table may need a tray or boundary to maintain his or her own materials.

- Labeling items (cubbies, tables) with print/braille labels provides a language-rich environment that supports early literacy.

- If the child is receiving prebraille instruction, keep a Perkins Brailler in the environment and allow sighted peers to explore with supervision.

- Place the child's cubby in an accessible location to promote independence. Label it with their name in braille and print.

- Provide books in print and braille to share with peers in the environment.

- If the child is receiving orientation and mobility services (specialized training in safe travel and movement), allow the child to keep his or her premobility device or cane by the door for easy access to use in the outside environment.

Consider the following when helping the child to learn about exploring the outdoors:

- Some children with visual impairment have a particular sensitivity to sunlight. If this is the case, make sure the child is wearing appropriate lenses or a hat to assist in the transition. Walk through the outside environment with the child to map out the various activities.

- Talk to the child about dips in the landscape such as the difference between grass and sand. Point out the ledge surrounding a sandbox.

- Add reflective or contrasting tape around potentially dangerous areas to caution a child with low vision.

- Allow the child to explore equipment. Try not to hover, but stand near an area to encourage safe exploration and act as spotter as needed. Talk with the child's parents about expectations and strategies. Often a child with a visual impairment will become comfortable with one activity, such as swinging. Encourage exploration and problem solving to introduce the child to new experiences.

- The child with visual impairment needs to be responsible for following the same rules and guidelines in the preschool environment as his or her peers. This is a valuable process that teaches the child appropriate interaction, safety, and readiness as well as providing the necessary foundation to fully understand how to interact with his or her growing world.

Young children who are visually impaired or blind will benefit greatly from an inclusive preschool experience. A best-practice approach includes the participation of specialists, such as a teacher of the visually impaired or orientation and mobility specialists who are familiar with early childhood education and child development to advise and support the general preschool staff. A best-practice approach also introduces the preschool teacher to the entire team of parents, teachers, specialists, and professionals as the child's primary teacher. Good team communication is critical to ensuring the child's successful inclusion experience.

Supporting Young Children with Physical Disabilities and Health Impairment

Sherwood J. Best and Sara Chen Ling

MARYANN

Maryann was a bright and adorable 3 year old when she entered a classroom for students with orthopedic impairments. She was diagnosed at a very early age with spinal muscular atrophy (SMA), a neuromuscular disease that is characterized by progressive muscular atrophy. At the time she came, Maryann used a stander with wheels. She had just enough strength in her arms to move herself very short distances. Eventually, she was trained by her physical therapists to use a power wheelchair successfully and safely. Like many other children with SMA, Maryann's intellectual ability was completely unimpaired, and in fact she appeared to be brighter and more sociable than most children her age. Beyond the specialized academic services and adapted physical education services provided by the school district, Maryann received physical, occupational, and equine therapy. She belonged to a very supportive family, which eventually included two younger brothers.

From the beginning of her schooling, mainstreaming or inclusion was a goal for Maryann's education. However, her physical disability significantly impacted her ability to participate in the classroom environment. So, when she turned 3, Maryann started in a special day class, where she had the opportunity to mature and develop the skills necessary for success in the general education classroom. One of these skills was self-advocacy. Maryann's teacher was familiar with many of the adaptations available to facilitate Maryann's participation. Maryann learned to use these adaptations independently, and she also learned how to use her words to ask for help when appropriate. Another aspect of Maryann's development with a disability was some frustration that

(continued)

resulted from her inability to do many things on her own. One way this frustration manifested was in her eating. She would often refuse to eat. The solution to this problem turned out to be finding alternate ways for Maryann to gain independence. Once she began moving around campus on her own using a power wheelchair and successfully completing schoolwork, her issues with eating quickly faded away.

After she gained confidence in the day class, Maryann started going to a general education preschool class just two doors down for half an hour every day. In order to facilitate this mainstreaming, the preschool teacher and the day class teacher agreed to also do reverse mainstreaming. That is, each day, Maryann would go to the regular preschool class, and four preschool students would come to the day class. This very nicely provided a way for students from both classes to become acquainted with each other. It also served as an opportunity for the regular education teacher's students to periodically receive more intensive instruction. Initially, the day class teacher had an instructional assistant go with Maryann to the preschool class. This instructional assistant was able to help educate the other preschool teachers and students about Maryann's disability, showing them what she could and could not do on her own. For example, Maryann was fully capable of sitting at a classroom table to complete a puzzle. However, due to her low muscle tone, if she was accidentally bumped by another student and knocked off her chair, she would not be able to catch her fall. It was also important for the instructional assistant to model and train others how to physically and safely transition Maryann from her wheelchair to the ground or from the ground to a classroom chair. Maryann's day class teacher periodically checked in with the preschool teacher, addressed concerns, and provided encouragement.

As Maryann approached her fifth birthday, the day class teacher began the process to transition her back to her home district for enrollment in fully mainstreamed kindergarten. At the time, Maryann was performing academically above grade level and had been participating successfully in the regular preschool class for a portion of each day, so full mainstreaming was a natural next step. Maryann's parents expressed a strong preference for her to attend her local, neighborhood school for the sake of Maryann's socialization. Representatives from her home school district attended her annual individualized education program (IEP) meeting and the upcoming transition was discussed. When the end of the school year neared, the day class teacher attended a transition IEP meeting at Maryann's home school and was able to see her future kindergarten classroom and playground.

These transition meetings and ongoing email communications proved crucial. The meeting at her home district was attended by the school nurse, kindergarten teacher, special education teacher, adapted physical education teacher, school administrator, and the occupational and physical therapists. Together, all were able to collaborate on ordering adapted playground equipment, problem solve Maryann's hygiene schedule, and discuss appropriate academic goals.

As a result, Maryann's gradual transition from a special day class to full-time general education was smooth. It required collaboration between many professionals and constant reevaluation of Maryann's abilities and needs. However, it was a complete pleasure to see her progress successfully. Maryann has just finished first grade at her neighborhood school. Her mother shares that they are often hosting sleepover parties

(continued)

(continued)

for Maryann's friends and that Maryann happily participates in a Girl Scout troop with a few other girls from her class. Every now and then, there is a small kink to work out. For example, when Maryann was in kindergarten, she initially sat in her wheelchair during carpet time. However, that meant she was not at eye level with all her peers, who were sitting on the carpet. This issue was quickly resolved, however. Soon, Maryann got to sit on the carpet and learn among her peers and her friends.

INCLUDING YOUNG CHILDREN WITH PHYSICAL AND HEALTH IMPAIRMENTS

The number of young children with physical and health impairments is growing. As a result of improved medical technology, infants who may have died before birth or who are born prematurely are surviving in increasing numbers. However, they may have lasting physical and/or health conditions that require careful attention and appropriate intervention. Many require medical surveillance at home and school. Therapy services and corrective surgeries are especially prevalent for young children with physical or health impairments, resulting in repeated disruptions of home life and activities at school.

It is important to reserve judgment about the cognitive capabilities of young children with physical or health impairments. They may exhibit uncontrolled movements of the head, arms, or legs. Sometimes they drool or lack bladder or bowel control when other children their age have achieved these skills. Sometimes they have imperfect or absent speech. It is not surprising that they may be perceived as unable to comprehend or respond to typical preschool activities. The danger of this perception is that young children with physical and health impairments go unchallenged to participate and achieve to their maximum capabilities. Critical keys to successful inclusion are adequate assessment and use of appropriate accommodations and adaptations to close the gap between the effects of impairment and potential accomplishments.

UNDERSTANDING THE IMPORTANCE OF FAMILY

Early childhood educators recognize the importance of family involvement and appreciate the contributions that family members make to their children's development. Family members often have valuable information and strategies to convey to teachers. Forging a positive, early bond with parents of young children with physical and health impairments shapes a productive relationship that lasts throughout the school experience.

Sometimes parents of young children with physical and health impairments appear to be too closely attached (enmeshed) with their children. They have difficulty separating from their children at school, contact the school throughout the school day, are perceived to be overprotective or overly cautious, place what feels like unreasonable demands on school personnel, and appear to be critical of any teacher behavior that does not meet their expectations. However, educators need to appreciate the dynamics of the child's condition and the effect on family interactions prior to school age. Infants and young children with physical and health impairments may have been seriously ill from the time of their birth. They may have been subjected to multiple medical procedures that caused pain and disrupted typical development. Members of their family observed that extreme watchfulness, specialized skills, and quick action were critical to their child's well-being (and even life). When these infants were discharged from the hospital, regimens of timed medication administration, breathing treatments, positioning, oxygen monitoring, and so forth became the responsibility of their parents. In addition to maintaining their child's health, their parental responsibilities include attending multiple medical and therapy appointments, hosting visits by professionals to their homes, and hearing the message that they are the pivotal adults for coordinating all such activities. It is no wonder that the very behaviors of attention, caution, and questioning they developed in their child's earliest days would be transferred to their behaviors and interactions with educators.

REALIZING THE IMPORTANCE OF COLLABORATION

Young children with physical and multiple disabilities receive many related services from a variety of therapists and other specialists. The occupational therapist attends to fine motor skills, activities of daily living, and sensory motor needs, while the physical therapist works on balance, posture, walking, and other gross motor skills. Both occupational and physical therapists assist with developing and procuring equipment such as braces, splints, and mobility items such as walkers and wheelchairs. Speech/language therapists support communication development and may also assist with feeding skills. They may provide assessment and help with making or purchasing augmentative and alternative communication equipment. The young child may also receive adapted physical education from a specialist who carries out a specially designed and modified physical education program. In addition to these pivotal groups of related services personnel, young children with physical and health impairments and their parents may interact with orthopedic surgeons, rehabilitation engineers, respiratory therapists, and other medical personnel. This is only a partial list. At different times in the child's life these specialists may be more closely involved than at other times. For example, immediately before and after a surgery the child may visit the orthopedist several times and receive extra physical and/or occupational therapy services. As surgical corrections taper off and the child acquires more refined fine and gross motor skills, services will decrease.

Particularly in an inclusive setting, the educator frequently serves as an informal case manager of service coordination among specialists. This can be a challenge. Educators must become familiar with the roles and activities of specialists in order to carry out appropriate therapeutic activities in the classroom. There are several reasons why educators should be aware of specialists' activities and skills. First, therapists may not always be available to provide direct support to young children whenever it is needed, so the educator may be required to assist. Second, acquiring vocabulary about other specialties creates opportunities for meaningful communication during individualized family service plan (IFSP) meetings and other points of professional communication. Third, parents may be more inclined to approach an educator with questions about their child's therapy services simply because the appropriate specialist is not available. However, if a parent is dissatisfied with some aspects of services that are not related to curriculum, the appropriate physical and health impairments specialist can address their concerns most effectively.

UTILIZING SPECIALIZED KNOWLEDGE AND SKILLS

Knowledge of generic intervention strategies optimizes the ability to support development in young children with disabilities. In addition, there is a body of specialized knowledge and skills that are critical for effective practice. These include knowledge about impairments, incorporating therapy goals into the classroom, physical management, maintaining health and safety, and logistics.

Knowledge of Specific Physical and Health Impairments

An important aspect of providing a safe environment for young children with physical and health impairments includes understanding the dynamics of their medical conditions and the implications of the conditions for development. Some physical conditions do not change much during the child's lifetime. For example, cerebral palsy is a stable (static) condition that is caused by damage to the developing brain. This damage usually occurs before birth but can happen during the birth process or even after birth when there is a lack of oxygen. Other conditions change over time. Muscular dystrophy is an example, and the young child with this condition may not have many early physical symptoms. However, physical signs appear as the child becomes older, and sometimes the first person who notices a change in the child's motor skills is the early educator. Some conditions are initially severe but stabilize over time. For example, young children born with cleft lips or palates may have several corrective surgeries as their facial structures mature. Finally, some conditions fluctuate between relative stability and potentially life-threatening episodes. Epilepsy is an example. Understanding the dynamics of physical and health impairments can help educators to anticipate and respond to potential medical needs and appreciate family responses.

Physical and health impairments affect typical development. Conditions that are neurologically based (caused by damage to the brain and other parts of the central nervous system) may result in delays in all areas of development. The presence of sensory impairments such as blindness or deafness compromises avenues for experiencing the world and learning skills. Some young children have conditions that are strictly orthopedic in nature. Although they may experience multiple painful and restricting surgeries, their brains are not involved and usually their cognitive development is typical. However, they may have been deprived of many physical and social experiences. Although they may appear mature in interactions with adults, they may be less comfortable with peers. In addition, the extent of their disability will require physical compensation and emotional adjustment. They will need to learn to cope with having a clearly visible disability. On the other hand, young children with health impairments (e.g., diabetes, arthritis) may appear to be physically typical but may actually be frail when compared to children with visible impairments.

Even though knowledge of disability dynamics is critical to supporting good health and development, educators should never make automatic assumptions based on a diagnosis. Breakthroughs in medicine and therapy are constantly shifting the boundaries of physical achievement in this population. However, the greatest negative effects of disability are the barriers that result from negative assumptions and lack of access.

Therapy Goals

Incorporating therapy goals into classroom routines provides multiple practice opportunities for young children with physical and health impairments. It reinforces their importance and can heighten achievement in areas such as fine motor and communication skills. Educators must become familiar with the fit and function of therapy equipment, not only to assist the child but also to decrease their own anxiety. Any display of anxiety or revulsion about equipment such as braces or artificial limbs is inappropriate. Since children must eventually learn to care for their equipment, they need to accept it and even incorporate it into a positive part of body image. Educators become more comfortable with children and their equipment when they learn basic principles of physical management.

Physical Management

Young children with physical and health impairments may lack the ability to move around the classroom or engage in other physical activities. When mobility is difficult, initiation decreases, and the child is less motivated to engage with play materials or other children. Although it is important to encourage independent movement, sometimes it is necessary for adults to physically move children, using appropriate principles for lifting, carrying, and transferring. Physical management also includes positioning and appropriate care of body and mobility equipment.

Lifting, Carrying, Transferring, and Positioning   Lifting involves picking up an individual; carrying means moving that individual from place to place; and transferring means shifting the individual's position while moving him or her. Positioning is the appropriate placement of the child in a variety of sitting and lying postures. Appropriate lifting practices reinforce the health and safety of the adult and the child, prevent back injuries, and optimize the child's movement efficiency and independence. Specific guidance and demonstration for positioning and handling a specific child should be provided by a physical or occupational therapist or a teacher specialist in the area of physical and health impairments.

The following describe basic principles of positioning. Place the child in positions that are normal and comfortable. Keep the knees and hips flexed. The child's feet should rest firmly against a flat surface when sitting in a chair. Sometimes a tray can be attached to a chair to provide a firm surface for resting the arms. If the child has tense muscles, place a rolled towel between the knees to keep them apart. Rolled towels can be placed slightly behind the shoulders to keep them flexed and prevent arching. If the child has loose, floppy muscles, place a rolled towel between the sides of the chair and the legs to keep the legs more together. The head should always be positioned without pointing up or down and facing straight ahead (neutral position). Sitting on the floor is fine as long as the child is not allowed to assume a *w* position with the knees bent and tucked on the outside of the body on both sides. Instead, have the child sit with both legs stretched out in front or crisscrossed, or tuck the child inside the embrace made by an adult's legs when sitting on the floor. The latter sitting position has the added advantage of the adult's body providing trunk support as the child leans back.

Children can also be placed on the side as long as their back has firm support and their knees are flexed. Placing a pillow or rolled towel between the knees keeps them in proper position. Periodically change the child from one side to the other. Placing the child on the back is less desirable, as it triggers abnormal motor responses. If you do position the child on his or her back, flex the hips and knees and keep them in that position with pillows or foam wedges.

Braces, Splints, and Other Appliances   Braces are worn on the legs and may extend all the way up to the hips. Shorter braces are called *ankle-foot orthoses*. They are made of durable and lightweight plastic and are left or right sided. They are worn over the socks and are snugly secured with a Velcro strap across the top of the foot or ankle. The foot of the brace is slipped into the shoe, which must be large enough to accommodate the brace. Braces need to be changed as the child's foot grows. Splints support the hands and wrists and help to keep them in proper position. They may also be held in place with Velcro straps. A third piece of equipment is the body jacket. It extends from the hips upward to just under the arms and encloses the back and front of the torso. The body jacket is made of rigid plastic and may be tightened with Velcro straps on the sides. It is worn over an undershirt or body stocking.

There are several general principles that apply to body equipment. First, they are custom made and must be changed as the child grows. Second, all equipment worn on the body should be checked for fit and comfort. Any excessive tightness, skin redness, swelling at pressure points of the equipment, or actual skin breakdown/abrasions should be brought to the attention of medical personnel and parents. Since many young children with physical or health impairments cannot adequately shift their weight to relieve pressure, they should be repositioned frequently to relieve pressure. It is a good idea to check the fit of body equipment by occasionally taking it off. Third, appropriate clothing should be worn with body equipment. Clothing should be loose fitting, comfortable, and made from breathable materials such as cotton. Clothing that is tight fitting or sweaty can irritate skin. Socks worn under braces and shirts worn under body jackets should be pulled snugly so there are no wrinkles to irritate skin. Finally, body equipment is prescribed by a doctor to be worn for a specific length of time to ensure maximum therapeutic value. Many children do not like to wear body equipment and ask to have it removed. Although all complaints of discomfort should be investigated, time compliance is critical. Distraction and rewards for compliance can assist children to wear body equipment.

Some young children with physical and health impairments have to wear limb or body casts as a result of surgery or injury. Some casts are lighter weight and still provide immobilization for healing, while other casts are heavier and remain in place for several weeks to keep limbs or joints in specific positions. Care should be taken to keep casts dry or they begin to deteriorate. The rim of the cast (where the edge of the cast meets the skin) should be kept as clean and smooth as possible. Often this area is where casts begin to deteriorate first, and children may pick at the cast rims or even push small objects down the inside of the cast. It is necessary to report if an object gets stuck inside the cast next to the skin. Check with the child's parents or appropriate medical personnel about elevating the casted limb to reduce swelling. Any unusual skin discoloration, excessive swelling, or coldness of fingers or toes should be reported immediately as these are signs of decreased circulation.

Mobility Equipment   Young children with physical and health impairments may use equipment for mobility, including scooters, tricycles, strollers, crutches, walkers, and wheelchairs. Mobility equipment provides freedom and independence to explore and the opportunity to exercise. Mobility equipment is available for young children and is increasingly designed to "grow" as the child grows. Attention to style, color, and other accessories add desirability and interest value. Selection of mobility equipment involves many factors, including the child's age, motor ability, physical endurance, and environmental situation at home and in the community. Equipment selection is the responsibility of the therapists, physician, and parents.

Wheelchairs are either manual or powered. Manual-drive wheelchairs are propelled forward by moving the big wheels on the sides of the chair with the hands. Good hand grip and sufficient arm strength are required to operate a manual wheelchair. Many are equipped with seating inserts to provide custom support. Power wheelchairs are becoming increasingly sophisticated and are sometimes even equipped with backup beepers and side-view mirrors! Direction and speed can be controlled by a joystick or switch. Power wheelchairs may be pushed manually by disengaging the motor from the wheels.

Typically, power wheelchairs represent independence and competence for their users. However, parents may view power mobility as a failure to achieve independence and a reminder of their child's physical limitations. Resistance to power mobility should be addressed from a team perspective.

There are several important considerations related to wheelchair use. First, children must be carefully taught to push their manual wheelchairs and/or "drive" their powered wheelchairs. If they are being pushed by someone else, they must be taught to keep their hands off the wheelchair rims so their fingers do not get caught in the spokes. They might want to wear special gloves to protect their hands and keep them clean. Second, pediatric wheelchairs are equipped with seatbelts, and these must be worn at all times, even when the child is not moving. Seatbelts are tightened low across the lap, not across the middle of the body. Third, pediatric wheelchairs are equipped with brakes. These must be locked whenever the child is staying in one place. Some brakes are located at the back of the wheelchair and are locked and unlocked with the foot of the person pushing the chair. Brakes may also be located on the sides of the chair and be manipulated by the young child. Fourth, if young children have a power chair, its speed should be set appropriately for safety and the terrain. Finally, endurance is a factor in wheelchair operation. Although the value of independent mobility cannot be underestimated, there are times when pushing the wheelchair for the child is more efficient and appropriate.

Maintaining Health and Safety

Health and safety are essential considerations for every educator. Young children with physical and health impairments may be especially vulnerable to illness due to lowered immune systems or general physical debilitation. The presence of trained medical personnel cannot be guaranteed at every school site, and educators are frequently the initial evaluators of children's health. They must have established procedures for handling and administering medication, meeting daily health care needs, and responding to emergencies.

Medication   Some young children with physical and health impairments take medications. These medications have been prescribed to be taken at precise times and sometimes interact with food or other medications. Medications should be brought to school and then stored in their original containers and in a locked cabinet. A simple written description of the visual appearance of the medication and its possible side effects helps with quick identification and response. Medications should be administered in a consistent location, such as a health office. A written chart listing the type of medication, dosage, time of administration, and person administering the medication should be kept with the medication and completed immediately after administration. The cabinet should also include a list of persons to call in an emergency, including paramedics, poison control, and family members.

Meeting Daily Health Care Needs   Young children with physical and health impairments have a variety of health care needs. Some of these are the same as those of typical children (e.g., assistance with toileting, hand washing). Other needs will be highly specialized and include procedures such as bladder catheterization, tracheostomy suctioning, oxygen monitoring, and tube feeding. It is not possible to describe the mechanics of all specialized health care procedures here, but there are some principles that guide best practices for all children who have these special needs. All specialized health care procedures should be provided by trained personnel. It is not necessary for a nurse or nurse's aide to provide such procedures, but physician permission, careful training, and compliance documentation are necessary.

All educators who work with young children with physical and health impairments should become familiar with standard precautions. Once referred to as universal precautions, these are procedures that protect all individuals from infection and contamination from infected bodily products. Standard procedures are critical in situations with young children who are not able to control their bodily fluids and who also interact with each other throughout the day. School-based standard procedures include hand washing, using gloves, and implementing environmental infection control procedures.

Hand washing is the most effective preventative measure for infection control. Hand washing should occur before and after visiting the restroom; before preparing food, eating, or feeding a child; before administering medications; and after touching contaminated surfaces. Good hand-washing procedures involve thoroughly wetting the hands, lathering and rubbing hands for an adequate length of time, and rinsing and drying carefully with disposable paper towels. The towel can then be held in the hand and used in turning the faucet off. The use of hand sanitizers does not substitute for hand washing. Instead, the best approach is frequent hand washing followed by using hand cream to keep skin soft and free of cracks. Gloves should be worn when diapering and feeding young children with physical and health impairments. Disposable, nonlatex gloves are the best choice because some children have latex allergies.

The final aspect of meeting daily health care needs is environmental infection control. Some germs remain active on environmental surfaces for several hours to several days, so daily cleaning is mandatory. A spray bottle filled with a solution of 1 part of household bleach to 10 parts of water is ideal for sanitizing surfaces. All surfaces that have been touched by children and adults should be cleaned with this mixture. After spraying, surfaces can be wiped with a disposable paper towel. Floors must also be cleaned daily and with disposable materials. All soiled cleaning materials should be placed into a plastic bag, which is then tied shut and placed in a covered receptacle for disposal.

Medical Emergencies   Understanding the dynamics of specific impairments can help prepare educators in the event of an emergency. Training in cardiopulmonary resuscitation (CPR) and basic first aid provides educators with tools for emergency response. A written protocol for emergency response is critical and should contain the following elements: 1) description of warning signs and symptoms, 2) specific short-term interventions and time for response, 3) contact and alternate contact information, and 4) plans for transportation. All adults who are involved with the target child should have basic emergency plan training to include 1) review of the plan and standard precautions, 2) rehearsal opportunities, and 3) identification of designated personnel to undertake emergency procedures. It is ideal to have the emergency plan written into a document called an *individual health care plan* that is part of the IFSP or IEP.

Young children with physical and health impairments should have the same opportunity as other children to attend the appropriate school program designated by the IFSP or IEP. Careful attention paid to their health and safety allows educators to focus on other aspects of their education.

Logistics

Successful education of young children with physical and health impairments sometimes seems to be less about actual instruction than logistics and management. These, however, are essential components of the child's educational experience. Careful attention to the practical aspects of management avoids accidents and reduces any negative physical and psychological impact of impairment.

Child Comfort   It is impossible for anyone to attend and interact to their greatest potential when they are physically uncomfortable. Attention to several aspects of child comfort will enhance the learning environment. The first comfort consideration is temperature. Some young children with physical and health impairments require warm and draft-free environments. Warm air rises, and adults who are standing may experience a different temperature sensation than children who are placed on the floor. Carpet helps to warm the floor area but must be kept very clean. Flooring should be inspected on a continual basis for any debris or dropped items such as paper clips, toys, and so on.

Many young children with physical and health impairments require specially adapted chairs that support the trunk, back, arms, and neck. Any seating system should allow the child's feet to make firm contact with the floor or other surface.

When feet dangle, the ability to control the trunk area is lost. Some seating systems are equipped with seatbelts, and these should be worn whenever the child is seated. Therapists recommend specially designed seating systems.

No one can remain comfortable when they cannot occasionally shift their position and move about. Principles of positioning were discussed earlier, but it must be remembered that children who cannot move themselves should be repositioned regularly (every half hour).

Managing Equipment Some young children with physical and health impairments have more than one piece of equipment. Walkers, wheelchairs, and special seating systems use up a significant amount of classroom area and create a trip hazard for other children and adults. If possible, park equipment outside the classroom door when it is not in use. Make sure to lock wheelchair brakes and keep equipment where it is safe and dry.

Competing Priorities The presence of many specialists at schools provides multiple opportunities for communication, collaborative interaction, and focused direct service for young children. Unfortunately, it also results in multiple and repeated interruptions for treatment, medical protocols, and appointments. Educators who understand the importance of maintaining predictable routines become frustrated when children are removed from their classrooms at times that are critical for student learning. They begin to believe that their classes have become waiting rooms with little purpose or educational value. However, there are several strategies educators can employ to address competing priorities. Communication is the first priority. Work collaboratively with related services personnel to establish core instructional times when children must remain in class. Ask therapists and medical personnel to enter and exit your classroom as quietly as possible. If you know a child will be removed from your class for therapy, seat him or her where removal from the classroom will cause minimal disturbance to other children. Do not interrupt instruction to discuss therapy activities or goals; these can be addressed during noninstructional time. Ask the therapist to provide direct services in the classroom while you teach. For example, if the therapy activity is passive muscle stretching, this might be possible to implement while the child sits in the circle with peers. Establish rules for interruptions from the office; if a child must leave to go home or to a medical appointment send him/her with an appropriate adult. However, you may need to convey important information during the transition provided by leave taking.

ENSURING INFRASTRUCTURAL ACCESS

Young children with physical and health impairments who use mobility equipment must have ease of access into and out of buildings throughout the school. The Americans with Disabilities Act of 1990 (PL 101-336) has provided standards for uniform accessibility, including slope of wheelchair ramps, drinking fountain height, and modifications of restrooms. Once inside the classroom, the child must be able to access all areas that other children use. This means that spaces such as reading corners need to be big enough to move into using a walker or wheelchair.

Accessibility also means getting out of a space. Plans for building evacuation should be made in advance, including assignment of personnel to remove children with limited mobility. All school personnel (and children) should participate in regular building evacuation drills.

Environmental and Object Modification

Modifying the environment includes 1) changing the location of materials and equipment, 2) modifying work surfaces, 3) modifying objects, and 4) special environmental controls.

Changing the Location of Materials and Equipment Young children with physical and health impairments need to be able to access their personal belongings such as backpacks. These can be hung on the back of the wheelchair but are not readily available to the child in this position. A small, zippered bag attached to the inside of one arm of the wheelchair can be used to store small items. Toy shelves should be arranged for easy access from the floor and toys placed inside plastic see-through bins.

Modifying Work Surfaces Children who use wheelchairs are often seated at a greater height than their peers. When it is time for small group activities, remove the arms from the wheelchair so it can be pushed up to the table. Another option is to transfer the child to a chair or seating system that is the same height as peers. If children remain in their wheelchairs, a tray attached to the wheelchair arms provides a raised work surface for object manipulation. Adjusting the tray from a flat to an angled surface helps to maintain the child's head in a neutral position. An inexpensive solution is to use a notebook binder placed on its side and secured to the table top. A large plastic clip can be glued to the higher end of the binder to secure materials such as paper.

Modifying Objects There are many ways to modify toys and other objects in the preschool environment. The first is to *stabilize objects* so they cannot be knocked away. When objects are stabilized the child can use both hands to manipulate them. Strategies include clamping the bases of objects to a surface, using masking tape, Velcro, or foam tape, or attaching suction cups. Another modification category is *boundary creation.* Place items inside shallow-sided boxes or plastic trays. If the container is a different color from the objects inside, the added visual contrast makes them easier to locate. The child can be placed within a padded boundary area (such as a ball pit) during vigorous play. Not only will play objects be contained within the area, the soft sides of the boundary will protect the child if he or she loses balance. Grasping aids are useful for children who experience difficulty grasping, holding, and feeling objects. Examples include wrapping tape or foam wrap around an object to make it bigger to grasp, attaching Velcro to a glove and objects that will be picked up, or designing a handcuff with a loop through which objects such as crayons or pencils are inserted.

Manipulation aids are used with children who find it difficult to move parts of objects because they lack isolated finger movement, pincer grasp, reach, or other refined motor skills. Ways to address grasp issues include using bigger toys that are easily grasped, attaching knobs or dowels to surfaces, placing a long handle on an object to allow push and pull, and widening the spaces between book pages with pieces of foam tape.

A final type of accessibility is achieved through the use of switches for battery-operated toys. If the child has some voluntary movement, he or she can operate a switch. There are many types of switches that can be activated using the hands, head, or other parts of the body. These switches interface with toys so that when the switch is activated the toy performs a function. Independent play, cause-effect, and means-end causation are all reinforced with switch use. A two-switch system can be employed to encourage turn-taking opportunities with typical peers.

Supporting Preschool Children with Autism in Inclusive Classrooms

Michelle Dean and Jennifer Symon

MS. MARIA

Ms. Maria worked in a fully inclusive preschool in Los Angeles. She experienced difficulties when a child with autism named Evan was placed in her class. During circle time each morning, Ms. Maria would introduce or continue a lesson on the weekly topic, which included reading a book to the students followed by an activity related to the story. While the other students were sitting on the rug in a circle, Evan would roll across the floor, sometimes over or on top of the other students. Other times he would reach into open containers on the shelf behind him and throw items such as blocks across the room. Ms. Maria tried a variety of strategies to motivate Evan to sit appropriately on the carpet and listen to the lesson. Unfortunately, Evan seemed to enjoy negative attention and would continue with his behavior. As a result, his classmates were often distracted and sometimes got hit and upset. What surprised Ms. Maria is that Evan didn't seem to care about the others. In order to continue the lessons, Ms. Maria would ask the assistant to remove Evan from the circle and to sit with him while he played quietly on the computer until the rest of the class was finished with the lesson.

By the end of the week, Evan completely avoided the rug during circle time, and he was allowed to go to the computer with the teacher's assistant. Much to Ms. Maria's dismay, the frequency of Evan's throwing behaviors increased, and he began to throw during other periods in the day. Consequently, Evan spent most of his time with the teacher's assistant and away from the class. Ms. Maria felt helpless and wondered if Evan might be better suited in a more restricted environment or a special education preschool where he could receive more individualized instruction. When an autism consultant came to observe the classroom several challenges were revealed. First, Ms. Maria knew very little about autism or about effective strategies to support Evan. Second, she had not been given access to Evan's individualized educational program and, therefore, was unaware of his current performance levels or goals. Third, she had no previous experience teaching a student with autism, and the district did not provide guidelines, additional supports, or training. Finally, Ms. Maria was unclear about the purpose of inclusion and had difficulty addressing Evan's behaviors while meeting the needs of the rest of the students in her class.

Significantly more children are being diagnosed with autism, and this has greatly impacted educational settings and become a catalyst for the evolution of preschool teaching practices. As more children with autism are placed in the same setting as their typical peers, preschool teachers are faced with new opportunities, responsibilities, and challenges. The depth and breadth of information about autism and potential educational strategies can be overwhelming and difficult to navigate. Autism is increasingly covered in the media in terms of increased prevalence, genetic findings, and intervention results. Often, equal deference is given to interventions that are and are not empirically supported. For teachers who are new to autism, it is difficult to parse valuable information and to implement best practices into the classroom.

To date, little is known about the preschool experiences of children with autism or the extent to which they are given accommodations and interventions in everyday public school settings. Likewise, few studies review teachers' practices or their knowledge of autism and appropriate educational strategies. Currently, many of the interventions that have demonstrated positive effects for children with autism—for example, discrete trial training (DTT) and pivotal response training (PRT)—were implemented in clinical settings or in structured one-to-one environments. Less is known about the implementation of treatment in natural environments, like general education preschool classrooms. Using focus groups to gain a qualitative understanding of early intervention practices in two Southern California districts, Stahmer, Collings, and Palinkas (2005) found that preschool and early intervention service providers did not feel sufficiently prepared to teach students with autism and expressed interest in receiving more training.

AUTISM IN THE CLASSROOM

The general education preschool classroom places great cognitive, behavioral, and social demands on children with autism. Rigid and repetitive behaviors and social and communication deficits are the core diagnostic criteria for autism, which differentiates this population from typical classmates. Independently navigating preschool classrooms poses significant challenges for children with autism. In particular, preschool classrooms place a heavy emphasis on cooperative learning and playing, following rules, and learning routines, which require social motivation and awareness. Unlike typical children, who are highly motivated by social acceptance and engagement, for a child with autism, implicit social expectations, group work, and novel engagement opportunities are overwhelming. Young children with autism have joint attention deficits that impact social communication and language development. Typical children use joint attention to cue others to look at and share enjoyment in a point of interest. Children with autism tend to not consider the feelings of others or use affect to communicate feelings with another person for the purpose of being social. Likewise, children with autism are less likely to acknowledge and respond to others' joint attention initiations. This lack of awareness of the perspective of others causes children with autism to miss out on important social and emotional opportunities framed within the preschool classroom.

The expressive and receptive language difficulties associated with autism interfere with a child's ability to be an active listener and to "check in" with

communication partners, pay attention to the teacher, or attend to important information. Likewise, it may be difficult to use words to express oneself and to get
personal needs met. Rigidity and repetition cause children with autism to prefer
routines and to avoid novel experiences. They have a tendency to fixate on details
without considering the main idea or the big picture. For instance, a preschool
child with autism may play with a specific toy in a way that is repetitive, such as
repeatedly pushing a key on a toy piano, opening and closing the door of a doll
house, or rolling a truck back and forth. It may be challenging for the teachers and
teacher assistants to engage the child and encourage him or her to participate in
the daily activities and lessons.

Children with autism have difficulties considering another's perspective
(Barron-Cohen, 1989; Frith, 2004) and with problem solving (Ozonoff & Strayer,
2001; Happe & Frith, 2006). These deficits impact children's ability to participate
and to be accepted in a preschool classroom. Furthermore, children with autism
have difficulty engaging in group activities, sharing, taking turns, and pretending,
which are salient features of unstructured time and play. A child with autism may
become aggressive if he or she is asked to share a toy with others, because the child
cannot read the facial cues of peers who are also waiting for a turn. Consequently,
children with autism have difficulty making friends and are often isolated during
play. Social isolation exacerbates the issue by depriving the child of these very
important learning opportunities.

STRATEGIES FOR SUCCESS

The focus of intervention for children with autism within an inclusion setting
is to maximize the child's independence. Considering their challenges, children
with autism are more likely to thrive in a structured environment that engages the
child's motivation and provides clear expectations and directions. First, adapting
the physical structure of the classroom can help children with autism spectrum
disorder independently stay on task, participate in group activities, and perform
basic self-help skills like going to the bathroom or putting a coat in a locker. Second, giving the child choices and including high-interest activities can help to sustain the child's motivation. For example, a child who is reluctant to join circle time
may be given the opportunity to choose to sit by a preferred peer, hold a favorite
object, or select a familiar song. There is a variety of evidence-based practices that
are socially appropriate and effective. Some interventions are fairly easy to implement, like visual aids and prompting, while others are more intense. For practical reasons, it is a good idea to start with simple, less intrusive, and easy-to-use
interventions.

Visual aids have been identified as an effective strategy used to create structure in the classroom. Such assistance includes visual directions and schedules,
choice boards, graphic organizers, and picture cards. A teacher will supplement
spoken language by using pictures, visual depiction of words, or graphics to highlight important pieces of information, step-by-step directions, or expectations.
Visual aids help to transform seemingly abstract directives into a concrete point of
reference. Thus, these tools support the different learning styles of children with
autism. Preschoolers with autism may benefit from concrete examples that expli-
cate classroom routines and expectations.

Preschool exposes children to group dynamics, academic language, multiparty conversations, and multistep directions. Because of receptive language difficulties, many children with autism miss great amounts of auditory input, like directions, rules, and expectations. Consequently, not knowing what to do throughout the day can increase anxiety and, as a result, undesired behaviors. Children with autism often do not have the expressive language skills or the social awareness to get their needs met like typical children. Therefore, these children are dependent on nonverbal behaviors, which are sometimes maladaptive, to assert themselves. By telling the children what will happen during the day, when it will happen, how, and what is expected of them, visual supports improve transitions by creating a clear ending to one task before beginning another.

Implicit rules are embedded within the structure of the preschool classroom. For example, environmental aspects, like finding a place to sit on the carpet or sitting at a table in small groups, require social awareness. Preschoolers without special needs can easily scan the room to look where others are sitting and choose a spot that is available and near a preferred peer. Children with autism, on the other hand, often fail to recognize expectations. In a situation like this, visual supports can make abstract concepts concrete by articulating social expectations and why they are important. Moreover, visual supports offer classmates a tool with a language prompt. So, when the student with autism misinterprets implicit expectations, his or her classmates can cue the student to follow the visual support rather than becoming angry or escalating conflict.

Ms. Maria Creates a Structured Environment for Evan

Making these kinds of simple changes in Ms. Maria's classroom environment allowed Evan to use more socially appropriate behaviors and to participate in classroom activities. Ms. Maria's classroom was Evan's first school experience, and he required more structure and classroom support to understand what was expected of him at school—including sitting on the carpet. Because Evan's individualized education program (IEP) highlighted expressive and receptive language deficits, Ms. Maria decided to implement visual aids to help Evan understand what was expected of him. Ms. Maria used visual supports to show the daily agenda, step-by-step directions to activities, and appropriate student behavior. First, she took photographs of all the centers and daily routines in the classroom, such as the table-time activities, carpet area, dramatic play, arts table, and outdoor playground. She then created a visual schedule that used photographs to depict each activity in the school day. At the beginning of each session, Ms. Maria reviewed the daily agenda with the entire class. Because Ms. Maria was implementing a picture schedule in a natural environment, she took pictures of students in her class appropriately engaging in each activity. So, when Ms. Maria pointed to "reading," the class would see a picture of the children in the reading area sitting with their legs crossed and holding books. Once she had reviewed the entire schedule, she would point to the first picture and transition into that activity. After the completion of each activity, Evan would remove the card from the schedule and place it in an envelope that was labeled "all done." Then Ms. Maria would point to the next picture and review the directions and expectations before allowing the class to transition to a new activity.

PEER-MEDIATED INTERVENTION

Peer-mediated interventions have been found to be effective ways of embedding interventions into daily classroom routines. To use this strategy, peers and classmates were trained to facilitate interventions within the classroom. Using classmates as intervention agents provides children with autism multiple opportunities to practice new skills and promote generalization and maintenance. Peer mediation has been used to increase social initiations and interactions and to build play skills like turn-taking, sharing, and other social engagement behaviors. Popular and empirically supported peer-assistance strategies include peer modeling, role-plays, verbal explanation, reinforcing, giving feedback, and the use of visual aids. Considering the developmental goals of preschools, interventions that are implemented in vivo, during play or cooperative activities, optimize peer engagement opportunities while reducing demands on the teacher (Chan et al., 2009).

INDIVIDUALIZED INTERVENTIONS

In addition to embedded classroom supports, children with autism often need more intensive, individually designed interventions. Because of the vast differences in children with autism and classroom cultures, careful observations of the child and the classroom environment are used to tailor the intervention for the child. While positive behavior support and incidental teaching interventions occur within daily classroom activities, other approaches use a more structured and controlled environment with one-to-one adult support.

Discrete Trial Training

DTT is a highly structured, one-to-one behavioral approach in which a clinician teaches an isolated or "discrete" behavior by 1) getting the child's attention, 2) requesting that the child perform an action, and 3) rewarding the action with a tangible item or social praise. In each session, the child participates in a series of trials in which a trainer very systematically presents a specific stimulus, a prompt if necessary, and a reinforcer if the child's response is acceptable. Training on each discrete behavior continues until the child can produce the response at an acceptable level of accuracy (e.g., 8 out of 10 trials).

Sarah

Because Sarah was minimally communicative, her individual education team agreed that she would benefit from more intensive language intervention. To work on her language development, Sarah would receive DTT for 30 minutes before school every day. Sarah and her speech teacher would sit across from each other at a table. The teacher would call Sarah's name to get her attention. Then she would point to a picture card and ask Sarah to say the word. If Sarah said the word, or an approximation of the word, she would get some cereal. If she did not respond, the therapist would model saying the word. Each session began with pictures of words that Sarah had said previously. Then the therapist would introduce new words. Sarah would have 10 trials for each word. The therapist would record her progress throughout each session.

Pivotal Response Training

PRT is also referred to as pivotal response treatment or pivotal response therapy. Because it is based on more naturally occurring setting events, and rewards for functional responses that readily generalize to "pivotal" skills such as communication and social initiation across multiple cues, it is very appropriate as an intervention in an inclusive setting for young children. PRT uses a child's interests to sustain his or her motivation and investment in the intervention. It also allows for a less structured environment by using multiple stimuli across varying contexts.

Holly

Holly had a difficult time participating in art activities. While some children enjoyed using various materials to color, paste, and paint, Holly became easily frustrated and gave up quickly. When she saw the paper and the craft materials out on the table, she became very upset, began to cry, and would knock them off the table. Holly seemed to enjoy other class activities; in particular, she liked puzzles, looking at princess books, and listening to music. Within the daily routine, children were allowed to select a quiet activity to play when they finished their writing. Knowing that writing was an important and pivotal school readiness skill, Ms. Delong realized that Holly needed an intervention to increase her motivation to write and to practice writing. First, Ms. Delong put the puzzles in a box and out of Holly's reach. Next, Holly was told that she would be able to play with the puzzles after tracing her letters. Then, when Holly was presented with her task, she was given a choice to write with a pink princess pen or a pink crayon. Then, Ms. Delong copied sentences from Holly's favorite princess book and asked Holly to trace the letters. When she was finished, she was also given an opportunity to trace a picture of a princess. When Holly was finished tracing, or trying to trace her letters, she was given access to her puzzles.

Not surprisingly, Holly chose to write with the princess pen. Because she loved princesses, she was highly motivated to trace words of the picture book and trace the picture of the princess. Once she was finished with the prescribed task, she was given immediate access to puzzles. As Holly progressed, Ms. Delong asked her to choose what book and what pages in the book she would like to copy. Over time, Holly stopped resisting writing time, developed fine motor strength, and was able to independently write letters.

COLLABORATION WITH PARENTS

One integral component of successful preschool inclusion is parent collaboration (Duhaney & Salend, 2000). In general, parents of children with autism prefer inclusion settings (Kasari, Freeman, Bauminger, & Alkin, 1999). Strong family involvement positively correlates with children's educational outcomes. Successful family involvement programs include parents in the process of goal setting and program development and evaluation.

After the responses collected from a focus group of early intervention service providers were reviewed, several common themes were identified. First, the most popular family involvement strategies used were communication notebooks, phone calls, classroom participation, structured parent education workshops, and trainings. Not all preschools incorporate parent involvement into their programs. In some preschools, a parent component was included in the weekly schedule. During that time, the providers were able to choose what method of communication to use. While a majority of participants in the study identified parents as being involved in the programming of their child, the quality of parent involvement varied. Teachers that worked in programs that prioritized family involvement had more positive perceptions of parent relationships compared to teachers who worked in programs without a parent component.

Ms. Williams and Kenny

Ms. Williams was worried about sending her son Kenny to preschool. She hoped that he would make friends, but at home and at church he was often in his own world. On the first day of school, she scheduled a one-to-one meeting with the teacher, Ms. Alvarez, after school the following day. Ms. Williams discussed her concerns about Kenny's lack of interest in others. Ms. Alvarez said that she noticed Kenny isolating at school too. Together, Ms. Williams and Ms. Alvarez began to brainstorm strategies to help Kenny make friends and play with others. First, Ms. Williams brought some of Kenny's favorite games to play at school. Next, Ms. Alvarez facilitated structured play activities using Kenny's favorite games with the other students. Then Ms. Alvarez would write what happened in the communication notebook each day and send it home in Kenny's backpack. Finally, Ms. Williams and Kenny would talk about the game and his new friends. Soon Kenny was playing games every day, and eventually he became open to learning new activities and playing with other children.

Conclusion

Research has identified several effective components of successful inclusion for young children with autism:

- Providers need to have knowledge about autism and understand that, as it is a spectrum disorder, the symptoms of autism present differently in each child.

- Collaboration with parents and other service providers maximizes educational opportunities by building a comprehensive intervention plan using multiple perspectives of the child.

- While there is no standard intervention that works for all children, or model of inclusion that is right for all classrooms, some interventions and classroom models have received empirical support and have been notably effective for improving outcomes for these children.

- Providing interventions in the natural environment increases the generalization and maintenance of skills.

As teachers and service providers embrace the inclusion of students with autism, it is critical to advocate for the use of best practices, professional development, and quality programming. Inclusive education offers children with autism opportunities to participate in a developmentally appropriate educational environment with typically developing peers. There is no single best inclusion practice for preschool classrooms that include children with autism. The interventions described here have received empirical support for fostering independence and promoting positive outcomes for young children with autism. By understanding the child and the environment, and working closely with families, teachers can choose interventions that are ecologically and developmentally appropriate.

Inclusion of Young Deaf and Hard-of-Hearing Children in Typical Preschool and Community Settings

Janice Myck-Wayne

Inclusion entails a commitment toward providing education, to the maximum extent possible, in the school or classroom the child would otherwise attend if no disability were present (Rogers, 1993). I have grappled with the issue of inclusion with young deaf and hard-of-hearing (D/HH) children. I have found myself being very proinclusion for all young children with disabilities, but less so with young D/HH children. As a teacher of the deaf and hard of hearing for the past 30 years, I have taught children from infants/toddlers to high school students with hearing loss (HL). The question of including children with HL, for me, has always been about children having access to a rich, developmentally and socially appropriate language environment. Within the field of educators of the deaf and hard of hearing, there exist concerns about access to full communication and social integration. Full inclusion is difficult, as it implies that the student who is D/HH will be able to participate in learning activities on an equal basis with hearing peers, uninhibited by communication and attitudinal barriers. The complexities of full access are heightened because deafness is a low-incidence disability, and inclusion may mean that the child with hearing impairment will most likely be the only such student in the classroom (Stinson & Lang, 1994).

What then makes inclusion unique for D/HH children? My perspective is focused on their unique needs, which primarily are concerned with language development and the child's need to develop the ability to use language to facilitate communication, develop critical thinking, be able to problem solve, and read and write. HL affects language acquisition. A child with a diagnosis of HL must be provided with access to language, whether it is through the auditory pathway or through a visual language such as American Sign Language (ASL). Research indicates that the earlier this process begins, the better the ability of the child to acquire language (Meinzen-Derr, Wiley, & Choo, 2011).

(continued)

(continued)

Inclusion of children with HL with their typical peers has been a debated topic. It garners almost as much debate as discussion related to the form of communication and amplification children diagnosed with HL should use. Added to the complexity of inclusion is that the degree of HL, the age of onset, early intervention, and amplification must factor into decisions about educational placements. The age the child was fitted with amplification must also be part of the equation. The educations of children who are deaf and hard of hearing can differ vastly because of the degree of hearing loss. Further complicating the issue is the fact that the research on inclusion of children who have HL is primarily focused on the K–12 population, not those in preschool.

Inclusion of children who are deaf and hard of hearing is complex, and the complexity stems in some part from the discussion of whether deafness is indeed a disability. Differing perceptions exist between the hearing and the deaf worlds (Ellwood, 1997). As an individual who is hard of hearing, the moderate degree of my HL allows me to function with minimal supports as a hearing person. Resistance to full inclusion by some in the deaf community (Cohen, 1995) stems from the notion that one outcome of inclusion is assimilating the student with HL and making them "normal." The deaf-world perspective, on the other hand, views deafness as normal (Komesaroff & Mclean, 2006).

ACCESS TO COMMUNICATION

Access to communication, either through audition or sign language, is seen as a barrier to successful inclusion. If full access is not achieved, social interactions between hearing students and students with HL are hindered, thus thwarting one of the benefits of inclusion. Cohen (1995) contended that many in the inclusion-for-all-children camp conclude that deaf children will improve their language skills by interacting with typical peers. Research by Ramsey (1994) actually found the opposite. Ramsey's study found that hearing children communicated with the deaf children by waving their hands in the belief that they were communicating. Intelligible communication consisted primarily of caretaker language in which the hearing children gave orders and used stern looks while saying "No." Social assimilation, which is accomplished through shared activity and conversation, did not occur for the deaf children in the inclusion setting in this case.

Often, interpreters are used to facilitate the differences in language. Winton (1994) found that the interpreter became an "artificial filter" between the hearing and the deaf children. The presence of an interpreter, according to Winton (1994) and Cohen (1995), denies the deaf child appropriate social interactions because every interaction requires a third person. In addition, some deaf children come to preschool without a complete command of any language and therefore cannot benefit from an interpreter. Antia and Levine (2001) point out that the use of interpreters with young school-age children is not appropriate, as "language is learned through interaction and exposure. The interpreter can only provide exposure, as the young child cannot be assumed to understand that the interpreter is functioning as the 'hands of the teacher'" (p. 371).

If one of the outcomes of inclusion is to include all children and develop social and emotional skills, this can often be counterproductive for young children who have HL. This is caused by the language barrier. Studies showed that contrary to social assimilation, the powerful social life that comes from shared activity and conversation did not exist for the deaf children (Cohen, 1995).

Access to communication should be a prominent consideration in the inclusion of young D/HH students in the general education setting. Antia and Levine (2001) present the major challenges for inclusion as language differences, modality differences, and language competence.

EXAMINING INDIVIDUAL NEEDS

In making the decision for inclusion, all decision makers, which includes the parent and all educators and professionals involved with the child, need to examine the environment. The environment must provide the intellectual, social, and emotional development the student with HL needs and to which he or she is entitled (Nowell & Innes, 1997). In order to determine if the environment is appropriate, subsequent questions need to be addressed. Nowell and Innes (1997) suggest that these questions include the following:

- What is the individual's hearing level and ability to use residual hearing?

- What is the individual's preferred mode of communication, and is it practiced in the environment?

- Will the individual have access to assistive devices?

- What is the level of direct communication that will occur in the environment between the individual, teacher(s), and peers?

- Will the individual's language abilities and needs be adequately addressed?

- Are there a sufficient number of other children who are deaf or hard of hearing of similar age and level with which the individual can socialize?

- Is the school/program staffed by certified and qualified personnel who are trained to work with the student who is deaf?

- Does the school provide a full range of assessment instruments and techniques designed for use with students who are deaf or hard of hearing?

- Are there personnel trained to conduct such assessments in the individual's preferred language and mode of communication?

- Will there be deaf or hard-of-hearing role models in the environment?

STRUCTURING INCLUSION

Kavale and Forness (2000) suggested that inclusion "appears to be not something that simply happens, but rather something that requires careful thought and preparation" (p. 287). The literature appears to support the use of co-teaching as a genuine alternative to segregated settings. Co-teaching offers an approach to address the social isolation of children who have HL in local school programs (Kluwin, 1999). Implementing inclusion in early childhood programs requires planning sufficient support and accommodation for individual children, particularly those with unique learning needs, since early childhood programs predominantly focus activities and experiences on the *whole child* (Winter & Van Reusen, 1997). Co-teaching, along with the appropriate supports, must be in place for children who are D/HH to realize their full potential.

CASE STUDIES

The following case studies demonstrate the complexity of including young children who are D/HH. No doubt, an entire book could be written on the experiences in facilitating inclusion of young children with HL.

Vivian

Vivian was diagnosed with a profound hearing loss at birth. Her parents, Jeff and Kristin, are both deaf. In fact, the majority of Vivian's immediate family is deaf. The family is part of the deaf culture. All members of the family, hearing or deaf, are fluent in American Sign Language (ASL). When Vivian was born, Kristin was working on her degree in social work and Jeff was an accountant. Vivian's maternal grandmother was a teacher of the deaf and hard of hearing and her grandfather was in academia. Vivian was referred to early intervention (EI) D/HH services at birth as part of her state's newborn hearing screen program. While the family did not view Vivian as having a disability and were not concerned about obtaining EI services, an individualized family service plan (IFSP) was written. Even though Vivian was fitted with hearing aids, the family did not promote auditory training or utilize speech services, although IFSP services included audiological monitoring, periodic developmental screenings, and transition planning and support from EI services (Part C, IDEA) to preschool (Part B, IDEA). All developmental and communication assessments conducted during the transition process measured Vivian above the expected age range. Given the family's primary language was ASL, it was assumed by school district personnel that Vivian's family would request placement in a D/HH special day class (SDC) in which ASL was used as the primary language. However, this was not the case. The family requested that Vivian be placed in a private preschool with her hearing peers and that an interpreter/instructional aide be provided to support Vivian's access to the curriculum and to promote social interaction. The family's rationale for this placement was that Vivian had extensive access to ASL, deaf role models, and deaf peers. They wanted her to have access to an academic-based preschool in order for her to continue her academic readiness and to be exposed to hearing children. Since Vivian was fluent in ASL, she was able to access the interpreter. The interpreter, though, did not assume the traditional role of interpreters, who act as a conduit to communication. The interpreter assumed a less formal role and became an "assistant" in the classroom. The interpreter promoted social integration by facilitating play while co-teaching lessons with the preschool teacher.

(continued)

(continued)

> In Vivian's case, the family viewed inclusion in the general education preschool as a means to support Vivian's academic-readiness development as well as her introduction into the hearing world. The family felt confident that she had a strong connection to the deaf world and positive self-identity as a deaf person.

Guillermo

Guillermo was identified with a moderate to severe hearing loss through the newborn hearing screen program. The diagnostic process to confirm his HL and obtain approval for hearing aids through the state's medical system took over seven months. His mother, Luz, lived with her mother and sister, while Guillermo's father, Henry, was deployed overseas. EI services began when Guillermo was 8 months old. He received weekly home visits from a D/HH teacher and consultation services from the audiologist and speech and language therapists. With his hearing aids, Guillermo had access to some speech sounds. Luz worked with Guillermo on using speech and sign language to communicate. His parents were pleased with Guillermo's progress in developing speech and language. At family gatherings, Guillermo interacted and played well with his cousins and adult relatives. At the D/HH EI mommy-and-me program, Guillermo participated in all group activities and music time. At the transition IFSP meeting to discuss Guillermo's transition into preschool, his parents stated that they wanted Guillermo to attend the local Head Start program with his cousin, Joaquin. The preschool assessment team assessed Guillermo at age level in all areas of development, except for language. The individualized education program (IEP) team recommended a self-contained D/HH class located 10 miles away from Guillermo's home. Guillermo's family declined the placement and pushed for him to attend the local Head Start program. Once the district agreed to the Head Start placement, the IEP was written to include the services of an itinerant D/HH teacher twice a week for a total of 60 minutes along with speech/language therapy (SLP) for 30 minutes once a week.

Two weeks after Guillermo enrolled in the Head Start program, the Head Start teacher told her administrator that Guillermo needed to be moved to a special education class. The teacher felt that Guillermo was distracted and did not follow the classroom routine. He was overly physical with the other students and did not follow directions. The only child he interacted with on a regular basis was his cousin, Joaquin. The parents called for a review of Guillermo's IEP. Upon further investigation, it was observed that Guillermo's hearing aids were not sufficient for him to "hear" the teacher in a classroom of 24 children. The Head Start classroom was considerably more noisy than the D/HH mommy-and-me class and his home environment. In addition, neither the itinerant nor speech-language pathologist had provided the Head Start teacher with suggestions on how to promote social interaction in small groups in order for Guillermo to make friends. No strategies on working with hard-of-hearing children had been provided. Consequently, his behavior became challenging, and his language skills regressed. The IEP team recommended a speaker system be installed in the classroom. The speaker system allowed for the teacher's voice to reach Guillermo

(continued)

(continued)

in different areas of the classroom. In addition, a boosted amplification system for his hearing aids and a teacher microphone were provided in order for Guillermo to access oral communication. The itinerant teacher's time was increased to two hours a week to support Guillermo's transition into the new setting. She arranged her schedule to arrive during small group activities and teacher planning time. In addition, the D/HH itinerant teacher co-taught one lesson every Friday. The SLP agreed to provide Guillermo's speech support in the classroom and include peers in the speech and language activities. The IEP team agreed to meet in two months to follow Guillermo's progress. After two months, the team reconvened. The family, Head Start teacher, itinerant teacher, and SLP reported that Guillermo was making progress in the Head Start classroom.

Andre

Andre passed the newborn hearing screen. When he was 6 months of age, his grandmother observed that Andre had stopped babbling and did not appear to respond to sounds or his music mobile in his crib. Andre's mother, Cheryl, was not alarmed, because he had passed the hearing screening, but at his next checkup she shared her mother's concerns with Andre's pediatrician. Andre was referred for an audiological examination and diagnosed with a profound sensorineural hearing loss. The audiologist referred Andre and his family to the cochlear implant center for evaluation. Andre's father, a radiologist, had read research about the effectiveness of the cochlear implant (CI) in facilitating typical speech and language development. A referral was also made to a local education agency (LEA) for EI services. Andre was approved for a CI and he had the surgery to implant the devices by 12 months of age. Meanwhile, EI services included twice-weekly home intervention services from a D/HH infant teacher and audiological consultation.

After Andre received his CI, his family sought to enroll Andre in an auditory-verbal therapy program (AVT). The family's insurance covered 80% of the once-a-week AVT sessions. Despite early intervention from both the district and the AVT, Andre did not progress in terms of oral communication and speech at the rate his family had expected. At Andre's IFSP transition to determine services for preschool, it was decided that he needed continued services of a D/HH teacher and AVT therapist to support his progress in the area of speech and language development. His IEP goals reflected the need for him to increase speech production and listening skills. It was determined by the team that Andre would attend preschool class for D/HH children with specific emphasis on oral/aural communication. This would provide him the support needed to develop his speech and language skills and increase his academic readiness. He integrated with hearing peers three mornings a week when the special education teacher and general education preschool teacher co-taught morning activities. The goals of the IEP reflected that Andre would be fully included in the general education preschool program in one year.

CONCLUSION

The literature on inclusion of children who are D/HH suggests that before a child is placed in an inclusive setting, a comprehensive assessment of the inclusive environment be made. In addition, the individual differences of each child need to be addressed. These differences can be addressed using the questions posed above by Nowell and Innes (1997) along with the child's communication system, use of amplification, and educational services and supports. While space does not allow for a fuller discussion here, it must be noted that the increasing use of cochlear implants with very young children is rapidly changing the kinds of supports needed and the recommendations for placement. This section has outlined some of the concerns and issues related to inclusion with young children who are D/HH, but it has only begun to approach the nuances and complexities of such inclusion.

RESOURCES AND REFERENCES

Visual Disabilities

American Foundation for the Blind. http://www.afb.org

Benjamin, S., & Sanchez, S. (1996). *Should I go to the teacher?* Portsmouth, NH: Heinemann Publishers.

California Department of Education. (1997). *Program guidelines for students who are visually impaired* (rev. ed.). Sacramento, CA: Author.

D'Andrea, F.M., & Farrenkopf, C. (Eds.). (2005). *Looking to learn: Promoting literacy for students with low vision.* New York, NY: AFB Press.

Holbrook, M.C. (Ed.). (1996). *Children with visual impairments: A parent's guide.* Bethesda, MD: Woodbine House.

National Association of Parents of Visually Impaired Children. http://www.familyconnect.org

Pogrund, R.L., & Fazzi, D.L. (Eds.). (2002). *Early focus: Working with young children who are blind or visually impaired and their families.* New York, NY: AFB Press.

Takeshita, B. (2009). *Developing your child's vision: A guide for parents of infants and young children with visual impairment.* Retrieved from http://www.low-vision.org

Physical and Health Disabilities

Americans with Disabilities Act (ADA) of 1990, PL 101-336, 42 U.S.C. §§ 12101 *et seq.*

Best, S.J., Heller, K., & Bigge, J. (2010). *Teaching individuals with physical or multiple disabilities* (6th ed.). Upper Saddle River, NJ: Pearson.

Romski, M.A., Sevcik, R.A., & Forrest, S. (2001). Assistive technology and augmentative and alternative communication in inclusive early childhood programs. In M. Guralnick (Ed.), *Early childhood inclusion: Focus on change* (pp. 465–480). Baltimore, MD: Paul H. Brookes Publishing Co.

Sadao, K.C., & Robinson, N.B. (2010). *Assistive technology for young children: Creating inclusive learning environments.* Baltimore, MD: Paul H. Brookes Publishing Co.

Autism Spectrum Disorder

Baron-Cohen, S. (1989). The autistic child's theory of mind: A case of specific developmental delay. *Journal of Child Psychology and Psychiatry, 30*(2), 285–297.

Brown, J., & Murray, D., (2001). Strategies for enhancing play skills for children with autism spectrum disorder. *Education and Training in Mental Retardation and Developmental Disabilities, 36*(3), 312–317.

Chan, J.M., Lang, R., Rispoli, M., O'Reilly, M., Sigafoos, J., & Cole, H. (2009). Use of peer-mediated interventions in the treatment of autism spectrum disorders: A systematic review. *Research in Autism Spectrum Disorders, 3*, 876–889.

Dawson, G. (2008). Early behavioral intervention, brain plasticity, and the prevention of autism spectrum disorder. *Development and Psychopathology, 20*(3). 775–803.

Dawson, G., Rogers, S., Munson, J., Smith, M., Winter, J., Greenson, J., Donaldson, A., Duhaney, L.M., & Salend, S.J. (2000). Parental perceptions of inclusive educational placements. *Remedial and Special Education, 21*(2), 121–128.

Frith, U. (2004). Emanuel Miller lecture: Confusions and controversies about Asperger syndrome. *Journal of Child Psychology and Psychiatry, 45*(4), 672–686.

Happe, F., & Frith, U. (2006). The weak coherence account: Detail-focused cognitive style in autism spectrum disorders. *Journal of Autism and Developmental Disorders, 36*(1), 5–25.

Individuals with Disabilities Education Improvement Act (IDEA) of 2004, PL 108-446, 20 U.S.C. §§ 1400 *et seq.*

Kasari, C., Freeman, S., Bauminger, N., & Alkin, M.C. (1999). Parental perspectives on inclusion: Effects of autism and Down syndrome. *Journal of Autism and Developmental Disorders, 29*(4), 297–305.

McGee, G.G., Daly, T., & Morrier. M.J. (2001). Walden early childhood program. In J.S. Handleman & S.L. Harris (Eds.), *Preschool education programs for children with autism* (2nd ed.) (pp. 57–190). Austin. TX: PRO-ED.

McGee, G.G., Morrier, M.J., & Daly, T. (1999). An incidental teaching approach to early intervention for toddlers with autism. *Journal of the Association for Persons with Severe Handicaps, 24*(3), 133–146.

Ozonoff, S., & Strayer, D. (2001). Further evidence of intact working memory in autism. *Journal of Autism and Developmental Disorders, 31*(3), 257–263.

Stahmer, A.C., Collings, N.M., & Palinkas, L. A. (2005). Early intervention practices for children with autism: Descriptions from community providers. *Focus on Autism and Developmental Disabilities, 20*, 66–79.

Stahmer, A.C., & Ingersoll, B. (2004). Inclusive programming for toddlers with autistic spectrum disorders: Outcomes from the children's toddler school. *Journal of Positive Behavior Interventions, 6*, 67–82.

Varley, J. (2010). Randomized, controlled trial of an intervention for toddlers with autism: The early start Denver model. *Pediatrics, 125*(1), e17–e23.

Deaf and Hard of Hearing

Antia, S.D., & Levine, L.M. (2001). Educating deaf and hearing children together: Confronting challenges of inclusion. In M.J. Guralnick (Ed.), *Early childhood inclusion: Focus on change* (pp. 365–398). Baltimore, MD: Paul H. Brookes Publishing Co.

Cohen, O.P. (1995a). *The adverse implications of full inclusion for deaf students.* Paper presented at the International Congress on Education of the Deaf, Tel Aviv, Israel.

Cohen, O.P. (1995b). Perspectives on the full inclusion movement in the education of deaf children. In B. Snider (Ed.), *Conference proceedings: Inclusion? Defining quality education for deaf and hard-of-hearing students.* Washington, DC: College of Continuing Education, Gallaudet University.

Ellwood, C. (1997). Re-visioning deafness: Supporting literacy in Auslan. *Literacy and Numeracy Studies, 7*(1), 77–88.

Giangreco, M. (2002). *Flying by the seat of your pants: More absurdities and realities in special education* (3rd ed.). Minnetonka, MN: Peytral Publications.

Individuals with Disabilities Education Act (IDEA) of 1990, PL 101-476, 20 U.S.C. §§ 1400 *et seq.*

Kavale, K.A., & Forness, S.R. (2000). History, rhetoric, and reality: Analysis of the inclusion debate. *Remedial and Special Education, 21*, 279–296.

Kluwin, T. (1999). Co-teaching deaf and hearing students: Research on social integration. *American Annals of the Deaf, 144*(4), 339–344, 580–591.

Komesaroff, L.R., & McLean, M.A. (2006). Being there is not enough: Inclusion is both deaf and hearing. *Deafness and Education International, 8*(2), 88–100.

Meinzen-Derr, J., Wiley, S., & Choo, D.I. (2011). Impact of early intervention on expressive and receptive language development among young children with permanent hearing loss. *American Annals of the Deaf, 155*(5), 580–591.

Nowell, R., & Innes, J. (1997). Educating children who are deaf or hard of hearing: Inclusion. *ERIC Digest* #E557. Retrieved from http://eric.ed.gov/?id=ED414675

Ramsey, C. (1994). The price of dreams: Who will pay? In R.C. Johnson & O.P. Cohen (Eds.), *Implications and complications for deaf students of the full inclusion movement.* Washington, DC: A Joint Publication by the Conference of Educational Administrators Serving the Deaf and Gallaudet Research Institute.

Rogers, J. (1993). The inclusion revolution (*Research Bulletin* No. 11). Bloomington, IN: Phi Delta Kappa.

Stinson, M., & Lang, H. (1994). Full inclusion: A path for integration or isolation. *American Annals of the Deaf, 139,* 156–159.

Winston, E.A. (1994). An interpreted education: Inclusion or exclusion. In R.C. Johnson & O.P. Cohen (Eds.). *Implications and complications for deaf students of the full inclusion movement.* Washington, DC: A Joint Publication by the Conference of Educational Administrators Serving the Deaf and Gallaudet Research Institute.

Winter, S.M., & Van Reusen, A.K. (1997). Inclusion and kindergarteners who are deaf or hard of hearing: Comparing teaching strategies and recommended guidelines. *Journal on Research in Childhood Education, 11*(2), 114–134.

Positive Behavior Supports

Preventing and Managing Difficult Behavior

Kathryn D. Peckham-Hardin, Ph.D.

The need for early childhood programs that support all children, including children with learning, emotional, and behavioral challenges, is clear. The early childhood years are marked by significant growth in language, social, and emotional skills. It is during this time that children learn how to play and get along with others, how to identify their emotions and the emotional states of others, and how to self-regulate their feelings and desires (Berk, 2007). While many children struggle during this period, a growing number of children experience emotional and behavior difficulties beyond what would be considered typical for this age group (Quesenberry, Hemmeter, & Ostrosky, 2011). This includes children who are at risk for developing serious challenging behaviors because of language, social, and/or emotional delays as well as those who enter early childhood programs displaying aggressive, disruptive, and other challenging behaviors.

Smith and Fox (2003, p. 5) define challenging behavior as "any repeated pattern of behavior, or perceptions of behavior, that interferes with or is at risk of interfering with optimal learning or engagement in prosocial interactions with peers and adults." In young children, challenging behaviors may take the form of disruptive behavior (calling out, running around), aggression (hitting, kicking, biting, and/or slapping others), refusal to participate in activities (says "No!," hides under table), having tantrums (crying, screaming, throwing self on ground), property destruction (tearing papers, breaking chalk/crayons/toys, throwing objects), self-injury (biting or hitting self), or withdrawal (plays alone, avoids interactions with others). Research to date suggests that the number of children with challenging behavior in early childhood programs represents approximately 1 in 10 children (10%), although some studies have reported rates as high as 20% and above (Carter, Van Norman, & Treadwell, 2011; Quesenberry et al., 2011). Prevalence rates for children who score at or above clinical levels for oppositional behaviors or early identification of conduct disorders range from 2–7% (Raver & Knitzer, 2002), although, again, others have reported higher rates, especially in low-income areas. Webster-Stratton and Hammond (1998) found that 23% of the 4-year-old, low-income children they studied scored within the clinical range for serious emotional/behavior disorders.

Children with challenging behaviors are at higher risk for being removed from inclusive settings (Hendrickson, Gable, Conroy, Fox, & Smith, 1999). Furthermore, these children are more likely to be expelled. Gilliam (2005) examined the expulsion rates in state-funded early childhood programs across 40 states. He defined expulsion as the "complete cessation of educational services without the benefit of alternative services" (p. 1). In other words, these children were not just removed from one setting and placed in an alternative setting, such as a self-contained special educational program; all services were ended. Of the almost 4,000 classrooms surveyed, he found that 6.67 per 1,000 children were expelled, a rate that is more than 3 times higher than children in the K–12 system (2.09 per 1,000 children).

Children with poor social and emotional skills and/or those who display challenging behaviors are more likely to be rebuffed by peers. Children learn important social skills such as cooperative play, turn-taking, and sharing through their interactions with other children. When children refuse to share or are aggressive toward others, their peers will slowly begin to avoid playing with them (Buhs & Ladd, 2001). Fewer interactions result in fewer opportunities to learn from others. Similarly, if a child is frequently removed from an activity because of disruptive behavior, learning opportunities are further reduced. Repeated negative interactions can result in further alienation and less learning. Furthermore, this cycle of negative experiences can also shape how the child comes to view school. Negative views toward school can result in reduced motivation to learn and learned helplessness (Algozzine, Daunic, & Smith, 2010; Dominguez, Vitiello, Fuccillo, Greenfield, & Bulotsky-Shearer, 2011). If challenging behaviors are not effectively addressed in these early years, children are at increased risk for poor outcomes in later life (Powell, Dunlap, & Fox, 2006). As Dunlap et al. (2006, p. 24) summarize, "early appearing behavior problems in a child's career are the single best predictor of delinquency in adolescence, school dropout, gang membership, adult incarceration and early death."

Teachers frequently cite challenging behaviors as a significant stressor and indicate the need for training and assistance to effectively address disruptive behaviors as a top priority (Carter et al., 2011; Cluines-Ross, Little, & Kienhuis, 2008; Raver & Knitzer, 2002). Teachers who find children difficult to teach are less likely to interact with them and may, over time, come to expect less of the child (Algozzine et al., 2010). Fewer interactions with adults and lowered expectations result in fewer opportunities to receive instruction, support, and positive feedback. These experiences can further lower the child's motivation to learn and, most importantly, to persist when things are difficult. Families and caregivers echo these sentiments. Parents talk of the stress that challenging behaviors can have on the entire family (Fox, Vaughn, Wyatte, & Dunlap, 2002), disrupting routines and creating feelings of ineffectiveness and social isolation.

In summary, there is a clear need to design early childhood programs that promote positive behaviors while simultaneously decreasing challenging behaviors. We know from current research that 1) nurturing and responsive caregiving are associated with positive outcomes in children; 2) children who demonstrate social-emotional competence in their early childhood years are more likely to experience success in later school years; 3) designing interventions based on assessment findings can decrease challenging behaviors; 4) comprehensive behavior support that includes strategies to prevent, teach, and encourage positive behaviors results in long-lasting changes; and 5) involving families in the process is critical (Dunlap et al., 2006).

PROGRAM-WIDE SUPPORT: A FLEXIBLE
AND RESPONSIVE TIERED SYSTEM OF SUPPORT

Programs that use a comprehensive approach with an emphasis on teaching, supporting, and reinforcing skill development have been shown to have a positive impact on children (Blair, Fox, & Lentini, 2010; Blair, Lee, Cho, & Dunlap, 2011; Hemmeter, Fox, Jack, Broyles, & Doubet, 2007). The response-to-intervention (RTI) model serves as an appropriate framework to address the needs of all children while building in a system of supports for children who are at risk for further delays/challenging behaviors and for children who display frequent and disruptive behaviors.

Response-to-Intervention Model

RTI is a comprehensive multilayered model in which "levels" or "tiers" of intervention are built into the system to ensure programs are able to meet the needs of all children. The National Center on Response-to-Intervention defines the three levels of support as 1) *primary prevention,* in which schools/programs use high quality curricular and instructional strategies that meet the needs of most children; 2) *secondary prevention,* the use of evidence-based intervention(s) of moderate intensity to meet the academic and behavioral needs of most children at risk; and 3) *tertiary prevention,* as providing intensive and individualized interventions to children who show minimal response to tiers 1 and 2. This model is typically presented as a triangle in which primary prevention serves as the foundation or bottom level of the triangle, secondary supports represent the middle, and tertiary intervention the very top of the triangle. Most children (75–85%) will respond positively to tier 1 or universal interventions and will not require supplementary supports. A few children (10–20%) will require additional academic, language, social, and/or behavioral supports designed to address specific needs. Finally, a small percentage (3–5%) of children will require intensive and individualized supports based on comprehensive assessment findings (Sprague, Cook, Wright, & Sadler, 2008). The essential components of RTI include 1) early screening to identify children at risk for poor learning and/or behavioral outcomes, 2) immediate intervention utilizing evidence-based practices to address specific needs, 3) systematic data collection to assess the child's response to the intervention, 4) modifying intervention/practices based on assessment findings, and 5) a built-in support system for teachers and staff to ensure interventions are implemented with fidelity (Sprague et al., 2008).

School-wide Positive Behavior Support (K–12)

School-wide positive behavior support (SWPBS) was the first model to apply the concept of a tiered level of support to address challenging behavior with school-age children in K–12 programs. SWPBS is a three-tiered approach in which the first level (universal/primary) focuses on prevention through universal strategies designed for all children. This includes the development of school-wide rules in which behavioral expectations across school settings (classrooms, hallways, cafeteria, bathrooms, and so on) are clearly delineated, systematically taught, and supported through school-wide rewards and other reinforcement systems. The second level (secondary) is designed for students at risk for developing challenging behavior in which additional academic and/or behavioral supports are provided. Finally, the third level (tertiary) provides intensive supports to meet individual student needs. Intervention is comprehensive and is based on functional behavioral assessment (FBA) data (Horner & Sugai, 2000; Sugai & Horner, 2006; Sprague et al., 2008).

This model of behavioral support is based on the following assumptions. First, we must teach before we can evaluate. While this may seem obvious when it comes to academics, the same principle has not always held for behavior. In other words, we cannot assume children understand the behavioral expectations or have a shared understanding of what it means to "be safe, responsible, and respectful" (Algozzine et al., 2010). Therefore, we must articulate the social and behavioral expectations, teach them, and then support positive behavior though the use of program-wide reinforcement systems. Second, challenging behaviors are communicative in intent, meaning there is a reason or purpose behind the behavior. Our goal is to understand that purpose and design interventions accordingly. Third, challenging behaviors occur within a context; there are environmental factors that influence the presence and absence of problematic behavior, as well as consequences that support or reinforce the behavior. These environmental factors are often referred to as *antecedents* and *consequences*. Fourth, intervention should focus on helping the person to acquire skills and alternative ways to get his or her needs met in a more acceptable manner. In other words, positive behavior support is an *educative model* in which equal emphasis is placed on building skills and improving quality of life as on decreasing or eliminating challenging behaviors (Carr et al., 2002). Finally, positive behavior support is data-driven model; assessments are used to design interventions, and ongoing data are collected to determine effectiveness (Horner & Sugai, 2000; Sugai & Horner, 2006).

PYRAMID MODEL FOR EARLY CHILDHOOD

The Pyramid Model outlined by Fox, Carta, Dunlap, Strain, and Hemmeter (2010) shares many conceptual similarities to the SWPBS model for older children, with some modifications to better reflect the needs of younger children and their families (Frey, Park, Browne-Ferrigno, & Korfhage, 2010). This model also has three tiers, but unlike the SWPBS model, the pyramid model identifies two distinct sets of interventions in tier 1 (see Figure 8.1). The primary goal of secondary supports in both models is to provide systematic instruction in needed areas, which may include specialized academic instruction; teaching adaptive, communicative, and social skills; and helping children/students learn to self-regulate their emotions and behavior. Finally, in both models, the third or tertiary level provides individualized supports based on FBA findings. Intervention at this level is frequently more comprehensive and includes strategies to prevent challenging behaviors from occurring through the manipulation of antecedents, skill building, teaching replacement behaviors, and positive reinforcement to support new behaviors (O'Neill et al., 1997).

In addition to the assumptions summarized earlier for SWPBS, Fox et al. (2010) outline additional assumptions specific to the pyramid model for early childhood programs. First, this model is designed to meet the needs of students with and

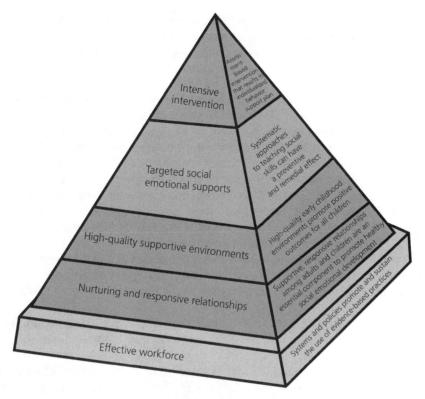

Figure 8.1. Pyramid model for early childhood. (From Center on Social and Emotional Foundations for Early Learning at Vanderbilt University. [2003]. *Pyramid model for promoting social and
emotional competence in infants and young children.* Nashville, TN: Author.)

without disabilities. This is not a special education model in which only students
with disabilities receive more intensive supports. Any child who is at risk for or
displays challenging behaviors is to receive the required supports. Second, inclusive settings in which children with and without disabilities learn, grow, and play
together are viewed as the most appropriate context. Children develop language,
learn how to interact with others, and learn to follow directions and regulate their
emotions within the context of interacting with adults, siblings, and other children.
Inclusive settings provide the rich context to promote these skills. Third, tier 1
serves as the foundation for subsequent levels; interventions in tiers 2 and 3 build
on strategies used in tier 1. The difference is primarily in the intensity and precision of the instruction. Instruction at these levels is more systematic to address
specific needs. Finally, families are viewed as an essential part of the process at all
levels of intervention.

Pyramid Model Tier 1: Universal Promotion

The strategies and concepts presented here are general or universal strategies
applied to all children in the effort to increase skills while simultaneously reducing the rate of disruptive behaviors through proactive and preventative measures.
These strategies represent what is known about effective instruction for young
children. Here they are focused specifically on the needs of early learners: social

and emotional development. Skills in these areas serve as the foundation for later years (Algozzine et al., 2010). There are two primary interventions in this level: 1) developing nurturing and responsive relationships with children and their families and 2) creating a positive, warm, and supportive environment.

Nurturing and Responsive Classroom   The early childhood years represent a time of tremendous growth. During these years, children are acquiring language, building extensive vocabularies, learning to identify and label their feelings and the emotions of others, developing relationships with peers and other adults, figuring out what behaviors are okay and those that are not, and becoming increasingly skilled at self-regulating their behavior as they become more and more independent in daily activities (Berk, 2007). Children do not develop these skills and abilities in isolation but instead within the context of supportive and responsive adults who encourage and reinforce their efforts (Fox, Dunlap, Hemmeter, Joseph, & Strain, 2003). Emotional support is especially needed for children who have, or are at risk for developing, challenging behavior. Dominguez et al. (2011) examined the relationship between nurturing/responsive settings and challenging behaviors and found that emotional support served to lessen the negative effects of problematic behavior.

There are many ways to develop meaningful and reciprocal relationships with children. Playing with children is a wonderful way to share moments of fun and excitement. Playtime is also a perfect opportunity to teach a variety of skills, including the sharing of thoughts and opinions (e.g., "This is fun! What do you think?"); identifying emotions (e.g., "I'm excited! What are you feeling?"); and problem solving (e.g., "The puzzle piece won't go in. Maybe if we turn it the piece will fit?"). Following the child's lead by showing interest in what he or she is thinking or doing is another way to establish rapport. Such interactions also provide a great opportunity to encourage language and cognitive skills. For example, a child is playing in the kitchen and picks up a plastic banana, raises it up in the air, and proudly says "banana!" The adult follows the child's lead by asking questions about the banana, talking about its characteristics (e.g., long and yellow), and asking the child what other kinds of fruits he or she likes. A third way to establish relationships with children is to learn things about them. One approach is to ask children to create books that talk about their favorite things, complete with photos of family members, pets, and friends. Then, highlight each child through a "star of the week" or similar program to provide the child the opportunity to share personal information with others. You can also learn about children from family members and other caregivers. Finally, when a child is absent, let the child know he or she was missed by making a special effort to welcome the child back.

It is equally important to build relationships with families (Fox et al., 2003). Families are entrusting the care of their children to people they do not know. It is imperative that they feel comfortable and know their child will be safe and well cared for. Take the time to talk with parents as they drop off or pick up their child; email or send brief notes home; and ask questions and share stories about the child's day during informal conversations with family members. Furthermore, through relationships with families, information about strategies that have been effective can be shared. For example, Mrs. Rubin (mother) shares with Ms. Ramirez (teacher) that Shane responds better to requests to clean up when he is given lots of choices and when the request is framed within the context of a game. She explains that after asking Shane to clean up, she engages him in a number of questions (e.g., "Do you want to start with the cars or the book?"; "How long—one song or two songs?"; "What song(s) should I sing?"; "Or would you prefer I count today?") Initially Shane gave a one- or two-word response and typically selected the first choice. However, Mrs. Rubin explains that now Shane often initiates the game by telling her his preferred method before she has a chance to ask any questions, and he is talking in more complete sentences (e.g., "Today, Mom, I want to put away the cars last!"). Thus, this strategy has not only resulted in fewer problem behaviors during cleanup and transitions but has also resulted in improvement in language skills. This information helps Ms. Ramirez in a couple of ways. First, she learns about a simple strategy she can use in the classroom. Second, she learns that Shane can talk in complete sentences when properly motivated, something that he is not currently doing at school. She will use this information to find additional ways to motivate Shane to use more complex language.

Positive, Warm, and Supportive Environment   In this second set of interventions, the goal is to create a positive and supportive environment that promotes language, social, and emotional competence within typical routines. This is done by establishing and teaching rules and behavioral expectations, creating predictable routines, and planning for transitions to maximize success.

Clear Rules and Behavioral Expectations   Preschoolers are learning so much about their world, including what is okay and not okay to do and when. For example, they learn they can run around and scream with joy when out on the playground, but in the classroom or inside the house they need to be less active (for safety reasons) and quieter (out of respect for others). They learn that they can push the buttons on the microwave but cannot reach in and take the food out without help. Young children learn these expected behaviors by being told what the rules are, by watching others model these behaviors, and through the positive and corrective feedback they receive from adults.

When designing rules, it is important to take the following guidelines into consideration. *First, state the rules in the positive telling children what to do, as opposed to what not to do* (Algozzine et al., 2010). For example, say "Ask a friend to share a toy" rather than "Don't grab toys from others." Algozzine et al. (2010) suggested teaching behavioral expectations using a *demonstrate, practice, and prove* model. Start by *demonstrating* the desired behavior and then ask the child to demonstrate the behavior to display their understanding of the rule. Next, arrange for opportunities to *practice* the expected behavior throughout the day during typical activities and routines. This provides children the chance to *prove* their ability to follow rules across different contexts and settings (maintenance and generalization). It will take time for children to learn and master these skills, and mistakes will occur. When mistakes occur, corrective feedback is needed. For example, Leticia asks Patti if she can play with one of the dolls. Patti says "no!" and grabs all of the dolls and starts to walk away. Help Patti understand what occurred. The teacher might say, "I know it is hard to share and sometimes we don't want to." This statement helps Patti understand the emotions she is feeling at that moment and why. Follow this by explaining the rule about sharing and asking Patti, "If you want to play with the doll later, what might you do?" This question encourages problem solving as Patti comes to realize she is not giving up the doll forever and that she can play with it again later by asking. The teacher might take this lesson a step further and ask, "How would you feel if Leticia wouldn't let you play?" This helps Patti to develop empathy as she comes to understand how her behavior impacts others.

A second consideration when designing rules is to create a classroom matrix that delineates the rules that are specific to a given setting or activity (see Table 8.1). For example, rules specific to centers might be "Clean up when done" and "Share materials." Rules specific to large group activities (e.g., circle time) might be "Raise your hand" and "Listen to your friends/teacher." By clarifying the expectations across settings and activities, children learn that behavioral expectations vary and that they need to alter their behavior accordingly.

A third guideline is to display the rules using both pictures and text (see Figure 8.2). Young children generally respond better to pictures than to text. Furthermore, the use of pictures will help *all* students, including younger children and children with disabilities who may have limited reading skills. Finally, place the rules at a child's eye level and place them in the place for which the rules apply. For example, place the rules associated with centers at each center, rules related to hand washing by the sink, and so on.

Predictable and Structured Routines   Most people like predictability. It allows us to anticipate and prepare for events. Predictability provides comfort, because with it we know that certain events are going to occur—especially events we enjoy and look forward to. Predictability helps us to regulate our behavior; for example, knowing there is a break coming up in 20 minutes helps us to remain focused and continue working. Young children are no different. Predictable routines provide children with a sense of security and help them feel in control of their world. Routines have additional benefits in promoting cognitive skills. For example, children learn there are many steps to most tasks requiring memory and that these tasks are often done in a particular order. Through this process they learn important time-related vocabulary, such as *first, next, before, after,* and *then*.

The term *routine* is defined simply as "a prescribed, detailed course of action to be followed regularly; a standard procedure" (Free Dictionary). In other words, a routine is a set of actions that is done the same way every day. As children learn the routines, they are able to complete them faster and with greater independence. The end result is more time engaged in tasks and less time getting ready for tasks.

Table 8.1.   Classroom behavior matrix

Circle time	Centers	Snacks	Waiting in line	Hand washing
Raise your hand	Share materials	Share snacks	Keep your hands to yourself	Two children at a time
Be a good listener	Help others	Eat only your food	Listen to the teacher	Take turns
Use inside voice	Finish your work	Throw your trash away		Put towels in trash
One person talks at a time	Clean up			

Share materials	Help others	Finish your work	Clean up

Figure 8.2. Presenting classroom rules using pictures with text.

Clearly, consistency is critical. Not only should routines be done around the same time every day but also done the same way each time. For example, if the morning routine is to 1) enter, 2) put backpack away, 3) go to a play area and play until the cleanup song is played, and then 4) come to the rug, then children should be taught to follow this same sequence each time. If necessary, break routines into steps and visually represent these steps using pictures (see Figure 8.3). The steps can be reviewed with the child ahead of time as a reminder of what to do or pasted onto a paper and numbered so the child can refer to the paper for guidance. Provide lots of positive feedback and be sure to reinforce attempts (e.g., "You started to walk toward your cubbie. Great! Keep going, you are almost there!").

Planning for Transitions to Maximize Success   Transitions are often reported as a difficult time and one in which challenging behaviors are likely. Factors that can lead to difficult transitions include 1) too many transitions, 2) too many children up and moving about at the same time, 3) uncertainty of what to do, and 4) down time as children wait for others. Taking time to plan for transitions can help to alleviate problems and increase child success (Hemmeter, Ostrosky, Artman, & Kinder, 2008).

1	2	3
Put backpack away	Play until clean up song	Come to rug

Figure 8.3. Presenting morning routine using pictures with text.

The best way to promote successful transitions is to keep children actively engaged to the maximum extent possible. As discussed earlier, *the first rule of thumb is to create a daily schedule that is carried out the same way each day.* Predictable routines create a sense of familiarity and help children to become independent as they learn the steps to daily tasks. For children who are still learning the daily routine, an individual schedule can be created as a visual cue to help them plan their day (Downing & Peckham-Hardin, 2001). The schedule can be in a simple book format, in which the child turns the page as one activity is completed to see what activity is next, or presented in a list, in which the child removes the picture once the activity is completed. *Second, limit the number of transitions.* Hemmeter, Ostrosky, Artman, and Kinder (2008) provide an example of how a daily schedule is modified to limit transitions by combining activities. For example, instead of snack time being a separate activity, they suggest that snack time be infused into centers as one of the options so children can eat when they are hungry. (See Hemmeter et al. [2004, p. 4] for the complete example). Hemmeter et al. (2008) also suggest altering the schedule by decreasing time spent in large group activities while increasing time for small groups/centers. Some children find large group activities to be particularly difficult (Blair et al., 2010; Blair et al., 2011), partly because such activities are typically more passive, requiring listening and watching versus being more actively engaged in activity. In contrast, longer center times provide more opportunity for children to be actively engaged, although this must be planned effectively. To prevent children from becoming bored, provide a number of options and allow for creativity and flexibility in how tasks are completed. For example, the task may be to draw a picture depicting a story the teacher just read. Some children may wish to draw while others may prefer to cut and paste pictures from a magazine. Different options provide children with choices and promote decision making. There are times when large group activities are necessary. To help ensure success, find ways to keep children more engaged; for example, infuse frequent opportunities to respond and move their bodies by answering questions or imitating body movements.

A third strategy to promote successful transitions is to limit the number of children who are up and moving around by dismissing small groups of children at a time. This can be done in a number of ways, including pulling sticks or names out of a can, calling on children who are wearing a certain color, or dismissing children by centers. There are advantages to using a random system. First, it requires that children listen for the relevant cues, thus increasing listening skills. Second, as children learn the system, they are less likely to engage in disruptive behavior such as calling out to the teacher ("Pick me!") or jumping up and down in their attempt to get noticed. Finally, a random system helps children to learn that sometimes they are first and other times they have to wait their turn.

A fourth strategy to planning successful transitions is to limit the time children are waiting without something to do. If there is only one sink available for washing hands, then dismiss children in pairs so they can share the sink as one child soaps up as the other rinses off. This teaches children to share supplies and to work cooperatively. As children wait in line to be dismissed for the day, arrange for an adult to be present to keep the children engaged. The adult can keep children engaged by singing songs, playing "Simon Says," or asking children with blue shirts to put their hands on their head, those with red shirts to cross their arms, and so on.

Finally, a fifth strategy is to arrange the adults in the room to maximize success. Placing adults in the middle of the room can help to direct students to the correct location or redirect those who may have lost focus. Similarly, standing in front of known distracters (e.g., the pet lizard's cage) can help decrease the likelihood the child will become distracted and lose focus. If transition times continue to be problematic, Hemmeter et al. (2008) suggest that a colleague or administrator come into the class and observe to get an outsiders' perspective. The educator should ask this person to note what is going on during transitions; specifically, what are children doing and what are adults doing? Are there too many children up at the same time? Are children waiting as adults prepare materials? Where are the adults positioned in ways to maximize success? Do children seem to know what to do? These questions can help to identify specific issues so that more precise plans can be put into place.

Pyramid Model Tier 2: Secondary Level of Supports for Children at Risk

While many children respond positively to the general or universal strategies described earlier, some children will need additional assistance. Tier 2 supports are designed for children who are beginning to display problematic behavior that is more intense and/or frequent than what is typical for children this age. Remembering that the RTI model is designed to provide early intervention before problems rise to the level of high concern, intervention at this stage is to provide more systematic intervention to build skills while preventing further escalation of problem behavior. It is important to note that the examples of direct teaching discussed below are skills all young children need to learn and acquire and should be part of the curriculum for all children. What is different in tier 2 intervention (from tier 1/universal) is that the instruction is more systematically delivered.

Systematic Instruction   Systematic instruction is planned teaching using modeling, prompting, shaping, and positive reinforcement to help children learn, generalize, and maintain skills and behavior over time (Westling & Fox, 2009). The first step is to clearly define the desired outcome: What do you want the child to do? This can be a discrete behavior, for example, asking for a turn, or a more complex skill, such as following multistep directions to complete a task. Next, while modeling the response, describe or explain to the child what is expected. When the child displays the desired response, provide immediate reinforcement. You may need to prompt the response by using gesture, verbal, and/or physical cues. Gesture cues include pointing to a general area to direct the student's attention or tapping the object you want the child to pick up. Verbal cues can be direct (e.g., tell the child "Ask for a turn.") or indirect (e.g., ask the child "What's next?"). Physical prompts are the most intrusive and should be used with caution. A partial physical prompt can include gently guiding the child's elbow toward the communication device to encourage him to push a button. A full physical prompt may include putting your hand under the child's hand and guiding the child to the desired object.

Using Systematic Instruction to Teach Skills: An Example   *Colin has difficulty when playing with others and will often take toys without asking. His behavior is beginning to impact his relationship with his peers, who often shy away from playing with him. Colin is receiving instruction in asking for a turn* *(target response). To teach this skill, the teacher takes Colin over to the toy cars, an activity she knows he likes and therefore will be highly motivated to perform. As Colin and the teacher watch Jesus and others play she says out loud, "This looks like fun. I want a turn playing!" The teacher turns to Colin and says, "Watch me. I'm going to ask for a turn," and then asks Jesus for a turn (modeling the response). As the teacher is playing with the car she again vocalizes that this is fun while waiting to see if Colin initiates asking for a turn. He doesn't, so she whispers in Colin's ear to "Ask for a turn" (direct verbal cue). When Colin makes the desired response the teacher says, "Great, you asked for a turn!" (specific praise) as she gives him the toy car (natural reinforcer).*

This example provides an illustration of the adult providing direct instruction. However, peers can also serve as instructional models. This is one of the advantages of an inclusive setting, in which children of varying skills and abilities play and learn together. Some children will be quite proficient at asking for turns and therefore serve as role models for others.

Jesse is good at asking, and so the teacher asks him to show Colin how he asks for a turn. One other peer is present, and after a few minutes Jesse asks for his turn. Jesse smiles, takes the toy, and begins playing. He talks to Colin and the other peer as he is playing. The teacher is standing behind the children as she waits to see if Colin will initiate asking for a turn. When he doesn't, the teacher prompts Colin from behind by whispering in his ear to ask for a turn (again, a direct verbal prompt). Colin asks and Jesse gives him the toy car (natural reinforcer). The teacher also praises Colin for asking (specific praise). The advantage of this approach in which the peer serves as the model while the teacher stands behind is that the interactions are child-to-child versus child-teacher-child. This is more natural and makes it easier for the teacher to fade her assistance.

It is important to note the possible need to "shape" the behavior by reinforcing closer approximations to the desired goal. For example, initially Colin may say "turn" or "please" as opposed to a full sentence. Another child may not say anything but instead show through nonverbal behavior (smiling and clapping) that he wants a turn. These approximate responses should immediately be reinforced; the adult may say, "Oh, are you asking for a turn?" to clarify the child's intention while further modeling the desired response and then immediately giving the child the toy.

Finally, the example with Colin assumes the child has sufficient oral language to ask and be understood by others. If the child has minimal or unclear speech, an alternative communication system will be needed. Augmentative and/or alternative communication devices provide students who do not communicate in traditional ways with an alternative way to communicate with others. Devices range in complexity from a picture exchange system (child hands a peer a card with a picture and text) to a communication device with voice output, in which the child pushes an icon and a voice recording is played. Sign language can also be used as an alternative communication system. However, the other children will need to be taught these signs so they can respond appropriately. The same general procedures can be used to teach a number of social skills such as initiating and maintaining interactions, sharing, cooperative responding, making comments, conflict resolution, and self-regulation of emotions.

Teaching Children About Emotions Many children have challenges with self-regulation. A way to support growth in this area is to teach children about emotions. Through this process, children learn to 1) identify emotions and the words associated with those emotions, 2) read others' emotional state of mind (develop empathy), and 3) learn how to self-regulate their own emotional state.

Identifying One's Own Emotions Children's initial vocabulary for emotions is small and consists primarily of emotions at different ends of the continuum, for example, the difference between being happy and mad (Joseph & Strain, 2003). The goal is to help children identify and label more subtle emotions. The first step is to help children understand what they are feeling and then provide a word to that feeling. Through this process children learn there are different emotions and states of mind while simultaneously increasing their vocabulary. For example, there are many words that represent being happy, such as *excited, joyful, pleased, cheerful,* and *delighted.* Adults can model this process by expressing their emotions. For example, while waiting for the computer to boot up the teacher explains to Christine, "This is taking a long time! I'm getting *impatient*," as she scrunches up her face in frustration. Pairing the word with the appropriate body language helps the child to identify what the feeling looks like and the word that describes that emotion. The teacher can expands this mini-lesson by modeling problem-solving strategies at the same time. She turns to Christine and says, "Let's find something to do while we're waiting" and asks Christine for suggestions of what they might do while waiting.

A similar strategy can be used to help children identify their own emotions. Graciela is making a necklace out of beads and she cannot find another blue bead. She begins to cry and pushes the container on the floor. The teacher first describes what she sees. She tells Graciela, "I see you are crying and you and have a sad look on your face." Again, the goal is to help the child learn to identify his or her own feelings and what those feelings look like. The teacher asks Graciela why she is crying, but Graciela just shakes her head and continues to cry. The teacher helps Graciela identify the emotion she is feeling by explaining, "You are frustrated because you cannot find the right bead." This explicit statement helps Graciela to understand what she is feeling and also addresses why she is feeling this way. Again, the teacher can encourage problem solving by providing some alternatives (e.g., "Maybe you can ask a friend for a blue bead.").

Identifying Emotions in Others Children also need to learn how to read others' emotions or states of mind. This helps them to develop empathy and compassion for others. The key here is to help children decipher body language, facial expressions, tone of voice, and other nonverbal cues that help us identify what others are feeling and thinking. Books provide a great avenue to teach this skill (Joseph & Strain, 2003). While reading a book, stop to ask questions, for example, "What is the bear feeling?" followed by "How do you know?" The first question focuses on identifying emotions while the second question encourages children to look for and describe the cues they see. For example, the bear is sad (emotion); he is crying (visual cue); he can't find his friend (contextual cue). Similarly, the boy is excited (emotion); it is his birthday and he is opening presents (contextual cue); he is smiling and ripping the wrapping paper (visual cues). Clearly, the teacher may have to support this process by asking leading questions and/or pointing out the relevant cues. Through repeated opportunities to practice this skill, children will become increasingly more proficient and will need less guidance and support.

Self-Regulation   Finally, through the process of understanding their own feelings and the emotional states of others, children learn to self-regulate their behavior. Self-regulation in this context means the child's ability to 1) identify his or her feelings and the feelings of others, 2) understand what these feelings mean (e.g., what is the cause and intent), 3) generate potential solutions, 4) make a decision, and finally, 5) act on that solution (Joseph & Strain, 2003). For example, through direct instruction, Graciela learns that she gets frustrated (emotion) when she can't find what she is looking for (cause); that she has options (ask a friend); and finally, that she can act on those options. For some children, modeling, prompting, and reinforcing these skills may be sufficient. Other children may need more concrete referents, especially if the child has difficulty immediately retrieving the appropriate word when already upset. For example, you might create a card (see Figure 8.4) with one row of pictures illustrating two to three different emotions (e.g., angry, frustrated, bored) and a second row depicting possible solutions (e.g., ask for help, look at a book, go to a quiet area). Limiting the card to

Figure 8.4.   Visual presentations to help with self-regulation.

just a few pictures means less options to scan, thus making it easier for the child to respond. When the child appears upset, the teacher can direct the child's attention to the sheet and say, "Show me what you are feeling." Pointing to the picture enables the child to respond quickly without having to recall and verbalize the correct words. If the child has difficulty identifying an emotion, the teacher can provide support by telling him what she is seeing. For example, while pointing to the emotion on the card that depicts frustration the teacher could say, "You pounded your hand on the table when you couldn't get the cap off the glue stick. Are you frustrated?" The teacher can then review the options with the child and encourage him or her to select one.

Pyramid Model Tier 3: Intensive and Comprehensive Behavior Support

A small percentage (3–5%) of children will require interventions that are individualized to meet unique learning and behavioral needs. Under the pyramid model, support plans are based on FBA data. The FBA process is designed to help us understand challenging behavior(s) in context by identifying the environmental factors that elicit and maintain the challenging behavior(s) of concern. These data are in turn used to design a comprehensive support plan that prevents challenging behavior while teaching and supporting desired responses.

Functional Behavioral Assessment   FBA is the process of gathering information about the challenging behavior(s) in order to design a support plan that addresses the needs underlying the behavior. The process begins by first clearly defining the challenging behaviors of concern in an objective and descriptive matter (O'Neill et al., 1997). For example, aggression may be defined as "kicking a peer or adult in the legs," self-injury as "biting arm and hitting head," and property destruction as "tearing papers and breaking pencils and crayons." The next step is to gather information about the when and why of the behavior. The *when* is frequently referred to as the behavior's *antecedents*. Antecedents vary widely by child and can include events like transitions from preferred to nonpreferred activities, wanting a toy, changes in the schedule, and being asked to complete fine motor tasks like cutting or stringing beads. The point is that the antecedent is, or the antecedents are, unique to that child. The *why* part of the equation is determining the reason behind or *function* of the behavior. Under the positive behavior support paradigm, challenging behaviors are viewed as communicative events—in other words, the child is communicating through his or her behavior. The goal is to understand the behavior *from the child's perspective*. The purpose or function of the behavior may be to communicate boredom, confusion, fear, frustration, displeasure, and so forth. It is through the process of gathering both pieces of information—when the behavior is most and least likely to occur and what events follow the behavior—that helps us determine why the behavior is occurring. From this information, the data is analyzed and hypotheses are formed. Information is gathered through interviews with relevant parties (e.g., family members, teachers, related service staff, paraprofessionals) and through direct observation in typical settings and routines.

Interview Data   The FBA process typically begins with the gathering of information through interviews with members of the education team (O'Neill et al., 1997).

As noted previously, the first step is to clearly define the challenging behavior(s) of concern. Once the behaviors are identified and defined, the remainder of the interview is designed to understand the environmental variables associated with the behavior: in other words, when the behaviors are most and least likely to occur (antecedents) and what happens after the behaviors occur (consequences). From these data, initial hypotheses are formed. The functional assessment interview (FAI) by O'Neill et al. (1997) is an extremely comprehensive interview assessment tool. What is particularly good about this tool is the focus on gathering pieces of information related to 1) antecedents, specifically when challenging behaviors are most likely to occur, and, conversely, 2) when challenging behaviors are not present or less likely (or stated differently, when positive behaviors are most likely). Both pieces of information help in understanding the environmental factors associated with the behavior. For example, if problematic behaviors are more likely during the early morning and less likely in the late morning and early afternoon, then time of day appears to be an important variable. It is important to include all stakeholders in the interview process, as varied perspectives help to create a more robust picture of the child. It is especially critical to include family members. Families not only know the child best, but because they interact with their child in a number of settings and contexts, they are likely to have a broader understanding of the child's strengths and areas of needs.

Observational Data   Direct observation is the process of observing the child within typical settings and routines. Data gained through direct observations often helps to further flush out the initial hypotheses formed from interview data and identify additional hypotheses as well. The *ABC observation chart* is a common assessment tool. The observer notes the antecedents, events that occurred before the challenging behavior (A); describes the child's behavior (B); and records the consequences, the events that followed the behavior (C). Data are typically taken in short intervals (e.g., 20–60 minutes at a time) and, as such, represent a slice of the child's day. It is recommended that information gleaned from the FAI be used to help determine when observations are scheduled to capture both positive and challenging behaviors. Another observation tool is the *scatter plot*, which notes the frequency of the challenging behavior across the day. The advantage of these data is that they provide a more comprehensive overview of the child's day. A disadvantage is that they do not provide specific information related to the antecedents and consequences associated with the challenging behavior.

Hypotheses Statements   As information is gathered and analyzed, hypotheses are formed. A hypothesis statement is a summary of the data that typically contains three pieces of information: the antecedent, the challenging behavior, and the function or purpose of the behavior (O'Neill et al., 1997). The format may look like this: W*hen/During* _____ (the antecedent goes here), *child will* _____ (description of the challenging behavior goes here), *in order to* _____ (the function of the behavior goes here). Several hypotheses may be generated, and interventions are designed around these hypotheses.

Functional Behavioral Assessment Example   *Jayden is a 4-year-old boy who displays destructive and disruptive behaviors. He has been identified as a child with a disability displaying moderate delays in language and cognition. Jayden's destructive behavior is defined as tearing and/or breaking papers, projects, or toys. His disruptive behaviors are defined as loud crying and screaming and running out of the room. FBA data was gathered and analyzed, and after a thorough discussion the following hypotheses were developed:*

1. *During large group activities like circle time (antecedent), Jayden will scream, cry, and get out of his seat (challenging behavior) in order to escape the activity (function of behavior).*

2. *When working on tasks that require intricate fine motor skills (antecedent), Jayden will tear or break materials (challenging behavior) in order to avoid the task (function of behavior).*

3. *When completing multistep tasks and unsure of what to do, Jayden will scream and/or break materials in order to get assistance.*

Further analysis of circle time revealed that problems were more likely when the teacher was reading a story and when giving verbal instructions for centers. Both lessons are language-based activities that require good receptive language. Jayden enjoys books, although he has trouble turning individual pages (tends to grab several pages at once).

Positive Behavior Support Plans Information gathered through the FBA process is then used to design an individualized support plan. Interventions at this stage are typically comprehensive and include strategies to prevent problem behaviors, build skills and teach replacement behaviors, and use positive reinforcement to support and strengthen new skills (O'Neill et al., 1997). A summary of the behavior support plan for Jayden is presented in Figure 8.5.

Preventive Strategies One goal for Jayden is to prevent the likelihood that disruptive behaviors will occur through the manipulation of antecedents including those activities or events that are associated with positive behaviors into the antecedents known to elicit problem behavior. Continuing with our example with Jayden, we know that intricate fine motor tasks and lessons with a heavy reliance on language are difficult events for him. The team identified the following preventative strategies. First, modify art and craft activities so objects are easier to handle. For example, if beading macaroni or other such materials, use larger size pasta to make it easier for him to manipulate the materials. Second, allow for partial participation: When cutting items, he cuts the larger pieces in which the lines to cut have been clearly delineated with a yellow highlighter, while someone else cuts the smaller pieces. (He and a peer could work out a deal in which one cuts all of the smaller pieces while the other cuts the larger pieces so both children benefit.) Third, insert page fluffers into books he reads often, making it easier for him to turn pages one at a time. A page fluffer is an object attached to the page to provide an extra space between pages. Fourth, at circle time when the children are listening to a story, provide Jayden with a modified copy of the book to include pictures that depict the concepts and vocabulary presented in the story. Provide adult assistance during this time to give him support and direct instruction. Fifth, at circle time when he is listening to instructions, provide pictures that portray

Hypotheses

Hypothesis 1: During large group activities like circle time, Jayden will scream, cry, and get out of his seat in order to escape the activity.

Hypothesis 2: When working on tasks that require intricate fine motor skills, Jayden will tear or break materials in order to avoid the task.

Hypothesis 3: When completing multistep tasks and unsure of what to do, Jayden will scream and/or break materials in order to get assistance.

Positive behavior support plan

Preventive strategies	Skill building/replacement behaviors	Consequence strategies
1. Modify art and craft activities so objects are easier to handle. 2. Allow partial participation, e.g., bold/highlight large areas to cut, adult/peer cuts smaller pieces. 3. Insert page fluffers in favorite books. 4. Provide modified copy of book read during circle time; provide adult support. 5. Provide pictorial directions for center activities. 6. Consult with OT regarding fine motor skills.	1. Teach Jayden to ask for help when frustrated or unsure of what to do; provide a "help card" as a concrete/visual cue. 2. Teach Jayden how to use pictorial step-by-step instructions to problem solve when unsure what to do. 3. Provide direct/systematic instruction to improve receptive language.	1. Provide specific praise when he asks for help. 2. Provide assistance when he asks for help. 3. Provide corrective feedback when he engages in challenging behaviors.

Figure 8.5. Summary of positive behavior support plan for Jayden. Key: fluffer, an object attached to the page to provide an extra space between pages; OT, occupational therapy.

the activities in each center. Provide adult assistance during this time to give Jayden support and direct instruction. Sixth and finally, provide pictorial step-by-step instructions when required to complete multistep tasks during centers. Pair Jayden with a peer who can provide assistance (show him what step is next and model the response). At home, the family will institute similar strategies, including presenting steps of activities in pictorial format for easier comprehension. The team also recommended consultation with an occupational therapist to discuss strategies to improve fine motor skills.

Skill-Building and Replacement Behaviors Once again the emphasis is on prevention by providing more intensive instruction to address language, social, and/or emotional delays and teaching alternative behaviors. With regard to skill building, the same procedures outlined in tier 2 apply here: specifically, providing direct instruction using systematic instructional techniques to teach communicative, social, and/or emotional skills. This can include teaching social-emotional skills such as turn-taking, initiating interactions with others, and self-regulation. The child may also need more intensive instruction to enhance expressive and receptive language and other fundamental cognitive skills (e.g., letter and number recognition, 1:1 correspondence, writing skill).

The teaching of replacement or alternative behaviors is specifically designed to address the function of the behavior by providing the child a different way of getting his or her needs met.

Continuing the example with Jayden, the function of his disruptive and destructive behaviors is to escape or avoid an activity because of frustration, confusion, or uncertainty of what to do. Thus, the replacement behaviors for Jayden will need to focus on this need. The team decided to work with Jayden to develop three skills: first, to ask for help (peer or adult); second, to follow step-by-step pictorial instructions; and third, to develop more effective vocabulary and language. Asking for help addresses the desire to escape the frustration of difficult tasks or the uncertainty of what to do. Following pictorial instructions serves as a problem-solving guide; when unsure of what to do he can refer to his individualized instructions. Although Jayden has some oral language, the team decided to provide Jayden with a concrete referent in the form of an "I need help" card. This is done for two reasons. First, a help card serves as a visual cue for Jayden to remind him that he can use the card when frustrated. Second, because he has difficulty accessing language, he is not reliant on verbal communication to ask for help.

The use of pictorial step-by-step instruction addresses Jayden's difficulty with multistep tasks. Learning to follow pictorial instructions will alleviate the uncertainty of not knowing what to do. Furthermore, learning to follow written/pictorial instructions is a lifelong skill that all children need to master and one that will help him throughout his school and adult career. Finally, concerning skill building, Jayden is to receive direct instruction during circle time to improve vocabulary and receptive language skills. Jayden's family note that he also has difficulty with some of the routines at home. They will also use more picture cards at home to help Jayden be more independent and experience less frustration.

Consequence Strategies   Strategies under this category include use of positive reinforcement to support and strengthen new behaviors as well as corrective measures when problem behaviors occur. Providing specific praise is a universal strategy that is employed in all tiers of support. Specific praise means explicitly explaining what the child did well: for example, "Thanks for waiting and asking for a turn," "I like how you shared the toy," and "Great, you followed directions and cleaned your table." Generic praise, on the other hand, is vague (e.g., "nice job" or "good work"). In addition to providing praise, some children may require more systematic reinforcement systems that are more concrete in nature: For example, if-then systems, in which the child sees that he or she can read a book after he or she has completed a specified activity, can be done in a number of ways. For example, the child has a card with four boxes; when all four boxes are filled the child gains access to the reinforcer.

For Jayden, the team identified the following strategies: 1) provide specific praise when he asks for assistance, 2) provide help when he asks for it, 3) provide specific praise when he uses his pictorial instructions to problem solve/complete a task, and 4) provide corrective feedback when challenging behaviors occur (review emotions and possible solutions, encourage him to identify and act on an alternative solution). Jayden's family will use these strategies at home as well.

Additional Specialized Strategies at the Tier 3 Level: Discrete Trial and Pivotal Response Training   Discrete Trial Training (DTT) and Pivotal Response Training (PRT) are specialized approaches that have been demonstrated to teach a variety of social, language, communicative, and play skills to children with autism (as discussed in Chapter 7) and other developmental disabilities (Koegel & Koegel, 2006; Jones, Carr, & Feeley, 2006; Rogers & Vismara, 2008; Stahmer, Intersoll, & Carter, 2003). Like positive behavior support, these strategies are also based on Applied Behavioral Analysis (ABA) and can be used as a stand-alone intervention or in conjunction with tier 3 interventions based on functional behavior assessments, as described earlier.

Discrete Trial Training   DTT is a systematic approach to teaching discrete skills and behaviors; for example, discriminating among colors, identifying objects either verbally or through gestures (pointing), and classifying items (Rogers & Vismara, 2008; Smith, 2001). DTT incorporates many of the components of systematic instruction, for example, clearly defining the target response, prompting and shaping behavior, and reinforcing correct responses. However, DTT is often presented in a more structured format that typically consists of 5 steps: 1) presenting the discriminative stimulus (S^d), 2) prompting or cueing to promote a correct response, 3) noting the child's response, 4) providing a consequence (positive reinforcement or corrective feedback), and 5) observing intertrial interval or wait time before the next instruction (Smith, 2001). Over time, step 2 (prompt/cue) is faded so the child is responding independently to the initial instruction or S^d, reducing the sequence to 4 steps.

In most descriptions of DTT, this strategy is used to teach a discrete skill in a mass practice trial format in which the child is asked to perform a given task several times in a row. An advantage of DTT is that instruction is well planned and provides the opportunity for repetition and practice, important components of learning (Westling & Fox, 2009). DTT can be used to teach important skills young children need to learn, such as behavioral expectations, routines, emotions, and self-regulation. For example, after reading a book on emotions, the child may be engaged in 5–10 minutes of intensive training in which he or she is repeatedly asked to identify the different emotions depicted in pictures displaying facial expressions. The repetition and relative fast pace of the instruction allows for multiple opportunities to make basic discriminations and to label the emotion. Similarly, a young child can be asked to demonstrate the routine of "clean up" several times within a 5-minute period. While the other children are cleaning up, the target child can be asked to engage in one explicit task—specifically, putting the blocks in the basket. The adult dumps the blocks out of a basket and gives the direction "clean up." The child responds by putting the blocks back in the basket. This routine is repeated several times in a row to provide multiple opportunities for responding.

Despite these advantages, the primary disadvantage of DDT is that instruction is teacher-directed and often done in isolation—meaning not in response to the natural cues of the environment. In the examples just cited, the child may learn to correctly label emotions as depicted in pictures but may not generalize this skill when looking at the facial expressions of peers or adults within the natural context of playing, talking, and sharing. Furthermore, simply labeling an emotion is not enough. The goal of instruction when teaching emotions to young children is for the child to identify his or her own emotions within the context in which the emotions are occurring. For example, when Graciela cannot find a blue bead, we want her to understand she is frustrated and that she needs to act on this emotion in an appropriate way—in this case, to ask for help or ask a friend for a blue bead. Similarly, for cleanup, after given the general instruction that it is time to clean up, we want children to put items away when they see an item on a table or the floor (the natural cue) versus when repeatedly given the verbal cue to "clean up."

Pivotal Response Training   In contrast, PRT is a naturalistic approach to teaching social, language, play, and communication skills (Koegel & Koegel, 2006) within typical routines. PRT focuses on teaching four "pivotal" skills that, when learned, result in improvements across a wider range of behaviors and skills. The four pivotal skills are 1) motivation, 2) responding to multicues, 3) self-management, and 4) self-initiation (Koegel and Koegel, 2006). Specifically, when a child's motivation to learn, to play, or to engage in social interactions is increased, the child is more likely to demonstrate overall improvements in a number of areas (e.g., language, joint attention, social skills, play skills). This same principle applies to learning the other pivotal skills as well: specifically, responding to multiple cues (e.g., the blue pen, the orange ball), using self-management systems that enable the child to self-regulate his or her behavior, and initiating social interactions with others (Harjusola-Webb & Hess-Robbins, 2012; Jones et al., 2006; Smith et al., 2010; Weiss & Harris, 2001).

PRT is done within the context of the natural setting; for example, when the child is playing with a toy during free time or when completing a cutting-and-pasting activity during centers. The primary strategy is to follow the child's lead while encouraging the child to engage in the target behavior—whether the target skill is to label an item, initiate an interaction, engage in joint attention, or share a toy with a peer. The components of PRT are 1) providing choice, 2) giving clear instructions, 3) reinforcing attempts, 4) using natural reinforcers, and 5) interspersing maintenance tasks with skills the child is just learning.

Because of the naturalistic nature of this intervention, PRT can be easily infused within typical routines. Continuing with the example of teaching emotions, this skill can be taught within the context of play. The child is playing with a toy doll and toy dog. Capitalizing on the child's interest, the adult talks to the child about the doll and dog. The adult then hides the dog under a box, pretends to cry, and says, "I can't find my pet dog!" After finding the dog the adult says with a big smile on her face, "I found my dog!" and then asks the child, "Am I happy or sad?" The adult may need to prompt the response by saying "I am happy!" to encourage the child to respond. Any attempt to describe the emotion (smiles, says "hap") is reinforced (e.g., the adults smiles and tickles the child to show her happiness). Similarly, the child can be taught to respond to the request "clean up" by giving him or her a choice: "Do you want to clean up the blocks or the paints?" Any attempt to respond is immediately reinforced: "Thanks for cleaning up. Now we can go to recess!"

CONCLUSION

The early childhood years are a time of tremendous growth as children learn about themselves, others, and the ever-changing world around them. Children need guidance and support as they navigate different environments, situations, and experiences. The level of support will vary by child, with some requiring moderate levels of assistance while a few will need more intensive intervention. The pyramid model discussed in this chapter provides a comprehensive approach designed to meet the needs of all children. At the core of this model are two primary interventions, providing 1) a nurturing and responsive setting and 2) a warm and positive classroom environment. Together, these strategies focus on creating a place where children feel safe to explore and have new experiences. Sometimes the child will succeed and other times he or she will fail. The adult's role in this process is to encourage, praise, teach, shape, and guide children through these experiences and help them to celebrate their successes and problem solve and persist when they are less successful.

While the vast majority of children will flourish and grow under such conditions, there will be children who will need additional help. Tier 2 of this model is designed to provide more assistance as needed. The RTI model serves as the conceptual framework in which early screening is done to identify children at risk of developing challenging, counterproductive behaviors. Intervention begins immediately, and ongoing outcome data is collected to evaluate the child's response to the intervention. Tier 2 strategies are often an extension of the interventions outlined in tier 1 but executed in a more systematic manner. Additional instruction in social skills such as turn-taking, sharing, initiating interactions, conflict resolution, or other important social skills may be needed. Finally, for children who display serious and persistent challenging behaviors, tier 3 interventions are needed. Interventions at this level are comprehensive and are built from functional behavioral assessment data. Throughout this process, teachers, family members, related service staff, administrators, and other members of the team work together to design behavior support plans, implement the resulting interventions in their respective settings, problem solve, and most importantly, come together to share successes. Specialized interventions such as Discrete Trial Training or Pivotal Response Training may be used in conjunction with the comprehensive support plan developed from assessment.

ADDITIONAL RESOURCES

ABC analysis chart: http://www.kipbs.org/new_kipbs/fsi/files/ABC%20Analysis.pdf
Discrete Trial Training (DTT) materials: http://autismpdc.fpg.unc.edu/content/discrete-trial-training-0
Functional behavioral assessment interview form: http://www.kipbs.org/new_kipbs/fsi/files/Functional%20Assessment%20Interview.pdf
Page fluffers: http://www.cde.state.ca.us/cdesped/download/pdf/db-PgFluffersFS.pdf
Pivotal Response Training (PRT): http://www.koegelautism.com/
Scatter plots: http://www.kipbs.org/new_kipbs/fsi/files/scatterplot-abc%20analysis.pdf

REFERENCES

Algozzine, B., Daunic, A.P., & Smith, S.W. (2010). *Preventing problem behaviors: School-wide programs and classroom practices* (2nd ed.). Thousand Oaks, CA: Corwin Press.

Berk, L. (2007). *Infants, children, and adolescents* (6th ed.). Needham Heights, MA: Allyn and Bacon.

Blair, K.S.C., Fox, L., & Lentini, R. (2010). Use of positive behavior support to address the challenging behavior of young children within a community early childhood program. *Topics in Early Childhood Special Education, 30*(2), 68–79.

Blair, K.S.C, Lee, I.S., Cho, S.J., & Dunlap, G. (2011). Positive behavior support through family-school collaboration for young children with autism. *Topics in Early Childhood Special Education*, *31*(1), 22–36.

Buhs, E.S., & Ladd, G.W. (2001). Peer rejection as an antecedent of young children's school adjustment: An examination of mediating processes. *Developmental Psychology*, *37*, 550–560.

Carr, E.G., Dunlap, G., Horner, R., Koegel, . . . Fox, L. (2002). Positive behavior support: Evolution of an applied science. *Journal of Positive Behavior Interventions*, *4*, 4–16.

Carter, D.R., Van Norman, R.K., & Treadwell, C. (2011). Program-wide positive behavior support in preschool: Lessons for getting started. *Early Childhood Education Journal*, *38*, 349–355.

Center on Social and Emotional Foundations for Early Learning at Vanderbilt University. (2003). *Pyramid model for promoting social and emotional competence in infants and young children*. Nashville, TN: Author.

Clunies-Ross, R., Little, E., & Kienhuis, M. (2008). Self-reported and actual use of proactive and reactive classroom management strategies and their relationship with teacher stress and student behavior. *Educational Psychology*, *28*(6), 693–710.

Dominguez, X., Vitiello, V.E., Fuccillo, J.M., Greenfield, D.B., & Bulotsky-Shearer, R.J. (2011). The role of context in preschool learning: A multilevel examination of the contribution of context: Specific problem behaviors and classroom process quality to low-income children's approaches to learning. *Journal of School Psychology*, *49*, 175–195.

Downing, J.E., & Peckham-Hardin, K.D. (2001). Daily schedules: A helpful learning tool. *TEACHING Exceptional Children*, *33*(3), 88–90.

Dunlap, G., Strain, P.S., Fox, L., Carta, J.J, Conroy, M., Smith, B.J., … Sowell, C. (2006). Prevention and intervention with young children and challenging behavior: Perspectives regarding current knowledge. *Behavioral Disorders*, *32*(1), 29–45.

Fox, L., Carta, J., Dunlap, G., Strain, P., & Hemmeter, M.L. (2010). Response to intervention and the pyramid model. *Infants and Young Children*, *23*, 3–14.

Fox, L., Dunlap, G., Hemmeter, M.L., Joseph, G.E., & Strain, P.S. (2003). The teaching pyramid: A model for supporting social competence and preventing challenging behavior in young children. *Young Children*, *58*, 48–52.

Fox, L, Vaughn, B., Wyatte, M.L., & Dunlap, G. (2002). "We can't expect other people to understand": Family perspectives on problem behavior. *Exceptional Children*, *68*(4), 437–450.

Frey, A.J., Park, K.L, Browne-Ferrigno, T., & Korfhage, T.L. (2010). The social validity of program-wide behavior support. *Journal of Positive Behavior Interventions*, *12*(4), 222–235.

Gilliam, W.S. (2005). Prekindergarteners left behind: Expulsion rates in state prekindergarten systems. New Haven: Yale University Child Study Center. Retrieved from http://info. med.yale.edu/chldstdy

Harjusola-Webb, S.M., & Hess-Robbins, S. (2012). The effects of teacher-implemented naturalistic intervention on communication of preschoolers with autism. *Topics in Early Childhood Special Education*, *32*(2), 99–110.

Hemmeter, M.L., Fox, L., Jack, S., Broyles, L, & Doubet, S. (2007). A program-wide model of positive behavior support in an early childhood setting. *Journal of Early Intervention*, *29*, 337–355.

Hemmeter, M.L., Ostrosky, M., Artman, K., & Kinder, K. (2008). Moving right along: Planning transitions to prevent challenging behaviors. *Young Children*, *63*(3), 18–25.

Hendrickson, J.M., Gable, R.A., Conroy, M.A., Fox, J., & Smith, C. (1999). Behavioral problems in school: Ways to encourage functional behavior assessment (FBA) of discipline-evoking behavior of students with emotional and/or behavioral disorders. *Education and Treatment of Children*, *22*, 280–290.

Horner, R.H., & Sugai, G. (2000). School-wide behavior support: An emerging initiative. *Journal of Positive Behavior Interventions*, *2*, 231–233.

Jones, E.A., Carr, E.G., & Feeley, K.M. (2006). Multiple effects of joint attention intervention for children with autism. *Behavior Modification*, *30*(6), 782–834.

Joseph, G.E., & Strain, P.S. (2003). Enhancing emotional vocabulary in young children. *Young Exceptional Children*, *6*(4), 18–26.

Koegel, R.L., & Koegel, L.K. (2006). *Pivotal response treatments for autism.* Baltimore, MD: Paul H. Brookes Publishing Co.

National Center on Response-to-Intervention. (n.d.). Retrieved from http://www.rti4 success.org

O'Neill, R.E., Horner, R.H., Albin, R.W., Sprague, J.R., Storey, K., & Newton, J.S. (1997). *Functional assessment and program development for problem behavior: A practical handbook.* Pacific Grove, CA: Brooks/Cole Publishing.

Powell, D., Dunlap, G., & Fox, L. (2006). Prevention and intervention for the challenging behaviors of toddlers and preschoolers. *Infants and Young Children, 19,* 25–35.

Quesenberry, A.C., Hemmeter, M.L., & Ostrosky, M.M. (2011). Addressing challenging behaviors in Head Start: A closer look at program policies and procedures. *Topics in Early Childhood Special Education, 30*(4), 209–220.

Raver, C.C. & Knitzer, J. (2002). *Ready to enter: What research tells policymakers about strategies to promote social and emotional school readiness among three- and four-year-old children.* New York, NY: National Center for Children in Poverty.

Rogers, S., & Vismara, L. (2008). Evidence-based comprehensive treatments for early autism. *Journal of Clinical Childhood and Adolescent Psychology, 37,* 8–38.

Smith, B.J., & Fox, L. (2003). *Systems of service delivery: A synthesis of evidence relevant to young children at risk of or who have challenging behavior.* Tampa, FL: Center for Evidence-Based Practice: Young Children with Challenging Behavior, University of South Florida.

Smith, I.M., Koegel, R.L., Doegel, L.K., Opendem, D.A., Fossum, K.L., & Bryson, S.E. (2010). Effectiveness of a novel community-based early intervention model for children with autism spectrum disorder. *American Journal on Intellectual and Developmental Disorders, 115*(6), 504–523.

Smith, T. (2001). Discrete trial training in the treatment of autism. *Focus on Autism and other Developmental Disorders, 16,* 86–92.

Sprague, J., Cook, C.R., Wright, D.B., & Sadler, C. (2008). *RTI and behavior: A guide to integrating behavioral and academic supports.* Horsham, PA: LRP Publications.

Stahmer, A.C., Ingersoll, B., & Carter, C. (2003). Behavioral approaches to promoting play. *Autism, 7*(4), 401–413.

Sugai, G., & Horner, R. (2006). A promising approach for expanding and sustaining school-wide positive behavior support. *School Psychology Review, 35,* 245–259.

Webster-Stratton, C., & Hammond, M. (1998). Conduct problems and levels of social competence in Head Start children: Prevalence, pervasiveness, and associated risk factors. *Clinical Child and Family Psychology Review, 1,* 101–124.

Weiss, M.J., & Harris, S.L. (2001). Teaching social skills to people with autism. *Behavior Modification, 25*(5), 785–802.

Westling, D.L., & Fox, L., (2009). *Teaching students with severe disabilities* (4th ed.). Upper Saddle River, NJ: Merrill/Prentice Hall.

Preparing for Kindergarten

Adaptations and Supports Across the Curriculum

The pressure to ensure that preschoolers are ready for kindergarten has steadily increased since the inception of the No Child Left Behind Act of 2001 (PL 107-110). This final chapter addresses preparing the preschooler with disabilities to enter kindergarten. Readiness for some children may be less about meeting core standards in language arts and mathematics and more about social and emotional competence. This chapter examines expectations for preschoolers and offers strategies to support kindergarten readiness.

In 1990, a set of national education goals was defined by the president and governors of all 50 states. The first goals stated that all children in the United States would start school "ready to learn" by the year 2000. Following much discussion, early childhood groups, including the National Education Goals Panel (NEGP, 1990), conceptualized a shared definition of *readiness* so they could address and measure it. Five multifaceted dimensions were agreed on to guide assessment and programming:

- Physical well-being and motor development

- Social and emotional development

- Approaches toward learning

- Language development

- Cognition and general knowledge (Zaslow, Calkin, & Halle, 2000, pp. iv–v)

The Common Core State Standards Initiative has moved forward the process of writing standards in English language arts and mathematics for K–12 grades. The standards initiative, a state-led effort, includes members of the National Governors Association Center for Best Practices and the Council of Chief State School Officers and has been adopted by the majority of states. Many states have explored the feasibility of offering universal preschool to ensure that all children enter kindergarten "ready to learn" (NGACBP, 2010).

Gronlund (2006) examined the benefits and potential drawbacks of early learning standards. They reinforce the potential for learning, establish expectations for children, and create a framework for accountability. However, early standards may be misused as they result in cookie cutter–style curricula with a focus on assessment results, emphasize accountability over individuality (resulting in inappropriate expectations for young children), and create high expectations of teachers without accompanying training and support. Early learning standards for preschool children are correlated with elementary school standards in many states, but Gronlund cautioned that for children younger than kindergarten age the primary tasks "are to acquire and refine foundational skills that will help them successfully learn the content and information in the later grades" (p. 10). The Council of Chief State School Officers and Early Childhood Education Assessment Consortium (2007) defines early standards as "statements that describe expectations for the learning and development of young children across the domains of health and physical well-being, social and emotional well-being, approaches to learning, language development and symbol systems, and general knowledge about the world around them." Early learning standards serve to underscore the importance of the development of foundational skills in preschool children, hence the inclusion of social, emotional, and physical development plus approaches to learning. In a joint position statement in 2010, the National Association for the Education of Young Children (NAEYC) and the National Association of Early Childhood Specialists in State Departments of Education acknowledged that standards are important to teaching and learning success but cautioned against narrowing early childhood learning standards to only two content domains (literacy and mathematics) while ignoring social and emotional development (NAEYC & NAECS/SDE, 2010). Additionally, the joint statement does not recommend that standards be used to deny entry into kindergarten.

Despite concerns expressed by many individuals and organizations, preschool instruction has become more and more focused on preparing children for the academic demands of kindergarten (Demchak & Downing, 2008). Children with disabilities will frequently need specific adaptations, carefully planned instructional strategies, and accommodations to achieve prekindergarten academic or social goals. Some children will need significant curricular modifications. Understanding what academic skills children will need to demonstrate in kindergarten helps teachers at the preschool level determine what readiness skills should be introduced in the pre-K classroom.

Demchak and Downing (2008) suggested that teachers who are aware of the demands and changes in kindergarten should modify the content and methods of instruction in the year preceding kindergarten in order to enable both sending and receiving teachers to understand the adaptations and teaching strategies that might be needed for children as they make this transition. It is no surprise that families also report that they want outcomes for preschoolers transitioning into kindergarten linked to expected behavior in that next environment to assist in a smooth adjustment and engagement (Dogaru, Rosenkoetter, & Rouse, 2009).

Rosenkoetter et al. (2009), in a review of literature related to children in transition from preschool to kindergarten, reported that the match between the sending preschool and the receiving kindergarten, as well as the direct instruction in preschool of kindergarten readiness skills, resulted in more successful transitions and outcomes in kindergarten. So, while heeding the cautions of possible overemphasis on reading and math preparedness and less attention spent on developing adequate social and emotional skills, we review the specific skills related to core standards in language arts and math and suggest modifications and strategies for preschool children with special needs as they begin the transition into kindergarten.

THE TRANSITION PROCESS FROM PRESCHOOL TO KINDERGARTEN

While typical children move from preschool to kindergarten without incident every year, the transition process for children with disabilities, if poorly planned, can result in a difficult transition into the kindergarten setting. Rosenkoetter et al. (2009) reviewed 50 studies on early childhood transitions and found a moderate to large amount of evidence for the following four findings:

1. High-quality childcare and developmentally appropriate classrooms lead to better social and academic expectations in elementary school.

2. Positive teacher-child relationships both before and after transitions are related to better cognitive outcomes.

3. Teachers and principals agree that good social skills are more important than academic skills as indicators for school readiness in young children.

4. Teaching the skills related to requirements in the next environment help with positive outcomes and adjustments for children.

Rosenkoetter et al. (2009) point out that for young children with special needs, the challenges and expectations of kindergarten entry are many:

- Do they follow classroom routines (standing in line, transitioning to activities)?

- Will they sit in chairs or on the floor for large group activities for up to 50 minutes?

- Do they follow multistep verbal directions and work independently in small groups?

- Will they socialize appropriately with peers and use words to communicate effectively?

- Are they able to care for themselves for toileting, dressing, and eating?

Rous and Hallam (1998) suggested that a child should not be expected to perform at a level for which he or she is not developmentally ready (e.g., working independently at a center for 10 minutes or following four-step directions). The teacher should assess how the child is *currently* performing and then plan *next steps* to move toward expected kindergarten behavior. Both early childhood education (ECE) and early childhood special education (ECSE) professionals in the preschool setting should be mindful of these skills and *directly teach them* during the last year of preschool. One school's transition planning practices are presented in the text box on next page. The following sections elaborate on specific steps to prepare preschoolers for the transition.

Planning Ahead for a Successful Transition

In our school district, administrators, school psychologists, and both regular and special education preschool teachers work with families, receiving schools (principals and kindergarten teachers), and other service providers to establish time lines and protocol for kindergarten transitions for preschoolers with disabilities. The process has been in practice for four years but continues to need revisions each year. Typically transitions begin in the early spring of the child's last year of preschool. Transition individualized education program meetings are scheduled and held at the child's school of residence.

When possible, kindergarten teachers are invited to observe the child in his or her preschool classroom. This often helps to reassure a teacher about the child's ability to follow routines, respond to adults and peers, and function in small and large group settings. Often, the first few days of kindergarten—with a new environment and different people and expectations—may heighten the anxiety of the child. The kindergarten teacher's first impressions may not be as positive as they might have been if she'd seen how well the child functioned in a familiar school setting last spring. Sometimes we run out of time before the end of the school year and we can't schedule classroom observations, but at least the receiving school personnel meet the parents and service providers before the new school year begins. If we can't schedule a teacher visit, we encourage the family to visit the new classroom and bring their child to meet the teacher during the school's open house, usually held in late spring. We also make transition books for children, taking photographs of their preschool class and teachers and their new school and teacher. Taking these books, written at the child's developmental level, home to read over the summer seem to help the child get ready, according to family reports.

We offer a range of options for kindergarten, ranging from special day classes for children with autism to special day classes for children with intellectual disabilities to regular kindergarten with supplementary supports and services. Over the past four years, we have found that preschoolers in our co-taught or blended preschools and those children who have received itinerant inclusion consultation have teachers who recommend regular kindergarten. In these classrooms, both the Head Start teachers and the early childhood special education teachers focus on teaching expected social behaviors as well as academic readiness skills during the last trimester before summer. The preschoolers who have attended more segregated special day classes and who have had few mainstreaming opportunities are typically recommended for kindergarten special day classes. Often, there are few differences in needs or disabilities in these groups of children, but their preschool experience seems to set the tone for transition discussion and placement.

—Special Education Teacher

SOCIAL AND EMOTIONAL READINESS

We cannot begin addressing academic standards without a discussion of social and emotional readiness for some children with disabilities. Hollingsworth (2005) summarized the concerns that we have observed in the inclusive classroom: the emphasis on academic preparation resulting in less attention paid to children's development in other domains, especially social skills. The expectations for children to sit longer, to attend to more involved, multistep teacher directions, to work independently in small groups and, generally, to behave like 5-year-olds when they are still in preschool contributes more pressure for the teacher working with preschoolers with special needs to prepare students not only for the academic demands of kindergarten but also for the emotional demands of this setting. The research review by Rosenkoetter et al. (2008) also reinforced the findings in several studies that teachers and principals view social skills as being more important for children's school readiness than academic skills. Children who do not have adequate social and behavioral skills when entering kindergarten have a more difficult time meeting academic expectations, and there is thus more frustration on the part of teachers, family members, and peers. The following skill sets are referenced in the Helpful Entry Level Skills Checklist developed by Byrd and Rous (1991) and are useful for assessing kindergarten readiness in young children:

- Following classroom rules

- Developing appropriate work behavior

- Using communication skills

- Having appropriate social and behavior skills

- Demonstrating ability to self-manage

The California Department of Education (Ong, 2010) suggested that three interrelated social strands—self, social interaction, and relationships—be addressed by teachers throughout the preschool experience. Children who feel proud and competent about themselves and their accomplishments, have opportunities to practice social interactions, and have the skills to relate to peers and adults in positive ways are more able and ready to learn academic skills as they move through preschool into kindergarten.

Chapter 6 addresses specific strategies to help teachers support the development of children with disabilities both emotionally and socially. Providing supportive environments and routines where children feel safe and organized is the first step toward preparing them for future learning. At the same time, expecting children to comply with classroom rules—with appropriate supports, accommodations, and modifications based on individual needs—should be emphasized as much as demonstrating achievements in academic standards. If young children are unable to meet social expectations in the kindergarten classroom, how will they meet the rigorous academic expectations? Deemphasizing the importance of learning these skills prior to kindergarten transitions will result in children having a more difficult time once they are in the kindergarten setting. The following vignette highlights the importance of addressing social and emotional goals as a child transitions into the kindergarten setting.

Chris

Chris has a diagnosis of autism. He enters kindergarten with basic academic readiness skills (e.g., identifies letters and colors, numbers to 20) but cannot work in small groups for more than three minutes at a time without adult prompts, struggles with fine motor skills like printing and drawing, has difficulty sitting in a large group setting for more than five minutes before beginning to yell loudly, and avoids transitions by running to the back of the classroom when peers line up to move inside or outside or from one center to another. Chris has difficulty expressing himself verbally and he talks very quickly and quietly and more to himself than others.

In preschool, Chris improved in his social and communication skills and tolerated sitting next to or lining up with peers and stayed in large and small group activities for up to 15 minutes at a time with adult verbal prompts. These achievements were met after several months in preschool and with much reinforcement and encouragement from his early childhood and special education teachers. Chris's transition into kindergarten has been difficult. His new teacher is welcoming but wary, especially because of his loud yelling behaviors when she is trying to teach the whole group of 28 children. She is concerned because he has also been hitting peers on the playground and becomes extremely agitated when she reprimands him for this behavior. His peers are beginning to avoid him.

Until Chris's social behaviors improve, he will make little progress in his academic goals. Although he needs help with his printing, he needs to be able to participate in the daily routine without multiple loud and distracting outbursts. The inclusion support team met to discuss Chris's school day and implement several strategies:

- They developed a picture schedule to give Chris a sense of the day and used it before every transition.

- They identified a quiet area in the back of the classroom where Chris could work with a classroom assistant—either previewing a book that would be read in large group later that day or doing some of the center work.

- The occupational therapist provided equipment and suggestions to help Chris with his writing (e.g., slant board, pencil grip, markers instead of crayons) and also talked to the team about helping Chris manage longer sitting periods by using a wiggle cushion to sit on and giving him sensory breaks throughout the longer group instruction periods by taking him outside the class for a walk or other motor activities.

- The assistant teacher was assigned to carefully observe Chris during recess periods and actively involve him in games with peers so that he didn't wander around and then hit children to get their attention. (The ECSE teacher postulated that this was the cause of the hitting behavior based on her observations.)

- The speech therapist offered suggestions for adults in the classroom to help Chris slow his rate of speech and use pictures to communicate his feelings and needs when they couldn't understand his words.

The inclusion specialist knew Chris would settle down once he began to understand the new set of expectations, but this was difficult to communicate to the

(continued)

(continued)

kindergarten teacher. After two weeks of implementing these strategies and concentrating more on Chris's social and emotional goals, the team began to see improvements. Once Chris began to adapt to the kindergarten routine, he sat for longer periods during centers and began completing more of the kindergarten academic work.

STRATEGIES TO SUPPORT
LANGUAGE ARTS AND EMERGING LITERACY SKILLS

Results of research on literacy skills in young children show the strong connection between learning critical emerging literacy skills during, and even before, the preschool years and becoming proficient readers in elementary school. Many children, especially those from low-income backgrounds, do not enter kindergarten with the prerequisite literacy skills necessary to learn how to read (Hawken, Johnston, & McDonnell, 2005).

Children with disabilities may have poor vocabulary development, which will make it more difficult for them to learn to read. Difficulty discerning sounds, words, and phrases has a huge impact on a child's ability to learn phonological awareness. For example, the ability to identify that *f* is the beginning sound in the word *fish* or understand that *cat* and *sat* are words that rhyme helps a child begin to understand how to put sounds together as he or she learns how to read. Not having this phonological awareness seriously hampers a child's ability to learn how to read during her kindergarten year.

The critical elements of emergent literacy are oral language (vocabulary, narrative skills, phonological awareness) and print awareness (McCathren & Allor, 2002). Literacy achievement in the preschool classroom is broken down into three main areas: reading, writing, and listening/speaking (Ong, 2010). Five domain elements are defined in the literacy knowledge and skills domain of the *Head Start Child Development and Early Learning Framework* (Head Start, 2010):

1. Book appreciation

2. Phonological awareness

3. Alphabet knowledge or print recognition

4. Print concepts and conventions: concepts about print and early decoding; identifying letter-sound relationships

5. Early writing

In slightly modified order these domains are used in the following sections to address both how and what typically developing children must learn and what modifications or accommodations should be considered for children with disabilities.

A multitude of strategies help children with disabilities increase both oral language and print awareness. Teachers using storybooks in a deliberate and planned manner to help emerging literacy skills in young children create enjoyable activities while effectively teaching children with short attention spans, poor vocabulary development, and lower cognitive skills than their typical peers. Previewing a story with a small group or on a one-to-one basis helps children become familiar with the characters and vocabulary used in the book. Using expansion, an adult builds on a child's one-word utterances about pictures in the story and expands to two words. Offering objects that represent two-dimensional pictures helps a child maintain interest in a story. Answering simple questions or discussing comments with more verbal children promotes maintenance of interest as the story is previewed. Reading aloud after prereading or previewing is done in a larger group with an adult modeling top-down and left-right reading while pointing to printed words in the story. Finally, children begin to recognize that sentences are made up of words and words are made up of sounds as teachers reference these points during story reading. Most important, these emerging literacy skills are built on children's interests and motivation.

Reading and Book Appreciation

A child begins to show an understanding of book knowledge and story appreciation when he or she

- Demonstrates interest in and looks at books

- Enjoys being read to

- Turns pages

- Recognizes front cover and orients book right side up

- Recognizes pictures

- Understands the beginning and end of books

- Understands that print in books represents language about the pictures

- Eventually understands story structure (beginning, middle, and end)

- Can listen to stories without pictures on every page

Book Appreciation Accommodations for the Child with Disabilities   Children with disabilities may need specific accommodations to begin to show an appreciation of books. For children with developmental delays and intellectual disabilities, using photographs of familiar people (e.g., family) and objects (e.g., favorite toys) while pairing them with the person or object can help children begin to make the connection between two-dimensional representations and real people or objects. Teacher-made simple 3–6 page family books (*My Family:* "This is Momma," "This is Papa," "Here is my dog") with laminated photographs for children to read at school and share at home are often more interesting than books with abstract illustrations or too many words.

Finding picture books with clear photos or simple illustrations of animals or people can be challenging (another reason to make personalized books). Using these types of books often and repeating the words and sounds as the book is "read" to a child is often very appealing and engaging for him. Lift-the-flap books or those with sound buttons encourage engagement as children physically manipulate the hidden picture or push the button to hear a related sound.

Children with visual impairments may need the addition of braille and/or large print materials to learn important preliteracy skills. They will benefit from a variety of modifications in the preschool setting to enhance their understanding of print and enhance book awareness. For a child with low vision, teachers need to enlarge words, pictures, and symbols; use bright and contrasting colors; arrange lighting to increase the visibility of pictures; and/or create noniconic symbols to mark environmental areas, cubbies, doors, and furniture. Some activities need to be simplified, and others need adult or peer intervention and support in addition to environmental modifications (Day, McDonnell, & Heathfield, 2002). The consultation and support of a teacher for the visually impaired is extremely important, especially for learning preliteracy skills. However, the ECE teacher can also begin to immediately use the following strategies:

- Use words and sounds as anticipatory cues or "symbols."

- Create books representing a child's own interests and experiences using tactile cues of actual objects/materials on each page of book and including braille symbols.

- Use recorded stories with interesting sound effects to teach appreciation of story structures.

- Encourage family members to tell or read bedtime stories as part of daily routines.

- Use favorite early childhood books with textures and sounds.

For the child who is deaf-blind, consider using familiar objects or tactile cues as "symbolic" anticipatory cues (e.g., plastic cup to hold as the story about snack time at school is read) and olfactory cues (e.g., smelling shampoo as a story about bath time is read).

The child with a severe motor disability will need to have pictures/photos incorporated into augmentative and alternative communication (AAC) training. Using computerized books, tablet readers, and e-readers as well as adding technology to support turning pages or finding favorite pictures are strategies that will help children learn to enjoy reading stories.

Children with autism may show more interest in books written about themselves. Illustrations and sentences should be kept at child's level of understanding and themes should be about scenarios that are meaningful to the child.

The nonverbal child can be taught to engage in looking at books and responding to questions and discussions by adapting dialogic reading strategies to allow the child to participate by using directed eye gaze, pointing, or other nonverbal responses (Zevenbergen & Whitehurst, 2003). The key elements of dialogic reading are presented in Figure 9.1. Dialogic reading also includes prompting strategies for developmentally young children. These include encouraging children to label pictures in the story, evaluating the child's response and suggesting alternatives if clearly incorrect, expanding the child's utterance, and encouraging the child to repeat the adult's expansion.

P.E.E.R

Prompt the child to label objects and talk about the story.

Evaluate the child's response; suggest alternatives if it is clearly incorrect.

Expand, by repeating the child's response and adding information.

Repeat, by having the child replicate the adult's expansion.

C.R.O.W.D

Completion prompts: "There was an old woman who lived in a _____."

Recall prompts: "Can you remember _____?"

Open-ended prompts: "Now you tell me something."

Wh prompts: "What/where/why are the _____?"

Distancing: Reference something outside the story. ("The old woman lives in a shoe, let's talk about places we live.")

Figure 9.1. Features of dialogic reading for preschool children. (*Source*: Zevenbergen & Whitehurst, 2003.)

Phonological Awareness

Children demonstrate the concept of phonological awareness when they have the skills to

- Understand spoken language
- Participate in familiar songs and rhymes
- Follow the beat/rhythm of music and chants
- Understand the concept of *listen* and recognize environmental sounds
- Recognize and produce animal sounds (e.g., moo, baa, oink, meow)
- Understand the concepts of a *word* and a *sound*
- Identify words that sound the same or different
- Segment/count the words in a short sentence
- Segment and blend compound words (e.g., backpack = back+pack and back+pack = backpack)
- Segment multisyllabic words into syllables (by clapping, etc.)
- Count the number of syllables in a multisyllabic word
- Segment and blend two-syllable words
- Complete familiar nursery rhymes
- Demonstrate understanding of the concept of *rhyme* (e.g., creates own rhyme)

1. Word awareness

2. Compound-word awareness

3. Syllable awareness

4. Rhyme awareness

5. Onset-rime awareness

6. Phoneme awareness

Figure 9.2. Developmental continuum of phonological awareness. (*Source*: Phillips, Clancy-Menchetti, & Lonigan, 2008.)

All children can develop these skills when preschool teachers include ample use of songs, nursery rhymes, books with repeated words, rhymes, and rhythms. When children are encouraged to clap to the beat of songs and rhymes and identify same and different sounding words during the daily routine at school, they become aware of the phonology of language. The development of this capacity is presented in Figure 9.2. Teachers can refer to and use words like *rhyme, word,* and *sound* often throughout the day to build awareness in preschoolers.

Phonological Awareness Accommodations for Children with Disabilities

For the child with speech and language disabilities, these skills can be very difficult to learn. If a child is having difficulty saying words or repeating sounds, it may be more important to use visuals than to rely on the child's ability to listen and discriminate sounds. As mentioned, for children having difficulty using spoken language to express themselves, very specific adult-directed teaching will be necessary. Speech-language pathologists can provide valuable information to teachers in this area and should be consulted. On a daily basis and in the classroom setting, using music and rhythm to encourage children to join in segmenting words (i.e., clapping out syllables), focusing on the sounds of names of peers or other high-interest words, and playing simple rhyming games with much repetition will set the stage for future growth as listening and speaking skills improve.

Print Concepts, Conventions, and Recognition

Children learning print concepts will

- Recognize print in everyday life (e.g., numbers, letters, their name, common words, and familiar logos and signs)

- Understand that print conveys meaning

- Understand conventions, such as that print moves from left to right and from top to bottom of a page

- Recognize words as a unit of print and understand that letters are grouped to form words

- Recognize the association between spoken or signed and written words

- Identify and name some letter sounds

Print Recognition Accommodations for the Child with Disabilities   To help preschoolers with disabilities learn to recognize print as meaningful, the following accommodations are suggested. For children with developmental delays and intellectual disabilities, teach salient environmental prints, such as McDonald's and stop signs. Use most-to-least prompting to teach discrimination of labels for a favorite food or toy. Teach children to recognize their own name labels on personal items (e.g., cubby, jacket, backpack). Start with larger photos and smaller print labels or names then gradually reduce the size of pictures and increase the size of words and names. Cover photos when asking children to identify and "read" the words; let the child see parts of the picture as prompts, if needed. Help the child with visual impairments identify his or her own chair or cubby with a braille label for her name or a specific texture symbol that will represent her name.

Children with autism respond well to visual schedules. Include printed words with pictures in picture schedules but gradually reduce the size of the pictures, making the words the more salient features. Focus on functional uses of print rather than simple automatic letter/word naming (e.g., provide opportunities to choose a favorite toy or snack by pairing a word card for the preferred item with a word card for the nonpreferred item).

Writing

Writing skills are demonstrated at the kindergarten level by children's knowledge of letters, sounds, and words used to write about people, objects, and experiences. Writing skills are also measured by use of oral and written English using appropriate conventions such as grammar and spelling (Ong, 2010). In the study of Head Start teachers, Hawken et al. (2005) found that, on a daily basis, the majority of teachers in the survey encouraged students to practice printing their names. Less often, children were encouraged to copy or print words or write in personal journals.

Alphabet Knowledge   Alphabet knowledge includes the names and sounds associated with letters. Children acquiring knowledge of the alphabet will

- Recognize that the letters of the alphabet are a special category of visual graphics that can be individually named

- Recognize that letters of the alphabet have distinct sounds associated with them

- Attend to the beginning letters and sounds in familiar words

- Identify letters and associate correct sounds with letters

Alphabet Knowledge Accommodations for the Child with Disabilities   To help preschoolers with disabilities learn to recognize letters in the alphabet and, eventually, words as meaningful symbols, the following accommodations are suggested. For children with developmental delays and intellectual disabilities, use small whiteboards to reinforce concepts of *word* and individual letters throughout the day. Encourage play with chalk, markers, whiteboard, paper, markers, or other writing media to practice letters. Avoid excessive rote repetition of alphabet; emphasize meaningful words like peers' or family names and favorite restaurant names or activities within the classroom (e.g., names of play areas).

For the child who is blind, spell the child's name frequently, out loud. Use hand-over-hand or hand-under-hand strategies to help him read the braille letters in his or her name; compare his or her name to another child's name printed in braille, focusing on the first letter of both names. Use key words when speaking to the child: *letter, alphabet, name, A, B,* and so on. Help the child explore patterns of braille dots.

For the child with high-functioning autism, print words on a small whiteboard (if he or she is reading) to foreshadow transitions (e.g., "Time to go outside," "Time to eat," etc.). For children not yet reading, use pictures from a daily picture schedule with words to predict "what comes next."

Early Writing (Name Writing, Invented Spelling)   When are young children "ready" to learn to write? Signs of readiness and emerging early writing skills are noted in the following observations of young children:

- Do children complete puzzles, hold crayons, color within the lines, print their first and last name?

- Do they draw recognizable pictures and use language to describe their illustrations?

- Are they able to print their names and other high-frequency words (e.g., Dolch words) by the end of preschool (fine motor/cognitive skills)?

- Can they recognize their printed name, the names of peers, and at least 20 sight words (commonly used words such as *I, like, the, see, you,* and color words, etc.)?

Children typically draw before they write. Baghban (2007) summarized children's drawing and writing development through age 7. Scribbles are the earliest prewriting skill that lets a child know that he or she can leave a mark on a surface. Typical toddlers react with delight when given tools that can make marks on paper or other surfaces. The cognitive awareness of producing something concrete based on one's actions is apparent when the young child scribbles, then stops to examine his or her work, then continues adding more marks. Children may scribble and label their drawing or may ask adults to tell them what they drew. When children begin to label their own drawings, they indicate a cognitive shift to abstract, representational actions: "I made a car." Typically, children draw people and other objects that are meaningful to them. By about 4 years of age, children are beginning to differentiate between drawings and writing. Drawings are helpful scaffolds as children begin to tell stories or write about their drawings. Children may confuse drawing with writing up to about age 7. For the child with special needs and possible intellectual delays, it is helpful to know the approximate stages of drawing in order to plan appropriate and meaningful goals:

- Children under 3 years old make random scribbles and may not differentiate what surfaces are appropriate for marking on. They begin to show an understanding that marks on paper and other surfaces carry meaning.

- Children ages 3–4 show more controlled scribbling, begin labeling their work or asking for others to tell them what they wrote, and start producing specific letters or objects if asked to do so.

- Children ages 4–6 print their names and show understanding of the alphabet, make different types of controlled marks in multiple directions to complete forms, and begin including letters in lines.

- Children ages 4–7 begin attaching sounds to letters and sounding out words to write.

     Children demonstrate writing readiness as they engage in

- Drawing lines, circles, crosses, and simple faces

- Drawing stick figures

- Pretending to write

- Writing their own name

- Copying letters

- Writing familiar names (e.g., "Mom")

- Using invented spelling

Writing Accommodations for Children with Disabilities

Teachers should provide opportunities such as easy, frequent access to art/graphic media and instruments (e.g., paints, brushes, markers, crayons) for all children and especially children with special needs on a daily basis at school. They can help children learn to intentionally use various media to make marks on surfaces and notice the effects (colors, texture, smell, etc.). Adults can draw objects for children to help them gain an understanding that real things can be represented with lines and shapes. Inviting children's requests ("What shall I draw?") and helping children draw faces, balls, Xs, and then encouraging them to label the drawings are all opportunities for developing early writing and communication skills.

For some children with disabilities, learning how to draw recognizable pictures may not evolve without guided practice from a teacher. A child may need to learn how to represent people by first being taught how to draw a circle then being verbally prompted to add eyes, nose, and mouth. As the child learns to represent faces, more body parts can be encouraged: hair, ears, tummy, arms, legs, hands, and fingers.

Children with motor disabilities will benefit from occupational or physical therapist consultation and possibly the use of equipment to help them hold writing instruments (e.g., using VELCRO® straps, hand grips, substituting easier drawing materials like markers instead of crayons that need more pressure to make marks). They may also need access to comfortable writing surfaces (e.g., slant boards).

Asking children to identify their work by making marks or letters for their names, attempting to draw pictures in journals, or adding their writing to group literacy activities with typical peers reinforces the importance of writing to communicate something about themselves, be it via ownership ("this is *my* work") or by communicating the beginning of a story ("my papa"). Over time, and when expected to on a regular daily basis, children with special needs will learn the importance and skill of writing.

LISTENING AND SPEAKING

Listening and speaking skills are measured by a child's ability to understand and follow directions, speak in complete sentences, and be able to use the English language to discuss information and experiences. Teaching preschoolers to use language to communicate their experiences with others, in addition to getting basic wants and needs met, includes the following:

- Language use and conventions: children use language to converse with others and to communicate wants, needs, and thoughts

- Learning and using a growing vocabulary: children learn to communicate, read, and understand what they are reading in subsequent years

- Understanding grammar: children comprehend what they hear in stories and put their thoughts and responses into sentences to begin to clearly express those thoughts (Ong, 2010)

English language learners simultaneously learning vocabulary and grammar in two languages may engage in a period of quiet observation in the classroom as the non-English speaking child observes and listens before beginning to use some English words mixed in with his or her first language before progressing to using grammatical morphemes and demonstrating a mastery of syntactic rules (Cook, Klein, & Chen, 2011). Vocabulary development will continue as the child uses and hears more language.

As teachers plan and prepare for daily lessons, awareness of speaking clearly, modeling accepted language styles and conventions, and teaching vocabulary can be embedded throughout all activities and across routines. Building both functional vocabulary and using specific vocabulary to teach children reading skills are extremely important. The prekindergartener needs to hear and understand literacy-related vocabulary including the names of letters, sounds that letters make, intentional use of words like *sentence, words, period, uppercase, lowercase, sounds*, and so on. Children entering kindergarten will be more prepared to engage in language arts curricula when they are familiar with this type of vocabulary.

The following vignette illustrates how a teacher might deliver an introductory lesson about the color blue. He models clear, concise language in sentences and talks about what he is writing. He employs functional and specific vocabulary and actions to highlight key words, which help both the typically developing preschoolers and the child with autism.

Mr. Ng

Mr. Ng is helping his 4-year-old students learn about the color blue. He asks the children to give him sentences using the word blue. He models a sentence for them, saying, "I am wearing a blue shirt." He prints the words on the whiteboard, using a blue marker to write the word blue and writing each word as he says it. He tells the children that he used an uppercase I for the first word and ended with a period. Mr. Ng uses this vocabulary as he writes down students' sentences. He recasts single words and phrases, volunteered by some children, into short but complete sentences and then asks the children to repeat the sentences with him. Mr. Ng also slowly sounds out words as he writes to illustrate that he is thinking about the sounds of each letter as they are printed so that he can make a word. He asks the children to print their names after their sentences to identify who said it, since the children are recognizing many names of peers in the class, if not other words.

Jamie, a child with autism, likes blue toys but doesn't say anything during this period. Mr. Ng asks Jamie's peers what blue toy he likes best. When they respond with "Legos" he asks one peer to give Jamie a blue Lego block and then writes a simple sentence on the board, but this time drawing a picture of the Lego block in blue marker instead of just writing the word. He encourages Jamie to point to the picture as Mr. Ng and some of the peers read the sentence. Later, Jamie is observed returning to the whiteboard and looking at the words printed in blue ink.

STRATEGIES TO SUPPORT DEVELOPING MATH SKILLS

Children learn mathematical concepts through planned hands-on activities embedded into daily routines. The National Council of Teachers of Mathematics and the NAEYC adopted a joint position statement in 2002 (updated in 2010). The collaborative statement emphasizes the need for high quality education for young children (3–6 years old) in mathematics in order to prepare them for proficiency in this area as they move into elementary school. The statement includes the following 10 research-based recommendations to achieve the goal of high quality mathematics education for young children (NAEYC & NCTM, 2010). Teachers and other key professionals should do the following:

1. Enhance children's natural interest in mathematics and their disposition to use it to make sense of their physical and social worlds.

2. Build on children's experience and knowledge, including their family, linguistic, cultural, and community backgrounds; their individual approaches to learning; and their informal knowledge.

3. Base mathematics curriculum and teaching practices on knowledge of young children's cognitive, linguistic, physical, and social-emotional development.

4. Use curriculum and teaching practices that strengthen children's problem-solving and reasoning processes as well as representing, communicating, and connecting mathematical ideas.

5. Ensure that the curriculum is coherent and compatible with known relationships and sequences of important mathematical ideas.

6. Provide for children's deep and sustained interaction with key mathematical ideas.

7. Integrate mathematics with other activities and other activities with mathematics.

8. Provide ample time, materials, and teacher support for children to engage in play in which they explore and manipulate mathematical ideas with interest.

9. Actively introduce mathematical concepts, methods, and language through a range of appropriate experiences and teaching strategies.

10. Support children's learning by thoughtfully and continually assessing all children's mathematical knowledge, skills, and strategies.

The position statement acknowledges the cognitive and emotional variability in the development of young children and stresses the need to deemphasize specific timetables for reaching defined skills or learning objectives. Rather, teachers need to know and understand that there is a developmental continuum for some mathematical topics with concepts and skills building on others, and children will achieve these skills as they become developmentally ready. Copley (2010) emphasized that young children have different ways to make sense of mathematical situations. They neither follow the same developmental sequence nor represent or solve problems in the same way, although there are general learning trajectories that teachers can use. The greater emphasis is on the *adult's understanding* of the developmental continuum and providing good teaching practices to meet individual children's learning styles and needs within the context of a mathematics curriculum.

It is important to know what constitutes early mathematics, especially as teachers plan adaptations for the child with disabilities in the inclusive preschool classroom (Eisenhauer & Feikes, 2009). Numbers, geometry, and measurement are central concepts in preschool curricula. However, data analysis and algebra (pattern recognition) can also be introduced and taught through play materials, games, and other early childhood toys such as puzzles and blocks. High-quality instruction of mathematical concepts during preschool helps children as they transition into more formal instruction in elementary school.

Preschool and kindergarten mathematics are related in the sense that preschool skills build a base for achieving kindergarten standards. Mathematics standards for kindergarteners include five areas:

1. Number sense and operations: understanding the relationship between numbers and quantity, simple addition and subtraction, and beginning understanding of estimation

2. Algebra and functions: understanding sorting and classification of a variety of objects

3. Measurement and geometry: understanding concepts of time and dimension (length, weight, capacity)

4. Statistics, data analysis, and probability: understanding simple patterning and collecting information about everyday objects

5. Mathematical reasoning: understanding how to solve problems and explain one's own thought processes

Teaching math to kindergarteners should be organized and systematic while also incidental and informal at times (Sarama & Clements, 2006). Helping children make connections between informal knowledge and explicit mathematical knowledge by encouraging children's play and using appropriate technology in the preschool setting will enhance a kindergartener's mathematical knowledge. During the preschool years, the following five areas are addressed as they build broad mathematical understanding for young children (Notari-Syverson & Sadler, 2008) prior to kindergarten: numbers and operations, geometry and spatial sense, measurement, algebra, and data analysis.

Numbers and Operations

Number concepts, including one-to-one correspondence, begin as preschoolers play with blocks and small manipulatives. Learning opportunities for one-to-one correspondence and counting occur across daily activities such as setting tables for mealtimes: One milk carton goes in front of each chair. How many chairs are at this table? How many spoons will we need? More math opportunities are embedded during circle time or small group periods by asking a child to count the number of peers or distribute materials such as bean bags or name tags to each child in the group. Preschoolers typically count to at least 8, add or subtract by 1, and match objects in one-to-one correspondence.

Geometry and Spatial Sense

The concepts of geometry are explored through manipulation of puzzles pieces and geometric shapes (two- and three-dimensional objects) into their correct slots by young children. Kindergarteners begin comparing lines, corners, and dimensions of shapes. Children begin identifying everyday objects by their shapes (the tire is round, but the paper is square). Block play provides opportunities to develop knowledge about spatial relationships that can be expanded to mapping classroom space and neighborhoods (how far, where, which way). Preschoolers begin to understand that maps represent space.

Measurement

Learning about measurement occurs as preschoolers play with water, sand, and other media using different-sized containers and comparing amounts they hold and as they make observations about time using clocks and temperature using thermometers. Measurement is a real-life task accomplished by mathematical knowledge. Comparing sizes and volume and measuring, using conventional (rulers, scales) and unconventional (hands, paperclips) units of measurement, all contribute to a child's understanding of the physical properties of objects.

Algebra

Algebraic concepts include understanding patterns (repetition of sequences of colors, shapes), equality (adding objects to each side of a scale to make them the same), and change (observing and measuring changes in plants as they grow).

Data Analysis

Analyzing data at the preschool level includes sorting and categorizing objects in different ways: "All the blue shapes go here and the red ones go there; now let's put all the circles in this pile and all the squares over there." Counting and representing results by graphing them ("Who likes green apples? How many children like red apples?") teaches representation of results of data collection.

Strategies for teaching the five areas described in the preceding paragraphs are summarized in Table 9.1.

Studies using different approaches to teach mathematical skills to children with disabilities indicate that longer, intensive instruction on a daily basis and across environments (home and school) results in better retention of math concepts than short, pull-out interventions. Using intentional teaching approaches across daily activities and routines, paired with ongoing assessment, yield the best and most long-lasting results (Notari-Syverson & Sadler, 2008). The use of scaffolding (supporting a child as he learns new skills), curriculum modifications (adjusting the curriculum to help a child with special needs participate and engage in problem solving at his level), and naturalistic teaching (following the child's lead, modeling, prompting) are deliberate approaches that can be used by teachers in the ECE environment. Adults can also encourage problem solving and logical reasoning by asking children to help in these instances. Demonstrating how symbols represent numbers and different ways of representing the world around them helps young children become familiar with mathematical reasoning and concept representation. A summary of teaching strategies for preschool mathematics is presented in Table 9.2.

A WORD ON EARLY SCIENCE EDUCATION

There is an increasing emphasis in the United States on the importance of science education, within the broader context of science, technology, engineering, and math (STEM) education. According to Katz (2010), early science education can be readily addressed through a project approach. The fundamental goals of science education include asking questions (*inquiry*), making predictions (*hypotheses*), and gathering information (*data collection*) to test the predictions. Within this context, young children learn that the basic academic skills of literacy and math and the cognitive skills of careful *observation, categorization*, and *comparison* have a purpose and "can be used in the service of children's intellectual pursuits" (Katz, 2010, p. 2). All young children, regardless of their background or disability, have an innate desire to explore and learn about their world. Katz cautions that early science goals should not be turned into "discrete bits of disembedded information" (2010, p. 2).

Science exploration in ECE could serve as an exciting and motivating context for learning that can support the intellectual development of every learner. This

Table 9.1. Intentional teaching strategies for early mathematical concepts

Instructional strategy	Numbers and operations	Geometry: shapes, space	Measurement	Algebra: patterns, equality, change	Data analysis: organizing and representing information
Ask guiding questions	"Enough for everyone?" "How many more?"	"How can we make a map of our block/town?"	"How can we decide who's tallest and who's shortest?"	"What's different?" "What made it change?"	"How do we know that more children like red apples?"
Explain rules	"Say numbers in the same order."	"Maps have different colors to show roads and buildings."	"We need to start at the zero when we measure with a ruler."	"Think about what might happen next in this pattern."	"Let's put all the things that go together in this dish."
Make more concrete (visuals/manipulatives)	Use fingers to represent numbers of objects.	Use different lengths of wood for child to create shapes.	Use length of string or ribbon to show students' heights on wall.	Create simple patterns using music and body movements.	Use blocks to represent votes, then build towers or lines for comparison.
Simplify/break tasks into smaller steps	Rote counting before one-to-one correspondence	Teach vocabulary related to shapes like open, curved, straight.	Start with measuring small items using numbers child is familiar with.	Start with simple ABAB patterns.	Start with comparing concrete, visual objects: "How many children are wearing pants?"
Adapt/modify materials	Slide manipulatives off paper as child counts.	Use nonskid mats for child to use when making designs with shapes.	Use cubes as units of measure instead of ruler.	Use pattern objects that are easy to grasp and manipulate.	Use large graph with big spaces to place actual objects being counted.
Child preference	Do counting activity with child-chosen objects.	Make/label shapes using food during meals.	Have children measure heads to make paper crowns.	Encourage child to choose sets of objects to make patterns.	Use child interests to collect data in the classroom.
Model	Show set of objects; have child take same amount.	Use different sizes/types of shapes when teaching.	Use different units of measure to show length: "The paper is as long as my arm."	Use completed models of patterns for children to replicate.	Show examples of different kinds of graphs.
Explicit prompts	Teach child to recount items before handing them to adult.	Teach songs about shapes; hum if child needs help to describe attributes.	Provide directions for using measuring tools.	Label objects in the pattern several times, then stop and wait for child to respond (dog, car, dog, etc.).	Use visual and verbal cues for children as they group objects into sets.

Source: Adapted from Notari-Syverson, A., & Sadler, F.H. *Young exceptional children* (Vol. 11, Issue 3), pp. 2–16, copyright © 2008 by SAGE Publications. Reprinted by Permission of SAGE Publications.

Table 9.2. Teaching strategies for preschool mathematics

Content area	Examples of typical knowledge and skills		Sample teaching strategies
	From Age 3 ———▶ Age 6		
Number and operation	Counts a collection of 1–4 items and begins to understand that the last counting word tells "how many."	Counts and produces (counts out) collections up to 100 using groups of 10.	Models counting of small collections and guides children's counting in every-day situations, emphasizing that we use one counting word for each object: ♡ ♡ ♡ "one ... two ... three ..." Models counting by 10s while making groups of 10s (e.g., 10, 20, 30 ... or 14, 24, 34 ...).
			Gives children a brief glimpse (a couple of seconds) of a small collection of items and asks how many there are.
	Quickly "sees" and labels collections of 1–3 with a number.	Quickly "sees" and labels with the correct number "patterned" collections (e.g., dominoes) and unpatterned collections of up to about 6 items.	
	Adds and subtracts nonverbally when numbers are very low. For example, when one ball and then another are put into the box, expects the box to contain two balls.	Adds or subtracts using counting-based strategies such as counting on (adding 3 to 5, says "five ..., six, seven, eight"), when numbers and totals do not go beyond 10.	Tells real-life stories involving numbers and a problem. Asks "how many" questions (e.g., *How many are left? How many are there now? How many did they start with? How many were added?*).
			Shows children the use of objects, fingers, counting on, guessing, and checking to solve problems.
Geometry and spatial	Begins to match and name 2-D and 3-D shapes, first only with same size and orientation, then shapes that differ in size and orientation (e.g., a large triangle sitting on its point with a small one sitting on its side).	Recognizes and names a variety of 2-D and 3-D shapes (e.g., quadrilaterals, trapezoids, rhombi, hexagons, spheres, cubes) in any orientation.	Introduces and labels a wide variety of shapes (e.g., skinny triangles, fat rectangles, prisms) that are in a variety of positions (e.g., a square or a triangle standing on a corner, a cylinder "standing up" or horizontal).
		Describes basic features of shapes (e.g., number of sides or angles).	Involves children in constructing shapes and talking about their features.

(continued)

Table 9.2. *(continued)*

Content area	Examples of typical knowledge and skills		Sample teaching strategies
	From Age 3 ────→	Age 6	
	Uses shapes, separately, to create a picture.	Makes a picture by combining shapes.	Encourages children to make pictures or models of familiar objects using shape blocks, paper shapes, or other materials.
			Encourages children to make and talk about models with blocks and toys.
	Describes object locations with spatial words such as *under* and *behind* and builds simple but meaningful "maps" with toys such as houses, cars, and trees.	Builds, draws, or follows simple maps of familiar places, such as the classroom or playground.	Challenges children to mark a path from a table to the wastebasket with masking tape, then draw a map of the path, adding pictures of objects appearing along the path, such as a table or easel.
Measurement	Recognizes and labels measurable attributes of objects (*I need a long string; Is this heavy?*).	Tries out various processes and units for measurement and begins to notice different results of one method or another (for example, what happens when we *don't* use a standard unit).	Uses comparing words to model and discuss measuring (*This book feels heavier than that block. I wonder if this block tower is taller than the desk*).
	Begins to compare and sort according to these attributes (more/less, heavy/light; *This block is too short to be the bridge*).	Makes use of nonstandard measuring tools or uses conventional tools such as a cup or ruler as nonstandard ways (e.g., *It's three rulers long*).	Uses and creates situations that draw children's attention to the problem of measuring something with two different units (e.g., making garden rows "four shoes" apart, first using a teacher's shoe and then a child's shoe).

240

Pattern/algebra	Notices and copies simple repeating patterns, such as a wall of blocks with long, short, long, short, long, short, long....	Notices and discusses patterns in arithmetic (e.g., adding 1 to any number results in the next "counting number").	Encourages, models, and discusses patterns (e.g., *What's missing? Why do you think that is a pattern? I need a blue next*). Engages children in finding color and shape patterns in the environment, number patterns on calendars and charts (e.g., with the numerals 1–100), patterns in arithmetic (e.g., recognizing that when zero is added to a number, the sum is always that number).
Displaying and analyzing data	Sorts objects and counts and compares the groups formed. Helps to make simple graphs (e.g., a pictograph formed as each child places her own photo in the row indicating her preferred treat—pretzels or crackers).	Organizes and displays data through simple numerical representations such as bar graphs and counts the number in each group.	Invites children to sort and organize collected materials by color, size, shape, etc. Asks them to compare groups to find which group has the most. Uses "not" language to help children analyze their data (e.g., *All of these things are red and these things are NOT red*). Works with children to make simple numerical summaries such as tables and bar graphs, comparing parts of the data.

Source: Excerpted from NAEYC, "Early childhood mathematics: Promoting good beginnings," position statement (Washington, DC: NAEYC, 2010). Copyright © 2010 NAEYC. Reprinted by permission. Full text of this position statement is available at http://www.naeyc.org/files/naeyc/file/positions/psmath.pdf.

is an ideal approach to inclusive preschool curriculum, rather than the current trend toward an increasingly more academic curriculum. Worth noting is a study by Marcon (2002) that examined the short- and long-term effects of different preschool curriculum models on school success. This study found that students in more academically directed programs initially demonstrated better knowledge of specific academic goals but poorer social skills than did children who attended child-initiated programs. However, in the longer term (by the end of 4th grade) academic performance of students from child-initiated preschool programs was significantly *better* than academic performance of the children who attended academically focused preschools.

An Example of Embedded Science, Technology, Engineering, and Math Goals

Katz described the following examples of a project approach to STEM goals. The project was simply learning about balls. Children brought balls to school. They studied and described the characteristics of the balls, learning key vocabulary (e.g., *sphere, spherical*). They also discussed the defining characteristics of a ball.

Students then posed specific research questions, for example, which ball will bounce the highest, which ball is heaviest, and so on. As the students made their predictions, the teacher would ask, "Why do you think that?" Students, over time, conducted different experiments to test each of their predictions. This required data collection and written records. Eventually each of their predictions was proven true or false. Students learned the important difference between opinions and facts.

It is easy to see how this activity simultaneously offers hands-on, interesting, active exploration, as well as the development of important mental structures, and opportunities to practice language, literacy, and math skills. One more added benefit was that the activities involved in data collection were done in small groups. This provided opportunities for cooperation and friendship.

INCLUSION STRATEGIES ACROSS THE CURRICULUM TO HELP CHILDREN WITH DISABILITIES IN KINDERGARTEN

The previous pages have provided an overview of preschool and kindergarten outcomes with strategies specific to language arts and mathematics curricula. The following suggestions are offered based on the authors' observations and experiences in the classroom setting and are specific to kindergarten transitions.

Transition Strategies

Effective and meaningful supports can begin prior to a student with special needs being included in a regular kindergarten. Offering teachers and paraprofessionals opportunities to observe the child in his or her existing preschool program, where the child is comfortable with the routine and the environment and knows his or her fellow classmates and teachers, gives them a picture that might look quite different from observations during the first week of kindergarten. The child, at that time, will be in an unfamiliar classroom with different peers and teachers; he or she may exhibit much difficulty with this change. Having observed the child a few months earlier may help the new teacher feel more confident in predicting and attaining future success as the student adapts to the new setting.

For the new kindergartener, a visit to his new class the week before school begins may help. Writing a transition story with accompanying photographs or line drawings about leaving preschool and going to kindergarten is a possible summer activity.

Paraprofessional Support

Paraprofessional support may be necessary at the beginning of the school year depending on specific child needs, size of classes, and existing available assistant support within those classes. Often, this support can be reduced by the end of the first trimester as the student and his or her classmates have settled into a predict-able kindergarten routine. The demand for, and use of, paraprofessionals or aides in kindergarten classrooms is an illustration of a common assumption: more adult support will help a child be more successful. Both administrative support and the knowledge and experience of itinerant inclusion specialists can help a transition team and the receiving kindergarten teacher determine the most effective types of adult support for specific children. (See Chapter 6 for more on paraprofessional support.)

Help for the Kindergarten Teacher

Training on specific disabilities or approaches to differentiated instruction can provide general overviews to teachers prior to beginning a school year. Although one-time trainings do not create lasting changes, they can offer opportunities for discussions of concerns and elevate feelings of effectiveness in new situations.

If an itinerant inclusion specialist is part of the support team, he or she should plan to be at the classroom the first day of school and visit often during the first month (especially if training and supervising paraprofessionals is necessary for this particular child). Leaving observation notes, providing contact information, and following through on kindergarten teacher questions or requests helps to build a supportive relationship.

Supports for Children in the Kindergarten Classroom

The following strategies to help children with special needs are broad and based on hands-on experience in kindergartens with 20 to 34 students in a classroom. These strategies are used throughout large and small work groups and complement specific standards-based academic work as described in the previous sections.

For children with autism or other disabilities that result in difficulty attend-ing for more than 5–10 minutes at a time, inability to sit and work independently during small group activities, sensory-seeking behaviors, and so on, the following strategies have helped:

- Cube chairs with low seats during carpet or large group periods when peers are sitting on the floor

- Lap or shoulder weights for children to hug or place on their heads, shoulders, or laps (If played with, weight is gently removed until child understands it is not a toy.)

- Favorite small toys, manipulatives, or stuffed animals that are kept in a box and offered to the child who may hold them in his or her hand during the group period (not played with)

- Air cushions or special carpet squares with child's name to define his or her sitting space

- Visual schedules that show what comes next so child is not asking or wondering when the period will end and what will happen next

- Opportunities for the child to take a break if the large group period is too long for that particular child (5 minutes may be too long for some children)

Teach the child to use acceptable language, signs, or pictures to ask to take a break. Do not allow a play time. Do provide a walk, sensory movement activity, or completion of a class job (e.g., distributing worksheets to small group tables). As the child becomes more used to the classroom schedule, slowly begin to increase the amount of minutes in the large group by acknowledging the child's request and signaling "one more minute" before allowing him or her to leave. Decrease the number of breaks as the number of minutes in the large group increase.

If a paraprofessional or teacher's aide is available during large group periods to provide support for specific children in the classroom, have the aide do the following:

- Provide a small whiteboard with markers and eraser for use by the child who is having difficulty focusing. The assistant replicates what the teacher is writing on the large board without talking (so the child can hear the teacher). The child can participate by erasing or using the markers to draw or print on the whiteboard. The opportunity to be more hands-on rather than passively sitting and watching can increase attention to the activity.

- Use an individual set of worksheets with the child and help the child focus on those worksheets as the teacher explains worksheets to the whole class. Try to use as little language as possible in order to encourage the child to listen to the teacher; point to areas of the worksheet that the teacher is discussing. Help the child point to or touch the parts of the worksheet being discussed. Often, children will visually follow their hands or fingers.

During small group periods:

- Seat child next to an adult monitoring that group; check that the child cannot easily leave the work area (place the back of the chair be against a wall or corner).

- Check that seat and table are a good fit. (Can the child sit comfortably, with good posture in the chair, and engage in fine motor work like printing or cutting with scissors?) If necessary, provide a taller chair, stool, or footrest so the child's feet are supported, and use a cushion or other support for the child's back if the seat or chair is too deep.

- Provide work breaks, if needed.

- Use visual timers to show the number of minutes left in an activity, if the child understands the concept of time.

- Allow the child to work in different areas of the classroom if sitting at a table is too difficult for too long (e.g., some children work better lying prone on the floor or working alone for part of small group time).

Based on determined accommodations for a specific child, help other adults in classroom understand and *consistently use* agreed-on accommodations such as the following:

- Using highlighter for child to trace words, names, shapes, or numbers.

- Using pencil grips, adapted scissors, or slant boards for paperwork.

- Understanding sensory concerns—such as touching glue or paint—and providing tools to help the child so that he or she does not need to use fingers.

- Providing written models of names or words close to the child's work for him or her to copy.

- Covering sections of worksheets with blank paper or folding worksheets to reduce visual overload and help the child focus on one task at a time.

- Noticing what motivates children to do their work and using these motivators. Sometimes these are as simple as a stamp, star, or happy face at the bottom of a completed work page or after each part is completed; sometimes the opportunity for free play upon completion of certain academic tasks is an effective motivator. Over time reduce the need to use as many motivators.

- Requiring reduced amount of work from child or different work due to child's disability (provide folders with prepared, modified work if different work is required).

A Few Words About Homework in Kindergarten (and Preschool) If Homework Is Required

The use of homework is often debated in schools and districts. Some districts encourage the use of homework from kindergarten on whereas other districts may limit the requirement, especially for younger children. Research is mixed and suggests that schools review homework policies for appropriateness (NEA, 2013). We will not debate the usefulness of homework here; instead we will offer strategies to help the child who may need accommodations if homework is a district policy.

- Consider modified homework after the first trimester if the child is not progressing in academic areas (e.g., send home name-printing practice rather than sentence or word practice; two pages of work rather than four).

- Use homework as a time to work on the very simple basics rather than trying to reinforce current standards if the child does not understand the math or language arts currently being taught.

- Speak with parents about the amount of time spent on homework and whether or not it is a struggle for both the child and family to complete all homework.

- Determine if a home-school reward system will help a child complete a manageable amount of work at home.

CONCLUSION

Standards-based expectations in academic areas including mathematics, reading comprehension, and writing skills result in the need for more accommodations, modifications, and accompanying support for children with significant disabilities in order to keep them fully included in the regular classroom. Kindergarten teachers have expressed feeling overwhelmed with the changes in expected academic achievement for their typical students; their willingness to welcome the child with a disability may be tempered by the need to teach so much more content during the academic year to their "typical" students. With dwindling state and federal funds in many districts, increased emphasis on academic standards, larger class sizes, and less adult support in classrooms, the challenges of meaningful and effective inclusion for young children with disabilities are many.

The individualized education program (IEP) team needs to determine what kindergarten setting will be most appropriate for each child based on goals and the supports needed to meet those goals. Sometimes placement in a regular setting will be recommended to help meet social and communication goals. At other times, a team may feel that placement in a regular kindergarten will help to meet all goals including academic development. Ensuring appropriate placement for children entering kindergarten is a challenge for IEP teams at times.

Working with elementary school staff can offer a different set of challenges from working with preschool staff. We have often heard kindergarten teachers express the need to measure the included child against his typical peers; they then feel a lack of success teaching that child if he or she has not met basic standards. This feeling tends to exist in spite of their knowledge of the IEP's modified academic goals and reassurances that the child is not being held to the same kindergarten standards as classmates. Clearly identifying a child's specific needs and reasons for being in the inclusive setting paired with consistent and responsive support for both teacher and child will lead to confidence and progress.

REFERENCES

Baghban, M. (2007). Scribbles, labels, and stories: The role of drawing in the development of writing. *Young Children, 62*(1), 20–26.

Byrd, M.R., & Rous, B.S. (1991). *Helpful entry level skill checklist—revised.* Lexington, KY: Child Development Centers of the Bluegrass.

Common Core State Standards Initiative. (2011). Retrieved from www.corestandards.org

Cook, R., Klein, M.D., & Chen, D. (2011). *Adapting early childhood curricula for children with special needs* (8th ed.). Boston: Pearson.

Copley, J.V. (2010). *The young child and mathematics* (2nd ed.). Reston, VA: National Association for the Education of Young Children and the National Council of Teachers of Mathematics.

Council of Chief State School Officers and Early Childhood Education Assessment Consortium. (2007). Appendix C. Development of state standards for early childhood education. Retrieved from nap.edu/openbook.php?record_id=12446&page=437

Day, J.N., McDonnell, A.P., & Heathfield, L.T. (2002). Enhancing emergent literacy skills in inclusive preschools for young children with visual impairments. *Young Exceptional Children, 9*(1), 20–28.

Demchak, M., & Downing, J.E. (2008). The preschool student. In J.E. Downing (Ed.), *Including students with severe and multiple disabilities in typical classrooms: Practical strategies for teachers* (3rd ed.). Baltimore: Paul H. Brookes Publishing Co.

Dogaru, C., Rosenkoetter, S., & Rous, B. (2009). *A critical incident study of the transition experience for young children with disabilities: Recounts by parents and professionals* (Technical Report No. 6). Lexington: University of Kentucky, Human Development Institute, National Early Childhood Transition Center. Retrieved from http://www.ihdi.uky.edu/nectc/home

Eisenhauer, M.J., & Feikes, D. (2009). Dolls, blocks, and puzzles: Playing with mathematical understandings. *Young Children, 64*(3), 18–24.

Gronlund, G. (2006). Adapted from: *Make early learning standards come alive: Connecting your practice and curriculum to state guidelines* (St. Paul, MN: Redleaf, Washington, DC: NAEYC, 2006). *Young Children, 63*(4), 10–13.

Hawken, L.S., Johnston, S.S., & McDonnell, A.P. (2005). Emerging literacy views and practices: Results from a national survey of Head Start preschool teachers. *Topics in Early Childhood Special Education, 25*(4), 232–242.

Head Start. (2010). *The Head Start child development and early learning framework: Promoting positive outcomes in early childhood programs serving children 3–5 years old.* Arlington, VA: Head Start Resource Center.

Hollingsworth, H.L. (2005). Interventions to promote peer social interactions in preschool settings. *Young Exceptional Children, 9*(1), 2–11.

Katz, L.G. (2010). STEM in the early years. Collected papers from the SEED conference, University of Northern Iowa. *Early Childhood Research and Practice* (15)1.

Marcon, R.A. (2002). Moving up the grades: Relationship between preschool model and later school success. *Early Childhood Research and Practice, 4*(1), 1–23.

McCathren, R.B., & Allor, J.H. (2002). Using storybooks with children: Enhancing language and emergent literacy. *Young Exceptional Children, 5*(4), 3–10.

NAEYC (National Association for the Education of Young Children) & NAECS/SDE (National Association of Early Childhood Specialists in State Departments of Education). (2010). *Joint statement of the National Association for the Education of Young Children and the National Association of Early Childhood Specialists in State Departments of Education on the common core standards initiative related to kindergarten through third grade.* NAEYC and NAECS/SDE.

NAEYC (National Association for the Education of Young Children) & NCTM (National Council of Teachers of Mathematics). (2002. Updated in 2010.). *Early childhood mathematics: Promoting good beginnings. A joint position statement of the National Association for the Education of Young Children (NAEYC) and the National Council of Teachers of Mathematics (NCTM).*

National Education Association (NEA). (2013). Research spotlight on homework: NEA reviews of the research on best practices in education. Retrieved from: www.nea.org/tools/16938.htm

National Education Goals Panel (NEGP) (1990). History of NEGP. Retrieved from govinfo.library.unt.edu/negp/page1-7.htm

National Education Goals Panel (NEGP) (1990). Legislation. Section 102. National Education Goals. Retrieved from govinfo.library.unt.edu/negp/page1-1.htm

NGACBP (National Governors Association Center for Best Practices), Council of Chief State School Officers. (2010). *Common core state standards.* Washington, DC: Author. Retrieved from http://www.corestandards.org/the-standards

No Child Left Behind Act of 2001, PL 107-110, 115 Stat. 1425, 20 U.S.C. §§ 6301 *et seq.*

Notari-Syverson, A., & Sadler, F.H. (2008). Math is for everyone: Supporting early mathematical competencies in young children. *Young Exceptional Children, 11*(3), 2–16.

Ong, F. (Ed.). (2010). *California preschool curriculum framework (Vol. 1).* Sacramento: CDE Press.

Phillips, B., Clancy-Menchetti, J., & Lonigan, C.J. (2008). Successful phonological awareness instruction with preschool children. *Topics in Early Childhood Special Education, 28*(1), 3–17.

Rosenkoetter, S., Schroeder, C., Rous, B., Hains, A., Shaw, J., & McCormick, K. (2009). *A review of research in early childhood transition: Child and family studies* (Technical Report No. 5). Lexington: University of Kentucky, Human Development Institute, National Early Childhood Transition Center. Retrieved from http://www.ihdi.uky.edu/nectc

Rous, B., & Hallam, R.A. (1998). Easing the transition to kindergarten: Assessment of social, behavioral and functional skills in young children with disabilities. *Young Exceptional Children, 1*(4), 17–26.

Sarama, J., & Clements, D.H. (2006). Mathematics in kindergarten. *Young Children, 61*(5), 38–41.

Taylor, J.M., McGowan, J., & Linder, T.W. (2009). *The program administrator's guide to early childhood special education.* Baltimore: Paul H. Brookes Publishing Co.

Whitehurst, G.J., & Lonigan, C.J. (2001). Emergent literacy: Development from prereaders to readers. In S. Neuman & D. Dickinson (Eds.), *Handbook of early literacy research* (pp. 11–29). New York: Guilford Press.

Zazlow, M., Calkins, J., & Halle, T. (2000). *Background for community-level work on school readiness: A review of definitions, assessments and investment strategies. Part I: Defining and assessing school readiness—building on the foundation of NEPG work.* Final report to the Knight Foundation. Washington DC: Child Trends.

Zevenbergen, A, & Whitehurst, G. (2003). Dialogic reading: A shared picture book intervention for preschoolers. In A. van Kleeck, S.A. Stahl, & E.B. Bauer (Eds.), *On reading books to children* (pp. 177–183). Mahwah, NJ: Erlbaum.

Index

Tables and figures are indicated by *t* and *f* respectively.